CLASSIC DIVES OF
THE WORLD

Horace Dobbs

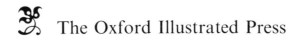

The Oxford Illustrated Press

Printed in England by J. H. Haynes and Co Limited, Sparkford, Nr Yeovil, Somerset.

Published by:
The Oxford Illustrated Press Limited, Sparkford, Nr. Yeovil, Somerset.

Haynes Publications Inc., 861 Lawrence Drive, Newbury Park, California 91320.

ISBN 0 946609 43 8

British Library Cataloguing in Publication Data:

Dobbs, Horace E.
    Classic dives of the world.
    1. Diving, Submarine—Handbooks, manuals, etc.
    I. Title
    797.2'3   GV840.S78

ISBN 0-946609-43-8

Library of Congress Catalog Card Number 87-82795

Books by the same author:

The Great Diving Adventure
Camera Underwater
Underwater Swimming
Snorkelling and Skindiving
Follow a Wild Dolphin
Save the Dolphins
Dolphin Spotters Handbook
The Magic of Dolphins
Tale of Two Dolphins

CONTENTS

To beautiful Fiona Jane

There is a pleasure in the pathless woods
There is a rapture on the lonely shore
There is society, where none intrudes,
By the deep sea, and music in its roar
I love not Man the less, but Nature more,
From these our interviews, in which I steal
From all I may be, or have been before,
To mingle with the universe, and feel
What I can ne'er express,
Yet can not all conceal.
                                    (Byron, *Childe Harold's Pilgrimage*)

AN INVITATION
by Horace Dobbs

Imagine I am your Fairy Godmother. With money and time no object I can grant you your wish to visit the most beautiful, spectacular and historic places in the underwater world accessible to skin divers: the classic dive sites and sights of the world.

Although I cannot do this for you in reality I can do it through the magic of the pen, the photograph and the printed page, i.e. this book. So settle down, make yourself comfortable and come with me on my magic carpet around the world.

Before we get going you are going to have to learn to dive and the amount of training you undertake will depend on how many of the sites you will want to explore for yourself. If you wish to get into the sea and be whisked around the Devil's Crown in the Galapagos, or sink into the cold treacherous waters of the Isles of Scilly, then you will need to have a full diving course. If however you just want to sample what the underwater world has to offer, on the Florida Keys say, then you might consider leaving your training until you reach your destination. Reading the next chapter, 'Taking The Plunge' will familiarise you with the basics on equipment and diving techniques. Right. You're ready. Climb aboard. Here we go.

We could start from anywhere, of course, but I think we will make our first excursion under the sea off the West Country. So let's start our journey in Plymouth which is where the Pilgrim Fathers set out from on their voyage to the USA, and where countless other adventures have begun. It was at Plymouth, on the Hoe, where Drake was playing bowls, that he was summoned by Queen Elizabeth to prepare to repel the Spanish Armada. But we are not going to commence by looking at an ancient Armada wreck. On DIVE 1 we are going to look at one of the casualties of the time when Britain faced another crisis initiated by a little man with a small black moustache — Adolf Hitler. After diving round the remains of a World War II wreck and cruising round the red reefs of Eddystone we are going to pop over the toe of England to the Bristol Channel for DIVE 2. There we will land on the tiny island of Lundy which first came to my attention when I was a schoolboy, as the place that issued stamps with puffins on them.

On Lundy I am going to leave you in the capable hands of one of the many guides who are going to escort you on your trans-world diving safari. His name is **Richard Oldfield** — who is far more widely known as the cartoonist 'Rico'. Very few divers in Britain will not have laughed at Rico's cartoons which have enlivened the pages of *Diver* magazine for many years. Although he is well known for his cutting wit, and his irrepressible Liverpudlian humour, Rico is a committed conservationist. Most of his cartoons spring from his detailed knowledge of the sea and the creatures and plants that inhabit it. It is obvious from his superb paintings of underwater subjects that he understands the sea. Rico is also a very keen photographer and he works very closely with **Christine Williams** who will also escort you on your underwater tour of Lundy.

From Lundy we are going to fly west, over Ireland, to one of the most westerly outcrops of rock in Europe for DIVE 3. It is called the Great Skellig or Skellig Michael. Of the many islands I have visited and explored in the world I put Skellig Michael at the top of the list for atmosphere. It has a romantic quality about it which seems to have no dimension in time. Having visited the Skellig I find the ancient Celtic legends all quite credible.

I was fortunate enough to be taken to the Skelligs (there are two islands) by **Des Lavelle** — a diver and the author of *Skellig — Island Outpost of Europe* (O'Brien Press, Dublin). As we chugged across the sea onboard his fishing boat from Valentia Island, Des regaled me and my companions with stories about the amazing history of the rock that towered out of the sea ahead of us. He did so in a soft Irish brogue, which is so much more poetic than the basic English language, lacing his commentary with the humour for which Kerrymen are famous. During our journey I asked Des where in the world he would go, given a free choice, for a holiday.

'I'd go to the Skelligs,' he said with a twinkle in his eye.

That comment says something about Des's love of the Skelligs. He and his charming wife Pat run a small guest-house and diving centre on Valentia Island. For Des, taking divers out to the Skelligs is work. It is also play. As he knows far more about the Skelligs than I do I will leave you in his capable hands before we set off on the next leg of our journey which will take us across the Atlantic Ocean to a location that could not be more of a contrast — no matter how hard it tried.

I refer to the low flat islands of the Florida Keys where — as they say in the song — 'the livin' is easy'. The glitzy, materialistic city of Miami was created during this century out of sub-tropical swampland and DIVE 4 is the place to come to if you are a diving softy. Just because it's easy it doesn't mean that the diving isn't rewarding. It is, with a wealth of corals and colourful fish to enchant your eye. Indeed, if you haven't much diving experience, but nonetheless would like to at least have a look into the underwater world of a coral reef — then this is where I suggest you begin. The water is like a luke-warm bath, so you will not require a wetsuit. Give me your hand and we will gently snorkel around on the surface. Look. There is a bronze statue of Christ of the Abyss. Firmly anchored to the reef beneath him, he is extending his hands up towards us, just as he has to the thousands of other divers who visit this site every year.

From diving for softies we are going to move onto diving for nutcases. These are people who not only swim underwater but do so in confined tunnels under the bowels of the earth. I refer to that unique brand of madmen known as cave divers. There are relatively few of them about, but those who take up this particular branch of diving usually become completely addicted to it. Although I have done some cave diving myself I must put you in the hands of a real expert if you are going to explore safely the deepest innermost tunnels of the 'Blue Holes' on Andros Island in the Bahamas. Unless you are very experienced it would be insane to attempt to dive the 'Blue Holes' without very careful pre-dive planning and in the company of divers who have experience in cave diving techniques.

You still want to go? Okay. But I hope you won't mind if I miss this one. For DIVE 5 I will leave you in the capable hands of Martyn Farr, the author of *The Great Caving Adventure* (Oxford Illustrated Press). He is one of Britain's foremost authorities on cave diving and has been on caving expeditions to many parts of the world, including China.

The next leg of our journey is a relatively short one in terms of miles but a long way off in terms of the diving experiences it has to offer. DIVE 6 takes us to the Cayman Islands. Although these islands are British Crown Colonies they have been Americanised to such an extent that you might almost think you were still on the Florida Keys. In view of this situation I thought it best to have an American guide to escort you. I was extremely lucky to procure the services of **Barbara Currie**, via my friend and fellow underwater cameraman, Stanton Waterman. He told me that although Barbara was an American citizen she had lived in Grand Cayman and had a great deal of diving experience which she was prepared to put at our disposal. So Barbara Currie is going to take you on DIVE 6 in the Caribbean where everything you could possibly wish for, including a dive in a submarine, is available if you've got the dollars to pay for it. And to gild this particular lily, Barbara has brought along the renowned underwater photographer and author of *Cayman Underwater Paradise*, **Paul Humann,** to record the scene.

I am going to insist on taking you on DIVE 7 for which we will have to cross the South American Continent. Our destination is the Galapagos Archipelago. This is one of the places I was desperate to return to after my first visit. So having you onboard will give me an excuse to whiz around the Devil's Crown again on a fast drift dive which is the underwater equivalent of a rollercoaster ride. Hold on to your hood!

The next stage on our round-the-world flight of fantasy takes us over the vast Pacific Ocean to New Zealand where we are to meet a long-standing friend of mine, **Wade Doak**. During the past decade Wade has devoted much of his time to the study of dolphins as those who have read his book *Dolphin Dolphin* (Hodder and Stoughton) will know. In 1984 Wade published his tenth underwater book entitled *Ocean Planet* (Hodder and Stoughton) in which he reviewed some of his innumerable diving experiences which started shortly after he was born when his mother dunked him into the sea and decided to call him Wade after the Norse giant who strode across the fiords to seize and devour young maidens. Wade was fortunate to live in a part of the world where the underwater life is prolific. He soon discovered that the Poor Knights Islands were one of the most rewarding areas to explore with camera and his deeply inquisitive mind.

Many of his underwater escapades have been shared with his charming and demure wife Jan, and their two children Brady and Karla. Wade and I have so much in common that from the moment we meet we do not stop talking. The more time I have spent with him the more respect I have gained for his knowledge and understanding of the sea, and the philosophy of life he has adopted as a result of his travels and underwater experiences. So it is with great pleasure that I will hand you over to Wade Doak for DIVE 8 who will take you

Round-the-world magic carpet ride to 17 classic dive locations

down his underwater staircase into the depths of the sea surrounding the Poor Knights.

When my first opportunity to visit the Great Barrier Reef, which has been described as the eighth wonder of the world, eventually came in 1981 I was really looking forward to it. But when I got there, after a 90-mile journey seawards out of Mackay, I have to admit that I was disappointed. Had it been my first dive on a coral reef I am sure I would have found it absolutely wondrous. But having already explored many seas, including the Red Sea and the Caribbean I felt let down. Several well-travelled British divers expressed the view that Australian spearfishermen were a greater plague than the much-publicised Crown of Thorns Starfish.

In the British Society of Underwater Photographers magazine *In Focus* (February 1986), Den Lewis wrote of his experiences as follows after setting out from Townsville and visiting one of the inner reefs called Grub Reef.

'On diving, I could not believe that it was the Barrier Reef. There was a distinct absence of fish and the corals looked dead. It was the same on the night dive at Faraday Reef, no crinoids, not even featherstars. No change at Myrmidon Reef, and John Brewer Reef was sand coated, but there were more fish, probably due to being fed by toursts in glass bottomed boats. Only when we reached Coil Reef and Wheeler Reef did things improve, with bright corals and plenty of fish.

That evening, the reason for the desolate reefs became apparent as the rest of the divers — Australians — unloaded 6-ft harpoon guns and went in search of unlucky victims. The same thing happened every evening, except when we dived on the wreck of the *Yongola,* which is a preserved area.'

Admittedly the diving did get better later. After expressing his severe disappointment he concluded his article as follows:

'Mind you, the Great Barrier Reef is a big place and I'm sure it has much to offer, depending on the time of year.'

In contrast to Den's view I had met several other equally experienced divers who were ecstatic about the Great Barrier Reef.

One of them was **Gilbert Dinesen.** He took up diving later than most, and is very modest about his considerable diving activities and achievements. I first met him on a diving expedition to Sardinia. On that trip I was impressed with his ability to find shells on the seabed and his encyclopaedic knowledge of them. Upon our return I visited his house and he showed me a vast number of sea-shells, most of them carefully labelled. It was the most impressive collection I had seen outside a museum.

Round-the-world magic carpet ride to 17 classic dive locations.

7

Gilbert's daughter, Zena, caught the diving bug from her father and eventually qualified in marine biology doing her Ph.D. on reef corals around Lizard Island. This was very convenient for Gilbert as it gave him a legitimate excuse to fly to Australia once every two years to visit his daughter — and go diving of course. It was apparent from the opinions I collected that to enjoy the best of diving on the Great Barrier Reef it is vital to know where to dive. So I invited Gilbert to take the role of guide on DIVE 9 on which we shall take a brief glimpse of the sea life on the greatest mass of living coral in the world.

Gilbert is not a photographer, but I was lucky to recruit the services of a young man, **Edward Childs,** to record the scene. Edward spent 10 weeks from July to September 1986 around Lizard Island recording the influence of divers on the marine environment while working on Operation Raleigh's Cape York Expedition. Here are three extracts from his Expedition Report:

1. Whilst the diving around Lizard Island might have been disappointing for some, no one could argue that the diving on the Barrier Reef itself was anything less than spectacular ... enhanced by the crystal clear water with visibility up to 35 m.
2. The current through Cormorant Pass caused our only diving incident when two diving staff members were carried away from the cover boat by an unexpectedly strong current whilst they were looking for an anchor and chain. They were located by the crew of *Triton* about three hours later when it was dark and they could use torches and a camera flash to signal the boat.
3. Cod Hole is an experience that is hard to describe as it is so unusual. In this one area of the Great Barrier Reef, about twenty Potato Cod congregate to be fed by divers. These fish, in excess of 90 kg, are very used to divers and will feed readily on anything, although they appeared to be more used to top quality food from the Lodge rather than our ration pack sausages. However, it was the Morays that made Cod Hole special for me. Their inquisitiveness was not echoed in other fish and to have a Moray come right up to your mask, wrap itself around your neck and try to get inside your wetsuit is a very special experience!

I don't think many divers will dispute the fact that Truk Lagoon is the greatest place to go wreck diving in the world. When I made a film there entitled 'Sunken Tombs of Truk Lagoon' I got to know the place fairly well. As our magic carpet is fitted with an in-flight movie I will let you see my modest masterpiece (it won a Gold Medal at the Brighton International Festival of Underwater Film) whilst we are on our way.

And talking of films did you see '2001 Space Odyssey'? It was co-written by your next guide **Arthur C. Clarke** who is going to look after you at your next port of call, which is Sri Lanka, or Ceylon as it used to be called. I first met Arthur at a Film Festival in Brighton in 1966. He had established a reputation as a science fiction writer. But it was his theoretical prediction that one day communications satellites could be put into orbit around the earth that was to have the most far-reaching consequences for the future of mankind. He is now one of the world's most respected space scientists. However, his amazing foresight enabled him to see the potential of inner space as well as that of outer space. He was a pioneer diver. And through the magic of this book I can take you back with him to one of his most exciting adventures in inner space. Most of us think of fish as being insensitive and stupid. But when Arthur C. Clarke dived in the turbulent and treacherous waters of the Great Basses Reef he discovered that the Giant Groupers that lived there were far from stupid. Indeed, he and his companions taught them tricks just like circus animals (which are invariably large brained mammals). Nowadays there are many parts of the world where fish, especially Groupers, will come out from their reef lairs and swim freely with divers. But at the time it was regarded as extremely remarkable. The forays that Arthur and his companions made from the Great Basses lighthouse were undoubtedly classic dives that have a special place in submarine history. So I am taking you back in time for DIVE 11.

The short film entitled 'Beneath the Seas of Ceylon' that Arthur C. Clarke and Mike Wilson made at the time for the Ceylon Tea Board became a classic. There is one sequence in the film which has remained in my memory ever since I first saw it over two decades ago. It shows a diver using a hula-hoop like a matador's cloak. A Grouper, called Ali Baba, charges at the hoop which the diver sweeps aside to cries of 'Olé' and the roar of a bullfight crowd on the soundtrack.

Despite a punishing schedule, Arthur continues to write. Using satellites that at one time were only the figments of his imagination he can now communicate directly with his brother Fred who lives in England. When he wants, Arthur can type the letters of a message on his keyboard in Colombo, and they appear on a visual display unit in his brother's house in Somerset.

I don't know if Arthur ever predicted that one day we would be able to dematerialise ourselves in one place and then rematerialise ourselves somewhere else. Until that happens (if it ever does) you will have to resort to using your imagination and my magic carpet. So let

me carry you away from Sri Lanka for DIVE 12 which is at a place called the Chagos Bank in the middle of the Indian Ocean. The uninhabited group of islands probably isn't even marked on your map, and if it is, it is in the wrong place. That is according to our guide on this site — **David Bellamy.**

I first met David in 1966 just after he had given his first major public lecture on pollution in the sea. I have to admit that I had half a mind to miss that particular presentation. But I stayed. And like everyone else in the audience it wasn't long before I was rolling with laughter and completely enraptured by his boyish

A diver explores the coral underwater wonderland at Ras Muhammed in the Red Sea. (Photo: Horace Dobbs.)

enthusiasm. What David said had a lot in common with my own views on the need to look after the marine environment. We worked together on Underwater Conservation Year which was the forerunner of the Marine Conservation Society. We became good friends and have remained so ever since, despite David's rise to the dizzy heights of what he disparagingly calls 'A tele personality'. He carries the grand prefix of Professor now and it sits well on his shoulders. To David, finding out about things is exciting, and learning about them should always be fun. So I will leave him to take you to a place no-one has ever dived before, and where the sharks may out-number all of the other fishes around you. If you want to find out more about the Chagos Archipelago I suggest you read David's book entitled *Half of Paradise* which was first published by Cassell in 1979.

I know you will be reluctant to leave David's company but it's time to move on to a land whose history goes back into the mists of the distant past. It is the Sinai — where Moses came down from the mountains with the tablets of stone. DIVE 13 is at the southern tip of the Sinai, at a headland called Ras Muhammed, where the precipitous cliffs plunge into the deep clear waters of the Red Sea. Above water it is dramatic; underwater the scenery is arguably the most spectacular you will find anywhere in the world.

At Ras Muhammed we are going to pick up my son **Ashley Dobbs,** who has dived the Red Sea many times. We have taken him onboard as he is going to pilot our magic carpet to its next destination for DIVE 14. Ashley was a competent scuba diver by the age of 11 and we enjoyed some of our first open water dives together in Mediterranean off the Island of Elba. Although they were very enjoyable, one of the memories I have of those dives was the lack of fish and the abundance of plastic bags on the sea bed. At the time we had no idea that Ashley would later be involved with setting-up diving holidays around the world for Bruce and Hedda Lyons at Twickers World. After that he formed a company called Vacance Gozo and went into the holiday business on his own. When he told me he had come across something exceptional in the Mediterranean, with lots of fish life, I wasn't exactly dismissive, but I was a little sceptical. Ashley informed me that the exceptional dive destination he had chanced upon was a small island called Gozo, which I had never heard of. It was close to Malta. I knew that many divers visited Malta every summer and heard jokes about the visibility at some sites beng limited by the number of divers in the water. So I knew that the Maltese islands must have some special attraction.

Later I had a postcard from Ashley in which he described a dive at night on Gozo at a location called the Inland Sea. Two dolphins (which were later helped to freedom) swam over his head as he sat 7 metres down on the seabed watching them weaving trails of phosphorescence above him. Not long after, I went out there to visit the Inland Sea myself.
myself.

When we arrived for our dive an Italian film crew were using the location. We watched as actors, dressed as mercenary soldiers and riding in an inflatable boat, appeared as if by magic out of a steep rock face. They then raced across the water before running their boat onto the beach. How they achieved this illusion will be revealed when you go for DIVE 14. However, I will give you a clue. The Inland Sea is in a limestone outcrop that was once above sea level.

The rocks of our next stopping place are of volcanic origin and you will need to be suited up before you drop into the sea at St. Abbs Head in Scotland, which is the location for DIVE 15.

From St. Abbs I am going to ferry you to a tiny island off the coast of Brittany. I dubbed it Dolphin Rock because it is the home of one of those very rare dolphins that befriends man in preference to its own kind. Dolphin Rock is the location for DIVE 16.

We are going to end our round-the-world tour near where we began — at the extremity of the West Country, in the Isles of Scilly. Many vessels, some of them laden with treasure, have ended their journeys here unintentionally. On our last dive, DIVE 17, we are going beneath the sea to search for gold and silver coins, and bronze cannons. Although many have been recovered there are still a lot left waiting to be uncovered. How Sir Cloudesley Shovell's treasure-laden ship, the *Association* came to founder in these treacherous waters in 1707 and how in 1966 it was first discovered by skin-divers, is a classic tale of diving adventure. You will have to decide for yourself whether it is the lure of gold, or the idea of reconstructing a piece of history, that drives divers to spend hours under the sea at a location as hazardous as this.

Well, in a nutshell 'That's it'. I hope you will now take up the offer and come aboard my magic carpet.

Enjoy your trip.

TAKING THE PLUNGE by Horace Dobbs

I have always maintained that anyone who is fit enough to go for a brisk walk is fit enough to take a look at what the underwater world has to offer. All you need is a pair of fins, a mask and a snorkel. With that basic equipment you can float on the surface, look down into Neptune's Kingdom through your mask, breathe through the tube and propel yourself gently through the water with your fins. In a location like the Florida Keys there are plenty of dive operators who will take out novices. There are platforms on the sterns of the dive boats, and once on site getting into the water is no more difficult than stepping into a swimming pool. Similarly when getting out — there is a ladder for you to climb up.

If the sea is calm, warm and clear, as it was when I first visited the John Pennekamp Coral Reef State Park in the Florida Keys, then you have nothing to fear. If necessary, one of the friendly guides will take your hand to reassure you. If you can't get the hang of finning they may even tow you along.

Even though you are just looking in I can assure you there is absolutely no comparison between peering down through a glass-bottom boat and actually snorkelling along on the surface. Everything is much clearer when seen through a facemask, and you can twist your head from side to side to follow the movement of fish. If you are worried about sinking then put on a lifejacket, or lifevest as they are called in the USA. Then you can't sink. An alternative is to wear the jacket of a thick wetsuit, which is made of sponge neoprene and spreads its buoyancy over your entire trunk. With such a suit on you will bob on the sea like a cork. Without weights you will find it very difficult to sink — even if you want to. So you will be quite safe, even if you can't swim.

I use the name *snorkel floater* for those who adopt this procedure. No matter how nervous of the prospect, I would advise everyone who visits a coral reef in warm clear flat seas to have a go at snorkel floating, in the company of an experienced diver. It is an experience you will never regret. To engage in snorkelling of any kind you need three basic items of equipment: mask, snorkel and fins.

The *facemask* enables you to see clearly down into the water. The faceplate should be of toughened glass and is best prevented from misting up by rubbing saliva across the inner surface with the fingers before a dive. It should be leakproof and a good fit. It may be necessary to try on several before you find one that seals comfortably to the contours of your face. One way of testing if a mask is satisfactory is to put it in position without putting the strap over your head. When you inhale gently through your nose the mask should be sucked onto your face and will not drop off if left unsupported.

A *snorkel tube* will enable you to breathe through your mouth when the mask is in place. The two rubber spigots should be clenched between the teeth with the rubber flange forming a seal when it is located between the gums and the lips. Getting used to breathing through the tube usually only takes a few moments. Don't bother with any gadgets on the tube to keep out the water. Use an open tube, and simply blow out hard to expel any water that gets in. The tube can be kept in position by sticking it up under the mask strap, or by having it attached directly to the mask strap. You can adjust its position until it fits comfortably.

A *pair of fins* completes your transformation from land animal to aquatic mammal. Most people prefer fins with a shoe fitting. If you have powerful legs you will enjoy thrusting yourself rapidly through the water with strong leg movements using fairly rigid fins. I personally prefer fins with much more flexible blades. The important factor to take into consideration when selecting fins is that they should not be too tight a fit. A pair that cramps your feet become agonising to wear after a short time.

Once you have mastered the use of the basic equipment on the surface it is time to consider snorkel diving. A smooth, clean, duck dive will send you on your way down into the sea. If you've got a generous waistline a *quick-release weightbelt* will make getting down easier, and staying down whilst holding your breath less energy consuming. If you are a confident swimmer, happy in water, then learning to snorkel dive should come naturally.

Once you have mastered snorkel diving you will be so fascinated by what you see that you will want to stay down for much longer than the time you can hold your breath. The

Decompression stop after a deep dive in Truk Lagoon. (Photo: Horace Dobbs.)

A diver using an amphibious camera and flash that is as easy to use underwater as it is in air. (Photo: Horace Dobbs.)

solution is to put on an aqualung and take down your own air supply with you. To the uninitiated there may appear to be a lot of mystique about aqualung, or scuba diving. In reality it is remarkably easy. You strap a cylinder containing high-pressure air *(definitely not oxygen)* on your back and breathe from a regulator that automatically delivers air to you at exactly the right pressure, according to the depth.

Although breathing from an aqualung is surprisingly easy underwater it is necessary to obey certain rules if you are to survive the experience. Thus it is absolutely essential to have a proper course of instruction.

The degree of tuition will depend upon your ambition as well as your physical capabilities. If you eventually plan to go diving in cold water at locations with strong currents, where the visibility may be poor, then a comprehensive course of diving instruction, which will enable you to cope safely with all of these eventualities, should be embarked upon. When you have completed the course you will be awarded a certificate which says so. It indicates that you know how to dive but it doesn't necessarily mean you are a safe diver. In that respect it is rather like a driving licence. You will be expected to produce it when hiring equipment, or before being accepted on a diving excursion.

Different diver-training organisations have different terms for various grades of diving proficiency. The bottom rung of the qualification ladder, that of a novice diver, indicates that you have had the minimum instruction to go diving under relatively undemanding conditions. Thereafter the grades change — letters, names, numbers or star ratings — as you progress, higher ratings being awarded only after you have completed appropriate qualifying dives under a variety of conditions. Even when you reach the elevated status of a diving instructor you will find you can climb even higher up the qualifications ladder. Long before you reach these dizzy heights you should have become familiar with words and terms such as: the bends, decompression sickness, bars (the type pumped into your air cylinder as well as those you lean on) and tanks which may also be referred to as bottles.

The loud use of these, as well as other jargon words such as 'viz' (underwater visibility) will set you apart from other sun worshippers on the beach, and may be especially useful if you are looking for a way of attracting the attention of a member of the opposite sex.

As this is a book on *where* to dive, not *how* to dive, I do not intend to detail here the effects of pressure on gas volumes, etc, which will help you understand the reasons why we follow certain procedures when swimming underwater. What I will do, however, is give you a little advice together with what I regard as a few essential rules. If you wish to find out more about why they are necessary I suggest you consult a diving manual.

When you go on your first dive with an aqualung you will quite naturally feel excited, and perhaps apprehensive. Thus your heart rate will probably be faster than normal, and you will use up your air supply quickly. However, after a while, as you become familiar with the experience of being weightless and you have got over the wonder of the fact that air really does flow into your lungs quite easily and automatically when you breathe in no matter how deep you are, then you should make a conscious effort to relax. If water seeps

into your mask, clear it by pressing the top of the mask against your forehead and exhaling through your nose. If your head is in an upright position the air coming into the mask will displace the trapped water. You should get to a stage where this procedure becomes second nature. If you don't a flooding mask

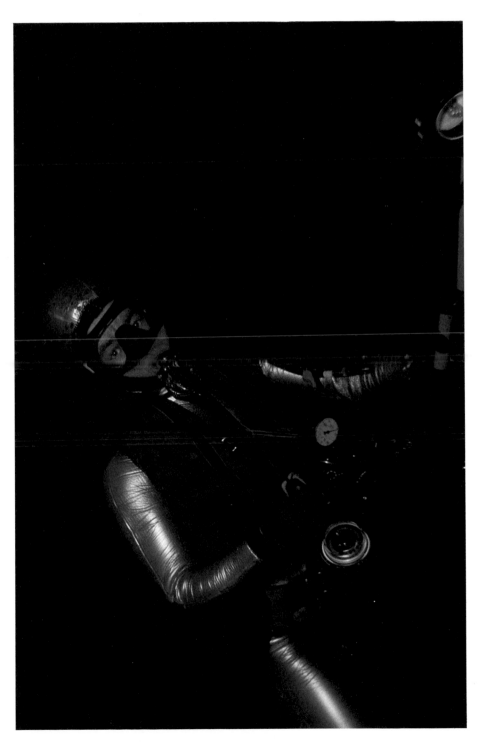

A warm diver is a happy diver. This diver is wearing a silver-finished wetsuit to keep out the cold. (Photo: Horace Dobbs.)

may cause you to panic. When this happens your first instinct will almost certainly be to rush to the surface. Should this happen it is vital that you remember and practise the most important rule of scuba diving. *Do not hold your breath when surfacing.* On the way up keep your throat relaxed so that the air in your lungs, which expands with the decreasing pressure, can escape. If you do not then your lungs may rupture causing a condition known as an *air embolism* – which can be fatal.

When you descend, whether snorkel diving or scuba diving, it is important that the air pressure on both sides of your eardrums should equalise. For many people this happens automatically and they hear their ears click as they sink down. If this does not happen spontaneously then ears become painful. It it easy not to notice the pain, or even to ignore it, during the excitement of your first dive. The pain is a warning that your eardrum is under stress. To relieve it you must clear your ears, which can usually be achieved by pinching your nose and blowing gently. Failure to clear your ears could lead to one, or both of your eardrums perforating. This is not as dangerous as an embolism, but it will stop you from diving until it has healed, and may impair your hearing. So my second rule is: *do not continue your descent, whether snorkelling or scuba diving, if your ears hurt.*

There are a host of other rules you may need to observe — depending upon the circumstances of a particular dive. But there is one that is essential if you are diving in deep water. It is: *watch your depth gauge.*

Once underwater and wearing an aqualung the sensation of depth is very subjective and is related to the underwater conditions. In murky cold water a depth of 10 metres can feel a long way down. On the other hand a depth of 40 metres can feel quite shallow when, for instance, the water is so clear that when you look up you can see your bubbles rising all the way to the surface. Under such circumstances it is very easy to descend to depths where *nitrogen narcosis,* known more descriptively as *rapture of the deep,* may cause you to act irresponsibly, or even stupidly. Be alert for this condition at depths below 30 metres. Do not descend below 50 metres unless you are fully prepared for the consequences.

At such depths you will also need to know how long and how deep your dive has been in order to ascertain whether or not you will need to make a decompression stop at the end of your dive. Decompression stops are necessary to avert another potential hazard — *the bends.* The time and depths of these stops will be detailed in the decompression tables which you must study before going on deep dives.

The length of time you can spend at various depths depends upon the size of your air cylinder, and the air pressure inside it. In Britain and the USA all regulators are fitted with pressure gauges which will indicate the internal pressure in the tank. Thus by watching your pressure gauge during a dive you can get a good idea of how much longer your air will last. In some parts of the world, particularly the Mediterranean, not all regulators are fitted with pressure gauges. A reserve system incorporated in the aqualung cylinder is used instead. It works on the principle that when most of your air is used up, the supply ceases until you pull the reserve lever, which opens a valve releasing the remainder of the air for your ascent. I don't like the system because I like to know at any stage of a dive how much air I have left. Also I am conscious of the fact that should I forget to ensure that the reserve lever is closed before a dive I might find myself in deep water with no air reserve. Although the air reserve system was quite common when diving holidays were starting up most centres now provide regulators with gauges — even when cylinders are fitted with reserves.

Diving standards and practices around the world are becoming progressively more unified. Even so, particularly in remote locations, a visiting diver may find himself presented with equipment with which he is not familiar. A regulator is a very personal piece of equipment. It is one of the items that comes high on the list when deciding what can be included in a miserly baggage allowance, for very unfairly, I think, the airlines do not give divers concessions for extra baggage that are available to participants in some other sports, such as golf.

No matter where I go in the world, if I am likely to find myself near water, I always pack a facemask, snorkel and a pair of lightweight fins, plus a Nikonos underwater camera. Thus if all else fails I know I can at least go snorkelling and take some pictures.

If you are going on a diving holiday it is important to take evidence of your diving capability with you. I strongly advise taking your diving logbook which contains full details of the training procedures you have undertaken and the types of dives you have done. Internationally recognised certificates are also available and their production should avert difficulties that may arise when it comes to hiring equipment, or being accepted into a diving group. A recent medical certificate indicating your fitness to dive may also be demanded. However, no matter how much paperwork you produce, some diving centres insist that you run through the basic procedures such as mask clearing and buoyancy control before they will allow you to join a group going off for a dive in the open sea.

Diving centres vary immensely in the standards they apply. For some it is a free-for-all with every man or woman for himself. Others will insist you stay very strictly in pairs. At some centres, in conditions of good visibility, a diving instructor will take down a group of up to twelve individuals and will keep his eye on all of them.

Experienced divers can make their air last much longer than novices and many like to extend their dives for as long as possible. Such divers feel cheated when told of the time limitations compulsorily imposed by some dive tour operators who insist the entire group all return to the boat at a specific time, regardless of how much air the various individuals have left. This is most likely to be the case in highly organised dive centres that cater mainly for American divers. At such locations everything from the time of departure to the ice in the cooler will be run like clockwork. The boat will be clean and tidy, the air of good quality and all equipment in tip-top condition.

On the other hand you may find yourself with a dive outfit in a remote tropical paradise that is run on somewhat more easy-going lines. At such places punctuality is unknown. The boat is unseaworthy, the air tastes oily, and having dropped you into the sea with a rusty cylinder on your back the skipper lights a reefer and sits back with a rum and Coke. He then abandons all further interest in you until you return — assuming you do of course. In the meantime he focuses his mind and his eyes (hidden behind silver reflective sunglasses) on a topless, bikini-bottomed nymph, lying on the foredeck browning parts of her body the sun doesn't normally reach.

Diving tour operators can be graded between these extremes and it must be said that the vast majority of them provide a good friendly service. However, the enforcement of what are considered by some as essential standards of safety and supervision may not be rigidly applied. If possible, therefore, it is best to be self-sufficient. When travelling to a new unknown destination it is preferable to go with a diving buddy you know, and who you can rely upon to give you a helping hand should you need it.

Also, before you depart I strongly advise that you check that all the equipment and services you need are available, particularly in remote destinations. Nobody wants to hump lead weights around the world, but it might be worth carrying your own life-jacket and diving knife. Ask well in advance what recharging facilities will be available — a good reliable compressor is obviously vital to keep cylinders recharged. Will you need a wetsuit? If you are a photographer will the chargers for your lighting equipment be compatible with the local electricity supply? If not you may need to take extra batteries. Can films be purchased and processed locally? Try to anticipate all of your needs and either take them with you, or get an assurance they will be available when you arrive. You are less likely to be disappointed if you expect the worst.

Your tour operator or travel agent should advise you on visas, which medicaments to take etc. Very few high street travel agents however, have first-hand knowledge about specific diving locations, and it is absolutely essential that you should check that the time of your visit coincides with good diving conditions. This may sound obvious if you are planning a dive at Flamborough Head in Yorkshire for instance, where you wouldn't expect to see your hand in front of your face for nine days out of ten in the winter months. But similar conditions may also prevail in tropical locations where pronounced seasonal variations can also occur. A strong onshore wind, which may be described as a pleasant cooling sea breeze in the brochure, and indeed might be quite pleasant for the non-diving holiday maker, could spell disaster for the diver. Such winds, in shallow-water regions, stir up the sand and silt, reducing visibility accordingly, as well as making boat diving very uncomfortable.

A non-diver's idea of clear water is also vastly different to the super clarity the experienced diver is looking for — and hoping for. So once again it comes back to getting as much information as you can before you depart. If possible, make your arrangements with an organisation that specialises in diving holidays and understands the needs of divers.

DIVE 1 ENGLISH CHANNEL: The Eddystone Reef and the Wreck of the S. S. James Eagan Layne by Horace Dobbs

A photographer peers through the seaweed-covered superstructure of the *James Eagan Layne*. (Photo: Horace Dobbs.)

During the Second World War the demand for ships of all kinds was enormous. German U-boats sank Allied ships faster than British yards could build them. So President Roosevelt stepped in and approved an emergency plan for the construction of new vessels. With the thrust that typified American industry at the time, production lines were set up based upon the same principles that had been so successfully developed for the mass manufacture of cars. 'Built by the mile and chopped off by the yard' was how the construction of the supply boats, called Li-

berty Ships, was described at the time. At the peak of production a complete ship was built from scratch in a few weeks.

The Liberty Ships were based upon a British design. They were slow and vulnerable; over 200 of them were sunk in World War II, 50 of them on their maiden voyages. Although the Liberty Ships were not designed for long service they had to be sufficiently seaworthy to withstand Atlantic gales. The Delta shipbuilding yard in Newhaven was created to build these disposable ships. Thirteen thousand people were employed in the yard which opened in 1941 and was closed in 1945. During that time it produced 32 Liberty Tankers, 24 Liberty Colliers and an impressive 132 Liberty Ships for carrying general cargo.

One of these was named the *James Eagan Layne;* she was launched sideways into the Mississippi River, on 2nd December 1944, just 40 days after work had started. The hull was not riveted, being made instead from steel-plates welded together. She was 422ft 8ins long, with a beam of 57ft and a depth of 34ft 8ins. Her draft was quoted with microscopic precision as 27ft 7^7/8ins. The *James Eagan Layne* was powered by two boiler engines, built by the Joshua Henry Ironworks of Sunnydale in California, which gave her a maximum speed of 11 knots. Allowing 16 days for fitting-out, the *James Eagan Layne* was ready for active service with a displacement of 7,176 tons on 18th December 1944. She was named in honour of a local seaman who lost his life as a result of his vessel being torpedoed.

When she set sail on her maiden voyage nobody could have forseen the ironic fate that was ahead of her.

She safely crossed the Atlantic and berthed in Barry, South Wales. Then, loaded with railway stock, pickaxe heads, jeeps, lorries and an assortment of spare parts for tanks, the *James Eagan Layne* set sail again to back-up the Allied invasion in Europe. She sailed round Land's End and into the English Channel, bound for Ghent in Belgium. But the *James Eagan Layne* never reached her destination. At noon precisely on 21st March 1945, as she passed over the submerged pinnacles of West Rutts near the Eddystone Reef off the Devonshire Coast, a torpedo ripped into her hull. Fortunately it was foggy and the U-1195 failed to hit her with another torpedo which would almost certainly have been a death blow. Tugs rushed to her aid to tow her into Plymouth, but their efforts were to no avail. When it was obvious that she would sink before reaching

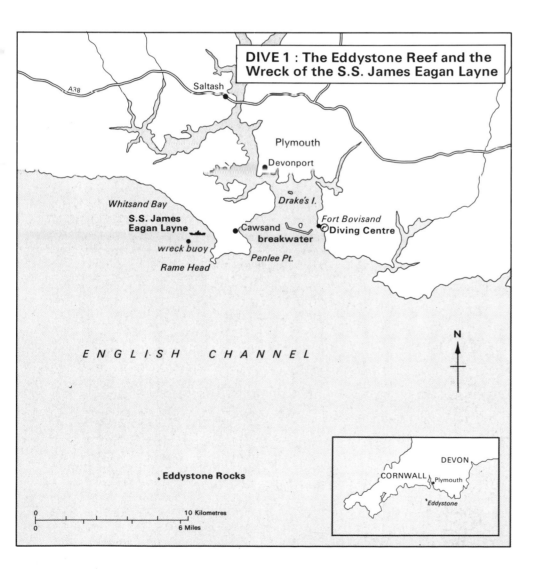

DIVE 1 : The Eddystone Reef and the Wreck of the S.S. James Eagan Layne

A diver hovers over an open hold on the *James Eagan Layne*. (Photo: Horace Dobbs.)

the dockyard the Liberty Ship was towed into Whitesand Bay which lies just to the West of Plymouth Sound. The exact location where she sank was recorded in the official record of wartime losses books of Lloyd's as: 50 13 3ON 4 14W. The crew of 42 and the 27 servicemen onboard were all saved.

The German U-Boat responsible for sinking the *James Eagan Layne* was herself destroyed sixteen days later by depth charges delivered from the *H.M.S. Watchman*.

The official accounts of the loss of the *James Eagan Layne* describe her as 'beached', although the charts indicate a depth of 24m at the place where she finally came to rest, sitting on the seabed on an even keel. Thus the hull was completely submerged at all states of the tide, but the top of the mast was always above the water and this enabled the wreck to be located easily. As she was well away from the major lanes used by shipping into and out of Plymouth the sunken vessel was not considered a hazard and was not therefore demolished. With other work of a much more pressing nature to deal with, salvage oper-

ations were not commenced until 12th May 1953. The scrap value of the vessel was far less than the cost of recovering it from the seabed. So after most of the cargo had been removed the *James Eagan Layne* was left as a monument to the extravagance of war. A wreck buoy was placed on the seaward side of the ship to warn passing ships of her presence.

To the undersea inhabitants of Whitesand Bay the *James Eagan Layne* was like a brand new piece of real estate — an artificial reef with living quarters for the myriads of life forms that were carried to the vessel as plankton in the currents. The outside of the ship was soon colonised by an immense variety of plant and animal life forms whilst the inside provided a safe refuge for fish. And with plenty of holes into which crustaceans could crawl, the *James Eagan Layne* became a popular place for inshore fishermen to set their lobster pots.

I first dived the *James Eagan Layne* in July 1967 on a filming expedition. The film, provisionally entitled 'Operation Nightdive', was commissioned by the BBC as a sequel to a very successful film entitled 'Neptune's Needle'

I had made with the Oxford Underwater Research Group and written about in *The Great Diving Adventure* published by The Oxford Illustrated Press. The new film was to be centred around the Eddystone Lighthouse and would reveal how life under the sea changed when darkness fell. We did not intend to confine our filming exclusively to the natural reefs of Eddystone. I also wanted to show what happened at night on an artificial reef in the form of a shipwreck, the *James Eagan Layne.*

The expedition got off to a very inauspicious start. The Brixham trawler which we had chartered to provide a floating base for the filming project, mysteriously developed engine failure the night before the diving team were to set off from various parts of Britain to converge on Dartmouth where she was berthed.

The situation was worsened when I was told when I arrived at fellow camerman John Eveleigh's house near Oxford that our above-water Bell and Howell camera wasn't working. After many phone calls we located an alternative Bolex camera which we could hire in Bath. We set off in pouring rain and arrived just three minutes before the shop shut.

The camera safely loaded in the car, we set off for a pub in Devon where I had arranged to meet those team members I had managed to contact. But by the time we arrived the pub was shut and there was no sign of them anywhere. Faced with the prospect of no divers, no boat and no bed I rang a friend who ran the Boatel in Cawsand, Cornwall, who offered to put us up for the night. It was 1.30 am when we got there and Frank had waited up for us. 'Have a drink on the house' he said with a cheery smile 'You both look as if you need it.'

A few hours later the sun rose into a clear blue sky. Roadside messages for the group were displayed by the AA and the RAC on the Exeter by-pass. Every possible contact was telephoned and asked to post a notice or pass on the message: 'Operation Nightdive members — come to the Boatel at Cawsand.'

That done, now all we had to do was find a boat.

A local fisherman, Tony Jago, agreed to put himself and his boat the *Nor Rocker* at our disposal, night and day, for a week. By lunchtime I had re-written the story and we started filming in Cawsand. By the evening the entire group had assembled and we squeezed them all into the Boatel. I outlined the film schedule to them. The first part of our plan was for John and myself to do a day's filming at Eddystone Lighthouse.

The reason for the presence of the Eddystone Lighthouse was the reef upon which it defiantly stood. The rocks were a hazard to shipping in the English Channel and most

On the bow of the *James Eagan Layne* there is a point where the seaweeds cease and Dead Men's fingers grow in profusion. (Photo: Horace Dobbs.)

specifically to vessels heading for Plymouth. I had become fascinated by the epic stories of the lighthouse and the men who designed, built and operated them which were dramatically retold in Fred Majdalany's book *The Red Rocks of Eddystone*. The first lighthouse on the site took 3 years to build and was completed in 1699. It was an elaborate and ornate structure with many features that would not have looked out of place adorning an onshore folly. It was designed by a Henry Winstanley who built palaces of entertainment, and enthusiastically applied his flair for exotic design and shownmanship to his plans for the first permanent lighthouse to be constructed on a tidal reef 12 miles offshore. When construction was complete the outside of the lighthouse was decorated and embellished in a manner appropriate to a great and ingenious showman.

When questioned, as he frequently was, about the ability of his lighthouse to survive winter gales, he would reply that he asked nothing better than to be inside it during 'the greatest storm that ever was'. On the 26th November 1703 his wish was granted. It was the night of the 'The Great Storm' — the greatest recorded storm in British history. By daybreak the next morning there was no sign that the lighthouse had ever existed apart from a few stumps of iron sprouting from the reef.

During our undersea forays we looked for pieces of wreckage that might have conceivably come from the first lighthouse, but found nothing we could positively identify. Such was the force of that and many subsequent storms that most of the stones used in its construction were probably scattered under the sea like chaff in the wind.

John and I spent a night in the present lighthouse which was built from interlocking granite blocks and completed by Douglass in 1882. We filmed the keepers at work during the night, and in the morning I stood alone on the platform surrounding the lantern on the top of the lighthouse. Inside the strong glass windows I could see the huge tower of lenses and prisms, partly draped with cloth to prevent them from concentrating the rays of the sun which was rising in the east. It was a beautiful moment. I held onto the red railings, looked down and was briefly mesmerised by the gently pulsing necklace of white foam that encircled the reef. From far, far below came the intermittent swish of the slowly heaving sea. The shadow of the lighthouse stretched like an unrolled purple carpet across the bright blue ocean. Close to the reef the sea was darker and I could see the forest of olive-green kelp above which shoals of fish roamed and were occasionally attacked by marauding seabirds that fell like white arrows out of the cloudless sky. In the middle of my reverie I was joined by one of the lighthousemen who came to see if any birds had been stranded on the platform during the night. He told me many birds used the lantern gallery as a rest-stop on their migrations.

Later that morning the *Nor Rocker* came dancing over the water from Cawsand to take us off. When we had filmed a free-flooding submarine that we towed behind the boat it was time to turn our attention to the *James Eagan Layne*. We motored round Rame Head and joined the small group of boats that were clustered round the king post, which projected above the water. It was the height of the season and holiday makers were taking advantage of the calm weather to do some fishing.

Our first task was to carry out a survey of the sunken Liberty Ship which we discovered was broken into two parts both of which rested on the flat sandy seabed, in a depth of just under 30 m. The seabed itself was typical of the area and was littered with broken shells and dotted with starfish. An occasional spider crab scuttled away when alerted by our presence.

Our newfound boatman, Tony Jago, fished for crabs and lobsters for a living. He worked the reefs around the Eddystone Lighthouse and knew the area intimately. With his knowledge of the currents, the times of slack water and the underwater topography he was able to take us into channels close to the rocks where other, less knowledgeable boatmen, would have been reluctant to venture. The reefs were rewarding to dive and in deep gulleys we found forests of Gorgonian Coral. Individual corals were roughly fan shaped with a maximum width of about two feet. They looked fragile, but were very tough and were firmly cemented to the rocks. Although they looked like branches of trees they consisted of colonies of animals that fed on the plankton suspended in the sea. To do this most efficiently they spread their fans perpendicular to the prevailing currents. Thus, although we dived at slack water we could tell in which direction the current would run by looking at the way the coral fans were arranged. Water selectively filters out the red component of white light. If a red disc is taken down it appears to turn purple at depths of more than 10 m. Yet some of the Gorgonian Corals we saw at depths of 20 to 30 m appeared to us to be distinctly red. The conclusion I drew from this observation was that the corals were somehow generating the light themselves. I wondered if they were absorbing high energy blue light (which is not strongly absorbed by water), converting it to red light, and utilising the energy released in the process.

Facing page: **A diver uses a knife to clear away encrustation. What he finds underneath may be rock or a bronze cannon.** (Photo: Horace Dobbs.)

Top left: **A Spider crab. The number seen off the Devonshire Coast varies considerably from year to year.** (Photo: Horace Dobbs.)

Top right: **An Edible crab. Will a diver take it home for tea or leave it to grow bigger?** (Photo: Horace Dobbs.)

Above: **A Dahlia anemone looks like a flower but is an animal that captures its prey with stinging tentacles.** (Photo: Horace Dobbs.)

The area also abounded with yellow sponges — but the colours were lost on the film, which we were shooting in black and white negative.

The bow of the *James Eagan Layne* pointed north and the rails provided excellent anchorages for luxuriant fronds of kelp and other seaweeds which barely moved in the still water. Most of the ship's surface between the holdfasts of the seaweeds was coated with barnacles and other small shellfish. But the iron was slowly oxidising and shedding rust which took with it the unfortunate molluscs that were clamped on top. The seaweeds stopped abruptly at about ten metres and gave way to a profusion of sealife that encrusted much of the outside of the hull — most prominent amongst them being Sea Anemones that covered the welded ironplates like a carpet of flowers. One pair of divers took with them a reel of fluorescent red plastic tape, of the type tied between posts to mark out road works. The red tape was attached to different parts of the superstructure to act as guide lines during our proposed night dive.

As well as our unexpected change in circumstances our filming plans also had to be flexible to cope with the vagaries of the weather. When the wind turned to the south west we had to abandon our night dive on the *James Eagan Layne* and filmed a huge Angler Fish in Cawsand Bay instead.

Despite all the setbacks, by the end of a week in Cawsand we had exposed enough film to provide the basis for a half-hour television programme. The film was processed, and during the evenings of the following winter I extracted all of the useable footage and spliced it together to follow a storyline. When I had done so and shown it to Brian Branston at the BBC we both agreed it could do with another unique component to lift the action at the end of the story and give it a more dramatic ending. I agreed to shoot some additional sequences during the summer of 1967 and was absolutely certain I had found the necessary magic ingredient when I heard about a friendly wild dolphin off the coast of Scotland. Thankfully, films are about creating illusions and by using artistic licence I could 'move' the dolphin to Cornwall, and have him swimming excitedly alongside the yellow submarine and over the kelp of the Eddystone Reef.

To obtain the highest qualification in the British Sub-Aqua Club — that of First Class Diver — one of the trials candidates have to undergo is to take a practical exam which consists of organising a diving expedition with a specific purpose. When a diver, John Holdsworth, applied to take the exam, I was appointed his examiner. With only the minimum of persuasion from me he agreed to organise a weekend diving expedition from

Yorkshire to locate and film the wild dolphin (called Charlie) who was rumoured to frequent the St Abbs/Eyemouth area in south-east Scotland. John hired a local fishing boat in the beautiful and quiet little village of Burnmouth and we set out in search of the dolphin.

We found Charlie off a reef in the entrance to Eyemouth harbour. He was most co-operative and swam up to my cine camera before swimming away to frolic with the divers. He mimicked their swimming motions and I felt for the first time the joy and excitement of relating directly to an animal which as a diver was superior to us in every way — whether we attained the elevated status of First Class Diver or not.

I had absolutely no knowledge at the time that a meeting with another dolphin off the Isle of Man would completely change my life and that I would eventually become known as 'The Dolphin Man' for my studies of these creatures in their natural environment and also write three books about them: *Follow a Wild Dolphin*, *Save the Dolphins* and *Tale of Two Dolphins*. What I did know was that I had got just the ingredient I needed to bring my television film to an exciting climax.

Once home, I edited the new footage I had shot into the rough-cut and sent it to the BBC. Brian Branston agreed that we had the basis for a really compelling programme. There was just one small snag. The BBC were going into colour and he had just received a directive from on high stating that all future program-mes must be made in colour. 'Operation Nightdive' which included, the *James Eagan Layne*, the Eddystone Reef and Charlie had been shot entirely in black and white. In many ways the saga of 'Operation Nightdive' was ironically similar to that of the *James Eagan Layne*. The film was torpedoed when the owner of the Brixham trawler welched on his agreement. We mounted a valiant rescue attempt and almost saved it.

I still have the rough-cut and it sits on a cupboard, rather like the *James Eagan Layne* still sits on the seabed — a snippet of history caught in a time warp. But who knows, perhaps, one day, it will be salvaged like the *Mary Rose*. From a diving standpoint the *James Eagan Layne* was a more interesting wreck to dive on than the flagship of Henry VIII before she was successfully raised from the murky waters of the Solent. But whereas the *Mary Rose* has been restored, and can now be seen by the general public, the *James Eagan Layne* exhibition is only open to the divers who are prepared to travel out to see her where she sank. It has been suggested several times that the vessel should be flattened, but protests that

she is a unique and irreplaceable piece of contemporary maritime history have thankfully prevailed, and at present her future seems fairly secure.

If left undisturbed the wreckage could remain for centuries, but the sea will decide first how long the *James Eagan Layne* will retain the overall contours of a mid-twentieth-century merchant ship. She is being eaten away by rust and wave action which can certainly be felt on the superstructure, especially at low water. In the winter of 1977 a storm of exceptional ferocity hit the West Country and tore out the marker post. When divers relo-cated the vessel they reported that miraculou-sly the hull of the *James Eagan Layne* was still there and intact, but it looked in many parts as if it had been sand blasted. Most of the exotic life encrusting the metal hulk had been swept away; but nature is remarkably resilient, and by the end of the summer the *James Eagan Layne* was completely recolonised.

I have visited the *James Eagan Layne* several times since 1967, and like so much of British diving, each dive was a different experience. On the way to the wreck from Fort Bovisand on 10th July 1973 I encountered a basking shark about seven metres long. We im-mediately diverted the inflatable, ran ahead of its line of movement and stopped the engine. The huge shark continued its progression without changing course and swam close to us. When it was well past we started the engine and used the same tactic again, but this time I slipped into the water with my camera as soon as we stopped. The shark swam directly towards me. I saw the huge mouth open wide and felt that I could have stood up inside it as the giant fish moved forward sieving plankton from the water. I took one picture of the gaping cavernous mouth and swam as fast as I could alongside the shark. I saw the gill slits open wide like a huge venetian blind, as the shark sped past me with barely a movement of its tail. I stopped finning and gasped for breath. As I remained still in the water I was briefly enveloped in a storm cloud of mackerel, flashing in the sunlight as they snapped at food particles. Then, as quickly as they had come, they were gone and the inflatable came and picked me up.

The visit to the sunken vessel was one of the dives on a practical course on underwater photography organised by the Underwater Centre at Fort Bovisand. It was the first opportunity I had to use the 15 mm lens introduced by Nikon for its Nikonos camera. Up to that time I had always used supplemen-tary lenses for wide-angle pictures. My partner and I dived at exactly slack water and the sea

Below: **This sponge and Gorgonian coral are firmly attached to a rocky outcrop.** (Photo: Horace Dobbs.)

Bottom: **The aptly-named Lion's Mane jellyfish.** (Photo: Horace Dobbs.)

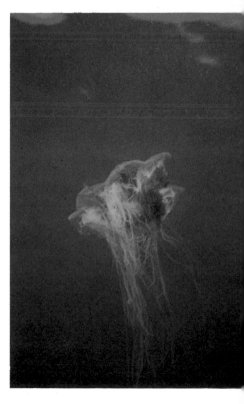

was calm. The seaweeds were still and when we reached the bows we allowed ourselves to drift slowly towards the seabed. When we reached the depth where the seaweeds stopped growing I took two pictures — one with flash and one without. The one taken with flash was covered with speckles of light reflected by the plankton suspended in the still water. The other picture, although not quite so rich in colours, was not blemished in this way and made a first-class cover picture for my book on snorkelling and skindiving.

Departure from the *James Eagan Layne* was delayed because my fellow underwater photographer, Geoff Harwood, lost one of his Nikonos cameras and we used our remaining air searching the wreck. Many months later it was brought up in a trawl net and because he'd had the foresight to put a sticker with his name and address on the inside, it was returned to him. Two years later he exhibited the lost camera at a photographic function we were both attending. One part of the alloy body had been rubbed away and the remainder was covered with the twisting calcarious tunnels of tube worms that usually only grow on submerged rocks. Despite the encrustations it still worked.

Several years after this incident I returned again to the *James Eagan Layne*, this time with a BBC film producer, Duncan Gibbins. We were working on a series of short films called 'Fish-eye view of Britain' which were eventually transmitted on a daily magazine programme called 'Nationwide'. We had already been out to the Eddystone Lighthouse on-board a diving boat called *British Diver* and I filmed Duncan at the interface, showing the lighthouse towering into the sky before pointing my camera downwards towards the kelp-covered reef beneath us. Duncan was relatively new to diving and the excitement and tension he undoubtedly felt was transmitted to me, and eventually through me to the viewers. His apprehension was most strongly expressed in his eyes when we sank through an open hatch into the hold of the *James Eagan Layne* which was still littered with assorted pieces of cargo. We moved slowly so as not to stir up the silt. The powerful light carried by Duncan pierced the gloom like a spotlight. Above us the opening through which we had passed was like a luminous green window framed in black. We found a crab, already minus several legs, pathetically trying to escape from the nylon fishing line in which it was entwined. Duncan patiently unwound the almost invisible cord and I filmed the released crab scurrying away amidst a pile of pick axe heads that were coated in brown silt.

A shoal of Pollack acted as our guide as we toured the spooky underwater scrapyard. Duncan found a spoked iron wheel about four feet in diameter. The uppermost surface was covered in soft brown silt. When Duncan gently raised it the powerful camera lights revealed that the underside was encrusted with sponges and bryozoans which glowed like jewels. When I turned off the lights we were plunged into darkness and we swam slowly towards the pale green glow that indicated the way out. We weaved our way between twisted metal spars and plates before drifting slowly upwards into the outside world which seemed unnaturally bright to our dark-adapted eyes.

Duncan definitely preferred it outside and shone his light onto the mass of marine life encrusting the welded metal sheets of the hull. Near the bow we found the tube through which the anchor chain once ran. Now the empty tunnel stretched from the hull to the deck and peering up through it was like looking towards the surface through an underwater telescope. When the movie lights were switched on the walls blazed with colour —revealing that this special ecological niche was fully colonised by sea life.

The film I made with Duncan was about shipwrecks and we compared the *James Eagan Layne* with other wrecks in the English Channel. One of them was the *Torrey Canyon* which resulted in the greatest ecological disaster in history from an oil tanker when she struck the Seven Stones between Land's End and the Scilly Isles and released thousands of tons of oil into the sea. In an effort to set fire to the oil slick the stricken vessel was bombed with incendiaries. When we found her remains in over thirty metres of water it was as if the giant tanker had been made of cardboard, torn up, and the pieces scattered over the seabed.

To get the feel of British wreck diving you could not do better than start with the *James Eagan Layne;* it is a classic dive.

But as always in the English Channel the diving conditions on site can be as unpredictable as the notoriously fickle British climate. If I was to recommend the best time to go I would say June and July. However there will be rare days in December when conditions are better than in the height of summer. So whenever you go it will be a gamble. It's just that the odds will be much more in your favour in mid-summer. Although the Eddystone Reef is well known it is visited by relatively few divers, and much of it remains to be explored.

DIVE 2 BRISTOL CHANNEL: Lundy Island
by Richard Oldfield and Christine Williams

In a pattern of islands like Great Britain, names like seas, channels, and firths skirmish frequently for importance in a patchwork of ocean mapped out by history and legend. Thus, the Bristol Channel, so named, holds a volume of water greater than places some men name seas. This wide wedge of estuary lies embraced, to the north, by the mountainous torso of Wales and to the south by the long limb of Devon and Cornwall. Far out in this channel, where its waters eventually merge with the Atlantic, lies a solitary island. Alone and exposed, and often wreathed in mist, Lundy seems, from the nearest mainland, a real fantasy island on the horizon.

Lundy is said to be an offspring of two old Norse words, *Lund* and *Ey*, which respectively mean 'Puffin' and 'Island'. Just three miles long, by under a mile wide, Lundy's spicy history belies its size. For at least three thousand years men have tried to make Lundy their home. Early colonists left their flint tools and Stone Age settlements to mark their passing. The Vikings too were to leave their mark in Lundy's legend; the island is spoken of in the famous Orkneyinga Saga.

The 16th century saw Lundy become popular as a pirate's paradise and many notorious rascals changed its fame to infamy. From then to this day its rocks have become storystones

Lundy Island from the south—a real fantasy island on the horizon. (Photo: Rico.)

filled with fact and fiction. Lundy's legends call about 15,000 visitors a year to explore her coves and rocks for the haunting echoes of piracy and shipwreck.

But Lundy has another face, a face that these tourists never see. Where her bleak outline plunges down to meet the sea, the story doesn't end. Lundy's ancient profile goes on to penetrate the hidden world beneath the sea. Here her battered boulders become densely populated reefs. Underwater her scars and crevices become caves and grottoes of hidden beauty dressed in a fairytale mantle of vivid and exotic marine life. Until the invention of the aqualung, this hidden landscape lay silently beneath the waves, waiting to be discovered.

The British Isles straddle so many oceanic frontiers that the underwater landscape is a picture of different territories and distinct communities. For example, the currents which sweep the south and west coasts are rich in the nutrients that support the gaudy array of species to be found in the Mediterranean and around the western coasts of southern Europe. These warm currents eventually mix with, and are cooled by, their colder Arctic counterparts, producing a unique cocktail. Lundy's strategic position makes it a wild frontier town, sheltering northern or Arctic species as renegades at the extreme south end of their distribution, and large proportions of southern Atlantic species at the extreme north end of their territories. So, the picture is one of Arctic species skirmishing with Mediterranean, a clash of national colour that presents subtleties and surprise.

Lundy's story as a divers' island began in 1969, when a close encounter with a marine biologist, Keith Hiscock, and a charming alien made news in the marine biology world. For beneath Lundy's waters Keith found a small visitor, far from home — the brilliant yellow Sunset Cup Coral that had previously been reported in only one other location outside the Mediterranean. Yet there it was off Lundy, thriving in profusion and soon quite a list of rare and unusual residents were found to be flourishing in the cool green depths.

Nowadays Britain's divers are an enthusiastic audience, for whom the inhabitants of Lundy are willing performers. For marine naturalists, underwater photographers and scuba-sightseers, the island's undersea residents can be counted upon to provide one of the most colourful shows to be found anywhere in north-western Europe. Most marine animals, Lundy's included, are invertebrates i.e. animals without backbones. The skeleton which holds us backboned creatures together against the force of gravity is a handicap for them. In the dense, supportive medium of water, where internal scaffolding is less necessary, animal life has found itself free to explore the outer limits of organic architecture. Of the stars on Lundy's stage, the real show-stoppers of this invertebrate clan, must be those exotic artistes — the corals. Although the water is rich in nutrients the prevailing temperature is too cool for the reef-building corals that occur in the tropics. So Britain's native corals are not reef builders, but they are true stony corals. They build individual limestone cups, which provide them with shelter and also earn them their common names, cup corals. The largest of these handsome animals living on Lundy is the beautiful Sunset Cup Coral *Leptopsammia* which grows to the height of an egg cup. Its body is furnished with a crown of tentacles, each studded with hundreds of tiny and deadly effective stinging cells. When you must live rooted to one spot you have to come up with some ruthless ways to go shopping for dinner! The Devonshire Cup Coral, *Caryophyllia smithi* although not as vividly hued as The Sunset Cup Coral, nevertheless achieves, with its delicate semi-transparency, a beauty of another order. The Star Coral, *Balanophyllia,* completes the trio. Although generally the smallest of the cup corals to be found in this area, it is no less of a living jewel than its neighbours.

The Gorgonion Sea Fans are another act in the coral circus. Britain's representatives of this elegant troupe don't grow to the enormous proportions of their cousins in warmer waters. They are, nevertheless identical in form and nature. From a single basic stalk they grow and branch, branch and grow, until the colony of tiny animals from which the whole fan is formed stands erect into the current. There they stand, like so many catchers mitts, their fingers spread across the prevailing tidal movement to filter the nutrients from the rich waters most efficiently. Growing at about a centimetre a year, a 300-mm fan needs 30 years to reach this height. Gorgonian Sea Fans are not uncommon around the south-west coast of Britain, but nowhere are they found as abundantly as on Lundy.

Still within the coral clan, soft corals, or Dead Men's Fingers, are common in British waters. The prince of these however, *Alcyonium glomeratum* which reaches a maximum size of about 30cm grows most abundantly on Lundy producing arguably the nearest vision to a tropical reef that British waters can produce. Again, not a single creature this, but a colony of small white anemone-like polyps, all living together in a crimson-coloured common supportive structure. Although it has the same survival plan as the Gorgonion Sea Fan it is visually much more opulent.

Dominated though the underwater world might be by invertebrate life forms, it's a fact that to moving animals like divers, other moving life attracts our first attention. Here Lundy's rock and crannies stand out again as a playground for the swimmers, the crawlers and a host of other animate underwater performers. Fish, crabs and lobsters are the divers' constant companions, while additional escort service may be provided by seals, dolphins and basking sharks. Perhaps not just basking sharks may be sharing the deeps of Lundy with visiting divers. Hartland Point, 11 miles away, just happens to be one of Britain's favourite Porbeagle shark fishing sites. 'Porbies' in excess of 300 lb are more than occasionally caught in the straits. Luckily, the same temperate water conditions which prove unfavourable to reef-coral growth also seem unfavourable to the nastier side of shark disposition. Still, it is possible encounters like this that add further spice to diving around Lundy.

As every diver knows, things that float on water often finish up under water. And being in a busy shipping channel Lundy has managed to collect for herself an impressive list of shipwrecks. The first recorded wreck was that of the sailing vessel *Wye*. Built in 1796 she was wrecked on Lundy that same year with the loss of all on board.

The most memorable on the list of Lundy's maritime misadventures must be the wreck of the battleship *Montagu*. So great was the navigational error that brought the *Montagu* to her end on Lundy's rocks in 1906, that the officer in command thought she had foundered at Hartland Point on the mainland. A navigational error, it was to turn out, of court martial proportions. Most of the ship's heavy armour was salvaged, but a great deal of her ammunition was left where now only divers can see. Twelve-inch shells still lay stacked in places under twisted bulkheads and plates. Some lie in the open, still live, an awesome reminder that some wrecks are look-don't-touch dives.

The wreck of *Robert* however, is the top contender for favourite wreck amongst Lundy's diving regulars. This 300-ton Panamanian cargo vessel was loaded with a cargo of anthracite duff from Cynheidre Colliery when she left Cardiff. Not long out of port she developed a list to starboard as her cargo shifted and she limped into Lundy's shelter on 22nd January 1975. The Clovelly lifeboat took off the crew who watched their vessel sink slowly, stern first, shortly after noon. The little 150-ft coaster now lies in about 90ft of water

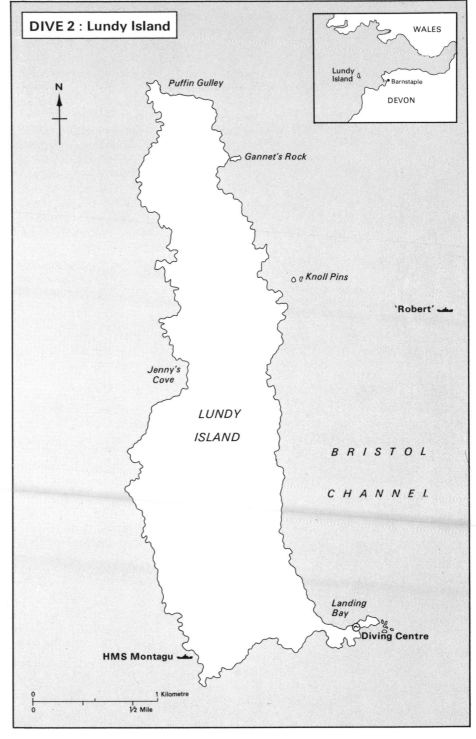

DIVE 2 : Lundy Island

just over a mile off Lundy's east coast. Still largely intact, the *S.S. Robert* rests on her starboard side. She is often buoyed, but, lying on an open gravel bottom the wreck is easily traced with simple sounding equipment. The wreck's proximity to Lundy has allowed her to become an outpost of the island's rich and colourful living community. Now the *Robert* is

a man-made reef, much of her surface obscured by forests of plumose anemones, and she is certainly a wreck you would regret having visited without an underwater camera.

We have often dived together around Lundy and have many happy memories of times spent exploring the outer rim where it descends into the sea. But there is one dive which shines out more brightly as a highlight than all of the others. It happened one sunny afternoon during a one-week holiday with a group of six divers. We eagerly loaded the boat and set off from Diving Beach on the east coast of this magical isle. A 10-minute journey gazing up at the cliffs and their birdlife brought us to the two inner Knoll Pins, clearly visible about six feet above the surface. We had to search carefully for our target — the outer pin. It was just visible below the surface. The boatman was conscious that he must not anchor as this would damage the slow growing delicate nature of the marine life.

Kitting-up was quick and easy and aided somewhat by photographers having, by tradition and sheer threat, the right to be the first

pair in the water! We checked our equipment and dropped over the inflatable side, holding on whilst bulky camera equipment was handed down to us. The boatman had placed us near to the outer pin. A gentle swim took us to the east side of a submarine, kelp-covered pinnacle.

Here, three metres down amongst the safety of the seaweed fronds, we check our cameras again and gaze out horizontally at the clear green water with its rainbow residents of jellyfish pulsating on some predetermined journey. We are now ready for the goodies waiting below. We carry with us powerful torches to show up the true colours. Rolls of film and fully charged flashes will enable us to relive our journey into this oasis when we are back home in Liverpool.

Signalling to each other we dive and, as the kelp forest thins and gradually disappears, we become aware that this really is a special place. Amongst the animals that live in this shallow zone are large and colourful invertebrates, anemones and sponges of pastel and brilliant hues. Soon we see the Gorgonion Sea Fans

Facing page: **Christine with a 12-inch shell on the wreck of the *Montagu.*** (Photo: Rico.)

Facing page, bottom: **Gorgonia Sea fans grow in profusion off Lundy.** (Photo: Rico.)

Below: **Christine gently handles an octopus.** (Photo: Rico.)

Top: **The extended feathery tentacles of a soft coral.**

Top, middle: **A profusion of Jewel anemones.**

Bottom, middle: **Sunset Cup corals.**

Bottom: **The Angler fish spends much of its time lying in wait for prey.**
(Photos: Rico.)

with their branching arms spread decorously across the current flow to catch their food.

We descend the outer face of this smaller seaward Knoll Pin to find a ledge favoured by photographers. Here we sit gently without disturbing the silt and look around this great amphitheatre of sea fans and red sea fingers. This is a classic setting for a wide-angle photograph with much delicate beauty in the foreground and a diver swimming down through a starburst of sunlit waters above. But today we are concentrating on close-up pictures. So after a brief sojourn, we travel on downwards across large vertical facets of granite. They are covered with Sunset Cup Corals. We hover beside the wall like humming birds and then delicately position ourselves to capture Nature's unbeatable artistry with our cameras.

Finning gently northwards, the vertical face becomes more sloping. Carefully choosing the areas to stop and stare, we notice that the life has become more stratified into special horizontal zones with hydroids and large yellow branching sponges. Several large male Cuckoo Wrasse with their brilliant blue colouration patrol this territory, friendly and curious, posing for photographs and pointing the way for the next stage of our dive.

We now leave the north face and turn westwards around the pin to face the island. This is one of the deepest parts of the diving area. At about 25 metres our journey is suddenly interrupted by a natural fault in the granite which severs this outer pin from top to bottom. It forms a natural fissure between one and two metres wide and about 12 metres long. This is the canyon.

Here the Knoll Pin Nature Trail gives the diver a choice. He can either swim through the canyon, or continue round the north end of the landward side. The latter route has its own special beauty with rare exotic beauties in grottos and overhangs, where great care has to be taken not to exhale bubbles which would upset the delicate balance of their environment. It almost has the flavour of a night dive, as the darkened crevices and grottos persuade some beautiful creatures to show their majesty in daytime. But we will save that for another dive. We have chosen the canyon.

Remembering to be careful about the easily disturbed sediment we enter in single file, pleased and relieved that all of the other divers have chosen the alternative route. We adjust our buoyancy so we float neutrally and move with the minimum of finning.

On our passage through the canyon there is much to see. Incongruous Sea Cucumbers, relatives of the starfish, wend their way imperceptibly along the base. Above them the walls are covered with Jewel Anemones in their irridescent colours and the special Devonshire Cup Corals. Whilst gazing at this variety of form and shade we see a slight movement which draws our attention to a large Angler Fish resting on the sediment, waiting for his prey. We slide a hand under him and lift him slowly clear of the silt. His open mouth and his grotesque features make a grand display for the camera. Then we gently replace him to continue spending his time with the lobsters, crawfish and octopus for whom this canyon is also home.

Continuing our journey and peering closely at the wall we see a splendid variety of sea slugs. None of them are more than a few centimetres long, yet the colours and patterns of their tiny forms challenge anything that science fiction can produce. But we will only be able to appreciate fully their extraordinary shapes and outlandish colours when we see our photographs enlarged.

We are nearing the end of the canyon. We check our air and find that our film has all too quickly been used. The gravel bottom of the canyon fills, angling us up towards the shallower kelp zone again. We glance upwards to see a shadow overhead. A large Tope, one of our British sharks, has been watching us from above. An instinctive reach for the camera reveals we are out of film. In any case he senses our interest and speeds smoothly out of sight.

Emerging back into the kelp zone, we can see the surface of the water and hear our boat engine. Signalling to each other we slowly rise, glancing below at the darkening scene. Surfacing, we see our diligent boatman looking for our bubbles. Marker buoys are not recommended on this site, so we are glad the sea has remained calm. He spots us as soon as our heads appear. Back in the boat with the other divers we exchange our experiences, excitedly trying to remember all the details of colour and interest along our 150-m route.

The dive ends, as all on Lundy must when the tide is in, with a climb up to the lighthouse above the Dive Beach. The group of de-kitted divers thin out in order of fitness up the tractor path that felt like a one-in-two incline on the first day of our holiday and has now reduced to a one-in-three.

At the top of our climb the east coast shoreline spreads out, hundreds of feet below. We stagger into the Marisco Tavern for a well-earned drink and revel in the memories of the dive just past. We plan the next — a night dive at Knoll Pins perhaps?

DIVE 3 ATLANTIC OCEAN: The Skelligs by Des Lavelle

The Skellig Rocks are two towering crags jutting out of the Atlantic about seven miles off the south-west coast of Ireland. Their isolation and frequent inaccessibility are part of their great attraction. Their magnificent seabird colonies add further magic. Their rich archaeological heritage is world-famous, and, if they need a further attribute, their diving opportunities are quite wonderful.

These various aspects of Skellig should not be taken individually. You must spend at least one whole day out there to experience just part of what the islands have to offer, above and below the water. But visiting these westerly outposts of Europe is subject to the vagaries of the weather, which is notoriously capricious. Even in the height of summer the sea conditions can make the boat journey uncomfortable, to say the least, and lying alongside the small jetty at Skellig Michael impossible.

There are plenty of good dives off the Kerry Coast with numerous inlets and islands to choose from according to the weather conditions. But the Skelligs is the destination all divers coming to the region want to reach. It is one of the classic dives of the world. So the question is will today be the day they can make it?

Looking out of the breakfast room window of the Valentia Island Diving Centre, one would bet that this MUST be the day for just any dive under the sun. The harbour, only 100 metres away, is mirror-calm. Not a cloud hangs in the sky. But these idyllic appearances do not necessarily add up to a perfect day on the Atlantic Ocean which lies restlessly outside the mouth of Valentia harbour on the south-west coast of Ireland.

While breakfast is being served, Des, the dive skipper, slips away for his almost ritualistic 'look at the weather' to see beyond the sheltered confines of the harbour and assess the true state of the Atlantic which, quite unpredictably, could well reflect the benign local conditions, or alternatively could well be rolling tormentedly from the effects of a storm seven or eight hundred miles away. The wavelength, the height, and the frequency of the waves, together with the local weather forecast, the state of the tide and a lifetime of local knowledge are all added together, and hopefully the print-out will be the right answer to everyone's question. And it is. The swell is down. The forecast is good. We shall sail at 10am.

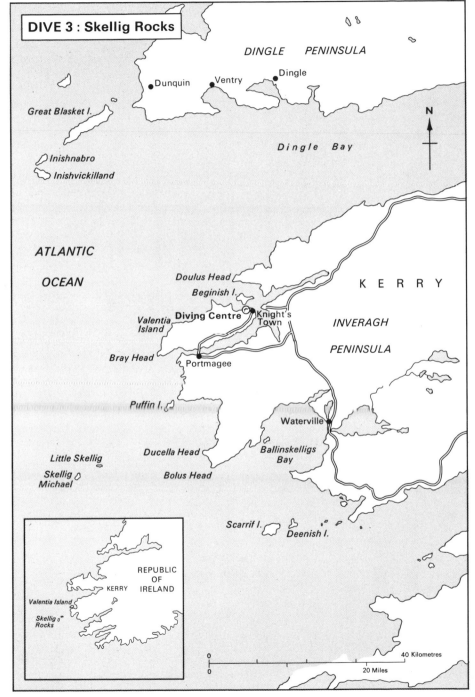

DIVE 3 : Skellig Rocks

Top: **Aerial view of Skellig Michael.** (Photo: Des Lavelle.)

Above: **Puffins on Skellig Michael.** (Photo: Horace Dobbs.)

Having imparted the good news that everything is 'go' the Skipper disappears again to attend to his own chores of fuelling and preparing the centre's diving boat *Béal Bocht* for the day's trip. This is the unspoken cue to get ourselves and our gear on board by the appointed time. No nursery, no pampering at Valentia Dive Centre. Just the very logical requirement that those who would dive the Atlantic must be of Atlantic calibre, must be able to operate the centre's compressors, must be able to take the responsibility of Dive Marshal, must be able to prod any would-be slowcoaches into line or assist any newcomers into the well-tried routine which keeps this small, family-run centre ticking over safely from Easter to mid-October and draws old clients back again and again.

The *Béal Bocht* is a ten-metre, 70-hp vessel, built in that sturdy displacement design which has evolved over centuries and takes every whim of the Atlantic into account. Capable of eight knots, she is fitted with radar, echosounder, VHF radiotelephone, medical oxygen, and a locker full of charts, local and national. On the two-hour trip from Valentia to Skellig, the skipper — pretending to abdicate all responsibility — is happy to give the least experienced members of the team every opportunity to practice the boat-handling and navigational skills which they have learned at long winter club lectures far from here. 'Our position is one mile south of Bray Head, our speed is eight knots and the tide is setting 350 degrees (true) at $1^1/_2$ knots. Assuming 4 degrees easterly deviation and zero wind drift, give compass course and E.T.A. Skellig.'

Bray Head falls behind. Puffin Island — a precious, 52-hectare bird sanctuary owned by the Irish Wildbird Conservancy, slides slowly by on the port hand, its citizens occupying the waters all around. Puffins to the right, puffins to the left, 10,000 pairs or more. Ahead, the twin peaks of Skellig Michael and Small Skellig beckon tantalisingly, seeming to come no nearer as we travel ever southwesterward!

'Shark!' shouts Hes from Holland, and all hearts beat a little faster as a dark blue triangular fin slips through the water — not with frightening speed, but with a studied laziness! No man-eater this, nor even a mackerel hunter. This is *Cetorhinus maximus*, the Basking Shark, a slow-moving monster of up to 10m in length which lives entirely on planktonic micro-life. The Basking Shark cruises this part of the coast in May and June; where from, nobody knows; where to, nobody cares. Once hunted for its liver and fins by Norwegian harpoon ships — and even by canvas-built rowing boats from Irish harbours, the 'Basker' now has relative peace to go on his annual pilgrimage with only the lesser hazard of salmon drift-nets to hinder him. Were we on a photographic shark hunt today — which is Hes's principal reason for returning to Ireland again and again — we would endeavour to plot the shark's course, motor some distance ahead, and deposit a line of diver cameramen across the expected path. With some luck, the shark at his slowest tick-over speed, which is still just too much for a hard-finning diver, would pass within camera range for some exciting photographs — provided that the sight of his cavernous, barn-door-sized mouth steadily approaching out of the gloom would not paralyse every finger and every limb!

'Gannets', said the skipper, pointing at the clouds of birds now obscuring the sky around the boat. This is the Small Skellig's claim to world fame, for every ledge of this ten-hectare, 150-m high crag is covered with gannets and gannets and gannets — 23,000 pairs of them! This island is another I.W.C. bird sanctuary — not that it needs such official designation, for Nature, in the shape of sheer cliffs and ever-moving sea has ensured that man shall never have a convenient foothold here. Small Skellig is strictly for the birds — and for the seals, the fifty or so Grey Seals, *Halichoerus grypus,* who find a home in the inhospitable caves and fissures around its base. Mere man, passing by in his little boat can but stare in humble amazement at this wonderful wildlife extravaganza.

Skellig Michael, final island in the chain, looms near at last. Two hundred and sixty

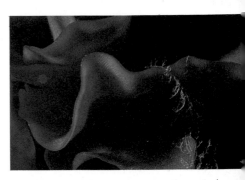

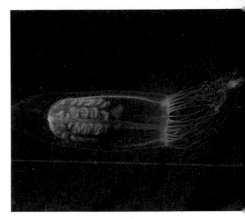

Top: **Ross Coral – Orange tinted and biscuit textured.** (Photo: Jos Audenaerd.)

Right: **A rare jellyfish pulses gently through the water off Skellig Michael.** (Photo: Jos Audenaerd.)

Below: **An adult Grey seal resting just above the water.** (Photo: Des Lavelle.)

metres in height, twenty hectares in area, this pinnacle of Old Red Sandstone is equally challenging in its steep cliffs. But mankind established a foothold here 1,500 years ago, constructing not one, but three stone stairways up the steep faces of the island, and, as a crowning triumph of the early Christian age, built a monastic village right at the top.

We land at a tiny jetty on the sheltered east side of Skellig Michael — a jetty built in 1820 as part of the Skellig lighthouse establishment, and maintained by them against all ravages of wind and weather ever since. After a two-hour boat trip it is a pleasure to be able to step ashore, stretch the limbs and enjoy the comfort of dry, steady land for changing into diving gear before venturing under water on the steep, stair-like faces of Skellig.

Wetsuits of 7mm thickness are the minimum requirement here. Dry suits are common too. The water temperature at the surface may be 16° in mid summer, but at the deeper levels — irrespective of season — it seldom exceeds 11 or 12°. Dive options are wide here at Skellig. Beside the jetty itself is a depth of 15m leading in steep steps to 30m or more . . . But who wants more when everything we need is at 25m or less —best light, best life, best colour, best temperature, best endurance? The main problem here for photographers is deciding which lens to take. Shall it be macro for anemones, wide angle for seals, or some lens in between? Michael from London has one solution: he dives with four cameras around his neck. At least he is ready for all occasions, but it does call for some acrobatic as well as photographic skills.

Billy and Leo from Dublin are into anemones.

Here at Skellig are avenues paved, wallpapered and roofed with Jewel Anemones in every conceivable hue of every imaginable colour. One could not begin to name them all, nor could one even describe the dazzling effect of playing a light along these multicoloured walls and ledges.

Jos and Danny from Belgium are on a seal hunt today — as they both have been on many frustrating days in past summer visits. It is an arduous quest — not in effort, but in patience, because the only way to catch a seal photographically under water is not to follow him — for this would be futile indeed — but to sink quietly to seven or eight metres, sit in a corner, and wait for the seals to come to you.

Come they will, but not in a slow, leisurely manner conducive to portrait photography. Rather they will dash momentarily into view, stare in wide-eyed, bewhiskered disbelief at the air-bubbling, light-shining, flash-popping creatures which have temporarily invaded their empire, and then, pivoting on a penny, slip away like the water itself through the cracks and fissures — only to reappear in a moment at a new vantage point for another tantalising glance. Total masters of their element, intensely curious and, fortunately, diver-friendly, they will sneak up behind a diver, peck at his fintips and suddenly disappear out of sight in less time that it takes for a man to look over his shoulder — much less focus and shoot a photograph.

Len and Diane from Penzance have found a small octopus and will follow it quietly around for the whole dive, admiring its variety of colour changes and camouflage skills as it settles on one background or another. The occurrence of octopus at this latitude (52 degrees north) is some small proof that the Gulf Stream is a very real influence on this coast.

On the other hand, tropical corals are rare, but at 30m on the southern face of Skellig there is adequate compensation for the colour-conscious eye in great cabbage patches of orange-tinted, biscuit-texture Ross Coral, *Pentapora foleacea*. And down here the detail-seeking microscopic eye will also enjoy the myriad of minute creatures living in their safe ecosystem within the coral's protective folds.

Clive, Rick and Bob from Surrey, wreck hunters extraordinary, are slowly circling the six cast-iron cannons and two ancient anchors which are all that can be seen of an unidentified 18th-century Skellig shipwreck. At 35m there isn't much time for more than a preliminary glance, and although the large gravel bed below the cannon ledges should be an interesting project, the chances of setting up a thorough survey operation are slim. Grids, lines, or anything placed on this exposed site could be gone without trace overnight in one brief weather change. In the absence of any real fact, Skellig divers opt for the romantic theory that this is the resting place of the *Lady Nelson* lost in this area with a cargo of wine — which was the source of much local inebriation when the God-sent kegs were washed ashore in great numbers!

'Freshening a bit from the northwest', says the Skipper. 'Don't think we'll get in another dive today'. But this throw-away comment bothers nobody. Shivering and changing on the Skellig jetty, everyone is agog with the day's anemones and congers and crawfish and pollack and jellyfish and lobsters — each experience outdoing the next. Gerrit and Reinalda from Holland have even seen a flock of guillemots — much more agile of wing underwater than in air — hunting a shoal of sand eels with much success. And everyone has at least one version of the seal-which-came-up-and-stared-me-in-the-eye-when-all-the-film-had-run-out story! Besides, for the moment there is Skellig island itself to explore, and an invitation from lighthousemen Brian, Mick and Aidan to join them for a cup of tea at the lighthouse.

Following the lighthouse roadway up along the cliff face of Skellig is another exercise in zoology: nesting razorbills, fulmars, kitti-wakes, guillemots and puffins line the way, scarcely stepping aside to allow the visitor to pass. And were it night time, a further 10,000 pairs of Manx shearwaters and equally as many storm petrels would fill the air, or wander awkwardly underfoot.

Night time is really what Skellig lighthouse is all about and today's keepers are maintaining a service which has guided mariners safely past these rocks for more than 160 years. A football-sized, three-kilowatt lamp is the heart of the lighthouse. Set in a cage of revolving glass lenses, this light sends out a beam of 1,800,000 candles which can be seen as a three-flash character 28 nautical miles away.

It is difficult to imagine that this lighthouse, though some 50m above the sea, is sometimes so besieged by waves that nobody can venture outdoors for fear of life and limb. Indeed, there is one record from 1953 when a wave broke the lantern's plate glass, extinguished the light, and injured the keeper by washing him down the tower's spiral stairs.

But on a fine summer's day there is no evidence of such extremes. A diesel generator in the engine room hums quietly to power the entire station. Two radiotelephone sets in the corner of the living room keep a silent audio watch on the happenings of local shipping. The well-used TV set and the microwave telephone link with the national network keep Skellig in touch with the world farther afield. Two recently-completed ships in bottles are the only visible clue that this is an old, old service and not a recently created 'high tech' office.

But if Skellig lighthouse has a long and interesting story, the island's other estab-lishment — the monastic site standing on the island's peak — boasts a history that goes back 14 centuries. To appreciate that we must climb higher. Upwards, ever upwards the steep climb takes us, step by stone step, to a 260m high pinnacle. Here one must gasp with both exhaustion and amazement, for nestled in a protective web of stone walls, terraces and gardens stands Europe's finest example of early Christian architecture: beehive-shaped stone dwellings, churches and monuments, shrugging off the years and the centuries without change or deterioration.

Questions that don't have answers abound up here. Who built this place? We know nothing about them. When was it built and how long did this work take? Nobody really knows. We say the 6th century only from the style of the architecture, but there were additions about the 10th century. Nor do we know how many builders were involved, nor how they contrived to exist on this austere outpost, nor why they decided to leave it in the 12th century.

Why they settled here in the first place may be more easily understood, because even in today's cold analysis, the character, the soul, the spirit of this strange place is tangible and real. Lucky indeed is he who could stand out here at daybreak, as the sun rises over the Kerry hills to the east, silhouetting Small Skellig island in jagged black, rousing the dawn chorus of kittiwakes to full voice, tinting the monastic site with a touch of golden daylight and cueing the ghosts of monks long gone to scurry out of sight into the crevices and shadows . . .

There is the sound of a boat's horn far below on the sea. The skipper is telling us that we have overstayed our time and must be away. True to expectations, the wind has come up, and as we head homewards into the spray of a freshening norwester only one question is uppermost in everyone's mind: will tomorrow be the day for another trip to the Skelligs?

DIVE 4 FLORIDA STRAIT: Key Largo by Horace Dobbs

A diver with the bronze statue of Christ of the Abyss in the John Pennekamp Coral Reef State Park in Florida. (Photo: Horace Dobbs.)

Facing page
Top: **Nancy peering between Fan corals.**

Middle: **Fish meander between the corals on all of the reefs in the underwater park.**

Bottom: **A shoal of Grunts drift lazily across the reef.**
(Photos: Horace Dobbs.)

On my first dive in the John Pennekamp Coral Reef State Park at Key Largo in Florida I thought I had found Paradise. That was in 1970. For more than a decade before then I had been experimenting with underwater photographic equipment and struggling to take pictures off the British coast. That doesn't mean that I did not enjoy diving in British waters. I did. But during the few days I spent in Pennekamp I saw and photographed undersea life in a profusion that staggered me. And when I saw the results I had more good pictures than from all of my other underwater photographs put together. I couldn't believe underwater photography could be so easy.

My visit to Key Largo also gave me a new perspective on diving. Up until that experience I had been brought up to believe that you had to be totally dedicated and capable of swimming at least two lengths of the pool with a 10-lb lead weightbelt wrapped around your middle before you could even touch an aqualung. Yet on the Keys I saw people swimming around under the sea who had never dived before, and who quite honestly would have been incapable of running up a single flight of stairs. Furthermore, although somewhat apprehensive, they were obviously quite safe. That was because the water was warm, shallow and clear. And they were well supervised.

My enlightenment came about as a result of

American friends offering to take my wife and me along with them on holiday when they found out we were visiting the USA on business. They lived in New York and were persuaded, without too much difficulty, that Florida would be a good vacation destination that year. Like lots of American families they used a camper van for both transport and accommodation when they went on holiday. They agreed to meet us at Miami Airport and drive us down to the Keys for a few days' diving.

Even now I can vividly recall stepping outside Miami Airport. It was the first time I had visited a tropical area in mid-summer and it was like walking into a blanket of damp heat. In those days temperatures were still measured in Fahrenheit in the UK as well as the USA — where they still are. As we cruised sedately south-west along the highway, the radio in our air-conditioned cab announced, 'It is ninety degrees and ninety-five per cent humidity here in downtown Miami.'

Fifty-five miles out of Miami we pulled off the US1 into the entrance of the John Pennekamp Coral Reef State Park where our hosts had reserved spaces for their camper and tent. At the entrance lodge we were greeted by a heavily built ranger who gave us a map so that we could find our allotted site beside the Marina Basin.

It was 8.30 in the evening East Coast time in the USA and 1.30 am in Britain. The sun set rapidly and the temperature fell to 80°. The humidity remained unchanged. The mosquitoes were ravenous. The electricity and water supply were rapidly connected to the camper from which the four children were reluctant to emerge for fear of being eaten alive. While they hid inside we set to work erecting, or more accurately attempting to erect the tent our hosts had brought especially to accommodate us. Progress improved when we discovered that the frame went outside, not inside. In the meantime I unwillingly gave away several pints of blood to the native inhabitants of the one-time swampland.

Almost opposite the entrance to the Park was the Carl Gage Diving Center. Its presence was advertised by a sign plus a diving tank and two vans with mini-submarines moored to their roof racks. By 10 o'clock the next morning the temperature in the sun outside the building registered 100 °F and the machine dispensing ice-cold drinks gobbled nickels like a Las Vegas fruit machine. A thermometer on the wall inside the building, which was air-conditioned and felt strikingly cool, registered 80 °F. However, it was the other items on display which were of much more im-

portance to me. It was a veritable cornucopia, guaranteed to delight the eye of a visiting diver. Cylinders, harnesses, lifejackets, watches, cameras, depth gauges, fins, masks, knives, demand valves, weightbelts and even an underwater scooter were displayed and available for purchase or hire.

I joined the mêlée of patrons of assorted shapes, sizes, age and colour who had assembled in the shop and were booking up the day's diving expeditions. We were served by a team of bronzed youngsters who, having made notes of our diving experience and qualifications, then attended to our individual needs. When these were completed we all lined up outside for 'Lifevest Drill', during which the man introduced as our Captain explained how life-jackets should be worn and inflated in case of emergency.

When these preliminaries were completed we set off in a convoy of cars for one of the boats which was moored about two miles from the centre. The air cylinders were soon stowed like a row of standing soldiers around the stern of the vessel. Packs of sandwiches and an unbelievable number of cans of soft drinks were deposited in the ice-box. The operation was carried out smoothly and swiftly. Within a few minutes of arrival at the jetty we were all onboard and one of the crew cast off. With our Captain Mike Voigt at the helm we were soon speeding across the blue-green sea to our first destination called Sea Garden which was about five miles offshore.

The party divided into three groups of about 10. I was assigned to a group led by Nancy. We put on snorkelling equipment — fins, mask and snorkels. Instant tuition was given to those who had not worn the equipment before. The experienced snorkellers stood poised on the gunwale, and then leapt into the sea with a mighty splash. The more timid and less experienced had to be coaxed to launch themselves into the water, but some just couldn't pluck up courage and retired at the last minute to mingle discreetly with the small bunch of non-diving passengers.

Our party of floating snorkellers clustered around Nancy like a family of ducklings as she moved away from the side of the boat. For security the novices kept closest to her. One large male straggled behind the party. Despite vigorous efforts he could not progress very fast through the water. That was because he used his legs as if he was pedalling a bicycle. Nancy was soon by his side. She showed him how to do the correct leg stroke — a kind of slow crawl.

The boat had anchored on the sand and that was all we saw at first. Then the reef appeared

out of the haze before us and became clearer and clearer as we approached. When we were directly over it the shallow outcrop revealed itself with crystal clarity. For the first time I saw the reality of a coral reef fairyland. Nancy snorkelled down 15ft to a Sea Whip coral with an Angel Fish flirting in its branches. She hovered momentarily and gently extended her hand, almost touching the fin of the fish with her finger. The fish idly moved to the far side of the bush-like coral and Nancy unhurriedly surfaced. We had just seen a Grey Angel Fish. She sounded again and again, pointing to something different on each descent. She obviously loved the sea and enjoyed her role as guide to Neptune's treasure-house.

Several times I snorkelled down with her and on one occasion saw my first Trigger Fish. It beat its dorsal and anal fins in unison, first to one side and then to the other, as it swam through the water in a manner in which I had never seen a fish swim before.

The party, myself included, were so entranced by what we saw that we were unaware of the passage of time or distance. Unknowingly we had idled our way around a giant circle until we were once again alongside the boat, which sat motionless on a sea without a swell. Submerged ladders attached to a platform over the stern made leaving the sea no more difficult than clambering out of a swimming pool. In fact in many ways it was much easier because the platform was at water level.

Soon all three snorkelling parties were back on the boat and the anchor was hauled in. The vessel shuddered as the powerful engine throbbed into life, and we skimmed out to the main reef for the next item on our itinerary — an aqualung dive.

Whilst the boat was speeding towards the reef the scuba divers (to use the American expression) collected together their equipment. Regulators, known in Britain as demand valves, were attached to air cylinders or bottles, which the Americans referred to as tanks. Staccato metallic hisses indicated that the divers were breathing briefly from their assembled equipment to check that their aqualungs were functioning properly. The more image-conscious divers strapped formidable-looking knives to their legs. Depth gauges and compasses were clamped to their wrists. The rotating bezels of their waterproof watches were twizzled and the water temperature gauges attached to their watch straps were scrutinised. They registered 105 °F out of the water in the sun.

The anchor went overboard. The engines cut. The white boat rolled very slightly in the

Facing page: **The shallow reefs of the Florida Keys are like gentle sunken gardens.** (Photo: Horace Dobbs.)

The statue of Christ of the Abyss is a popular prop for underwater photographers! (Photo: Horace Dobbs.)

most imperceptible swell. The water looked cool and inviting.

We again formed groups - smaller ones this time. Nancy lined up her team along the gunwale and checked each person in turn. Having completed her inspection we all sat, one by one, on the side of the ship. Then, in time-honoured fashion, at a signal from Nancy, we plummeted backwards into the sea. As soon as one person was clear of the boat the next person, already in position, dropped over the side. The sun, impinging upon large rising bubbles, flashed as if reflected in a mirror. We drifted down into the coral pleasure-garden. The density of life on the reef was phenomenal. The fish were as colourful and a hundred times more abundant than the birds in a sub-tropical forest. Shoals of Grunts and striped Pork Fish flowed over the top of the reef as smoothly as flotsam on a stream. Every speck of the reef base was composed of living Stony Coral, or was covered with sponges and other exotic forms of sea life. I wasn't wearing a wetsuit and didn't need one. The water was like a luke-warm bath. I was exactly neutrally buoyant and moved through the sea with a minimum of effort. I felt totally relaxed. Breathing easily I had no sensation of being an alien intruder. For a time I was just one of the many creatures drifting weightlessly in a sun-filled, peaceful fluid world.

The diversity of the new undersea life I saw around me was more than I could assimilate in one dive. When I eventually left the water there were some clear images but many were just impressions. It was not until I had referred to books and especially my photographs that I was later able to put together even a modestly comprehensive picture of coral reef life. For instance I remembered clearly two distinct types of Angel Fish. Some, which I did not recognise, were small and their black bodies were marked with bold yellow bands. They appeared completely different from the Queen Angel Fish which I did recognise immediately for they wore cloaks of exquisite royal blue hues and on their heads they bore crown-shaped markings. Yet I later discovered that the small striped fish were juvenile versions of the Queen Angel Fish. I also found out that some small yellow fish I saw were juveniles of the Bluehead Wrasse which, as their name implies, had bright blue heads.

Some of the corals that grew out of the reef like bushes were flexible and waved with the motion of the sea. They were obviously related to the pink and red Gorgonion Corals I had seen off the British coast. The giant Sea Fans, whose name described their shape, were lavender-coloured and looked fragile, but in reality were surprisingly tough.

A coral I was able to identify immediately was the Brain Coral — so called because of its overall cranium shape and the complex patterns of fissures on its surface that bear a remarkable resemblance to those on the surface of a human brain. These unyielding rock-hard structures were one of the reef building corals which, when they died, would provide a sound and solid foundation for other forms of reef life to grow upon. Another coral I recognised the instant I accidentally brushed against it was the Stinging Coral or Fire Coral. It was as if I had touched a stinging nettle. Tube sponges were also easy to recognise. They remain in one spot and spend their lives pumping water through their bodies. Later I read that this was achieved by means of countless flagella, and that a single four-inch high sponge filters 25 gallons of water a day.

By gaining such knowledge I appreciated the life-style of all of the stationary reef dwellers, including the stony corals and the sea fans. In the process of filtering their food from the soup in which they were immersed they were clarifying the water, thereby making it much easier for me, an alien intruder, to see what was around me.

I was intrigued by the diversity of the shapes of the fishes and the specialisation of their feeding habits. Fishes like the Pork Fish and the Grunts I could easily understand. They congregated in great shoals and were the shape I expected fishes to be, with a mouth size in proportion to the rest of the body, like say Mackerel or Herring. Thus they were equipped to swim after smaller fish and catch them in flight. Fishes like the Butterfly Fish, Angel Fish and Tangs were not equipped to feed in this way at all. They had tiny mouths relative to the size of their bodies. Likewise the Trunk Fish which had the appearance of whistling errand boys. These fish were solitary, or in pairs, and spent their time weaving in and out of the reef pecking at minute specks of food on the surface coral. It was wonderful. I just watched and marvelled at it all.

With Carl Gage I also visited two wrecks. One was that of the *S.S. Benwood* which sank in 1943 and provided the foundation for a new reef. After 27 years it was well colonised and inside I saw a fine specimen of what was considered one of the most vicious and feared denizens of the deep. It was hidden deep in the wreck and I finned slowly towards it. I put a flashbulb in my flashgun and was pleased when it popped, as my flash had an irritating habit of misfiring. The fish remained unmoved by the sudden but short-lived burst of light. I was pleased to have got a picture of such a

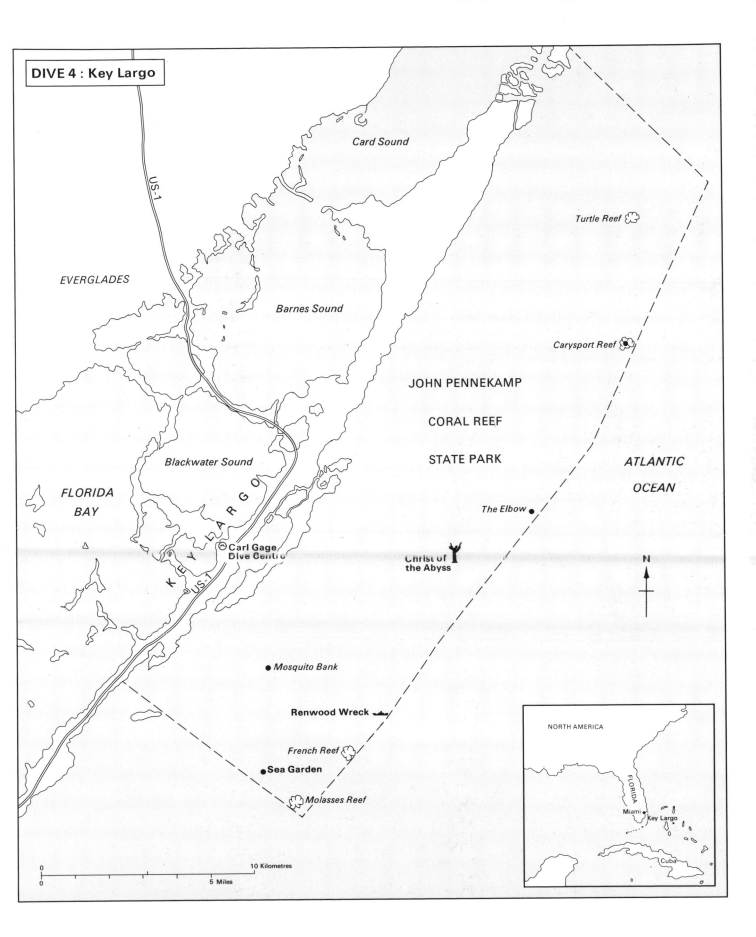

DIVE 4 : Key Largo

Card Sound

US-1

Turtle Reef

EVERGLADES

Barnes Sound

Carysport Reef

JOHN PENNEKAMP

CORAL REEF

STATE PARK

Blackwater Sound

ATLANTIC

OCEAN

FLORIDA
BAY

The Elbow

Carl Gage
Dive Centre

Christ of
the Abyss

N

Mosquito Bank

Renwood Wreck

French Reef

Sea Garden

Molasses Reef

0   10 Kilometres
0   5 Miles

NORTH AMERICA

FLORIDA

Miami   Key Largo

Cuba

villain and retired gently whilst I was still intact.

Months later, when I was back in England, I put on a slide show at a diving club. My grand finale, the close-up picture of the fearsome Barracuda, fell flat when a member of the audience cried out, 'That's not a Barracuda'.

'What is it then?' I retorted.

'I don't know but it isn't a Barracuda', came the reply.

Anxious to prove the clever-dick wrong I hastily flicked through a book on coral reef fish and found that my heckler was right. My Barracuda wasn't a Barracuda at all. It was a harmless Snoek, which I later learned was sometimes caught commercially and canned. I have since seen hundreds of Barracuda, usually hanging almost motionless in great shoals in the open sea. Barracuda certainly have the appearance of extremely efficient and ruthless predators. I can imagine that to see them feeding on a shoal of pilchards would be an awesome spectacle. However, despite their ferocious appearance I have always found them to be timid and quite unaggressive. Now I am familiar with both Barracuda and Snoek I find it hard to believe that I could ever have mistaken one for the other.

Another wreck I visited was outside the Pennekamp Park. It was the Spanish galleon *San José*. She was one of a fleet of 21 ships, including 4 Men-of-War, that were struck by a hurricane off Plantation Key in 1733 when carrying a huge quantity of treasure to Europe. When I saw the remains of the *San José* they looked like the skeleton of a half-buried whale, its ancient encrusted ribs protruding from the vividly white coral sand 10 m down. Two discarded metal mesh baskets were the only signs of the salvage operation that had taken place after her discovery two years earlier. The *San José* did not yield a rich reward for the treasure hunters because it was salvaged shortly after it sank. Nonetheless some silver coins were recovered. They were called 'pillar dollars' because of the Pillars of Hercules pictured on them. Like the rest of the group I foraged in the coarse sand to see if Lady Luck was dealing aces my way. But all I found were a couple of Sand Dollars — the empty shells of a native echinoid, or sea urchin.

The wreck's largest and most easily identifiable artefact rested on the seabed nearby. It proclaimed the presence of the *San José* as boldly as a barber's pole. It was the huge anchor. The sea was so clear and still, the sun so bright, and the sand so white, that the stock cast a clear shadow on the seabed. Within the curtain of shade under the anchor stock hovered a small shoal of Grunts. They were the only apparent sign of fish life on the sandy desert of the seabed that extended flat and

I thought these two large fish were fearsome Barracuda when I took the picture. Later I discovered they were relatively harmless Snoek. (Photo: Horace Dobbs.)

featureless to the limit of visibility in all directions.

During our short stay on the Keys I joined my wife and our American friends on a trip in a glass-bottomed boat. I was very disappointed. The coral reef looked drab and dreary compared with what I had seen when out diving. It was as if we had walked around the outside of a cathedral and looked at the stained glass windows, which to be appreciated must be seen from the inside. I resolved I would have to take them all down inside the sea to show them what they had missed.

The next day we hired from the concession inside the park a small vessel called a Patio Boat. It consisted of two floats joined by a platform on which were chairs. This stable and comfortable accommodation was covered with a canopy supported on a light framework. It was a kind of waterborne 'Surrey with a fringe on the top', but instead of a horse it was powered by an outboard motor and was steered with a wheel instead of reins. It was just right for our party of four adults and four children. The ladies organised cooler boxes filled to the brim with food, drinks and ice, whilst the men sorted out the diving equipment, some of which I had hired from Carl Gage's Dive Shop. The excitement mounted as we loaded everything onboard in preparation for our two-family diving adventure.

We were soon skimming smoothly across the water with everyone, including the children, having a go at being captain and steering the boat. After travelling for about two miles through mangrove trees we reached the open sea.

'I knew from my trips with the dive boats that when viewed from the sea, to the inexperienced eye the shoreline looked like a continuous green band of mangrove in which it was difficult to identify any features, including the channel that would lead us back into the lagoon. However, within the Underwater Park four of the reefs were clearly marked with towers. So we used them as reference points together with my underwater compass to plot and steer a course to our chosen destination, the Christ of the Abyss statue, which lay hidden under the sea.

After a little searching we located the bronze statue on the seabed close to a shallow reef. We could see it from the surface. Through the clear water we saw Christ looking up towards us, his arms extended as if to invite us into the sea. We anchored nearby and first explored the region by snorkel. Two of the children jumped overboard as soon as we stopped. They were like ducks on the water and flippered hither, thither and yon across the surface of the sea.

The adults however, were less impetuous. Neither of the ladies was a strong swimmer. They first had to accustom themselves to wearing a facemask and breathing through a snorkel tube on the surface. Once this was mastered they lowered themselves gently into the water. Holding my hand they floated on the surface of the sea alongside the boat looking into the coral garden beneath them. When they were comfortable doing this we moved off with very gentle finning movements to explore the nearby reef.

My wife, Wendy, had snorkelled and briefly dived before in the Mediterranean. So when she had recovered from her snorkel trip we put an aqualung on her back and a weightbelt round her middle, before she once again lowered herself, this time even more gingerly, into the sea. At least she didn't catch her breath with the cold which is the reaction most European divers have when they first enter the sea in their home territory.

She had already prepared her facemask in the usual manner, by spitting in it and rubbing the saliva over the inside of the face plate, to prevent it misting up, before I adjusted it to make sure it wouldn't leak. Then we both allowed ourselves to sink down very slowly into the soft all-enveloping sea, breathing in and out as we went.

Once she had got used to breathing, and appreciated once again that it was as easy to inhale and exhale under water as it was on the surface, she relaxed. Her confidence quickly built up until she was finning along happily,

Since my visit to Pennekamp Park what were once considered dangerous creatures have become tame. Here, Captain Slate, who runs a dive centre, feeds his pet Barracuda 'Oscar' in an unorthodox way – with the dead fish held between his teeth. (Photo: Stephen Fink.)

well fairly happily, on her own. She knew I expected at least this much of her as I told her I wanted her to model for me before we submerged. Weightless in the water, she hovered in various poses around the most photographed prop in the Pennekamp Park — the statue of Christ of the Abyss.

Our presence had not gone unnoticed by one of the residents of the reef, a Nassau Grouper Fish. He followed me around like a puppy and when I stirred up the sand with the wake from my fins he darted forward to snap up any unfortunate sand dwellers I inadvertently revealed. I was very pleased that spearfishing

To human eyes a Puffer fish looks comical when it blows up with water – a defence mechanism which is intended to frighten off predators. (Photo: Horace Dobbs.)

had been banned in the Park, for if it had not he would have been skewered long before he had a chance to make friends with humans.

After I had taken some pictures we did a gentle circuit of the reef before I delivered Wendy back to the Patio Boat where our host Norman was waiting to help her back onboard after she had removed her weightbelt and aqualung. Then it was his turn to join me under the sea.

Norman had taken a few scuba lessons prior to setting off for Florida. He enjoyed putting into practice what he had learned in the swimming pool a few weeks earlier. Whilst we were down several other boats arrived. We stayed below — that was the safest place to be when they were on the move. I was enjoying being warm and weightless in a three-dimensional pleasure playground. I peered into a small cave and at the back saw a Squirrel Fish — its large eyes indicating that it spent much of its time in the darker recesses of the reef. As my own eyes adjusted to the lower light intensity I could see the inside of his home more clearly. A tiny fish, with vivid, fluorescent blue stripes, that lived up to its name of Neon Goby, flitted around like a housewife cleaning with a feather duster. I loved peering into such mysterious nooks and crannies. The reef was full of them. I felt as bemused and excited as I did when I first visited a fairground as a child. But being at this underwater fair was even better — all of the sideshows were free.

I escorted Norman back to the boat. My camera was out of film so I handed that in before I sank once again beneath the boat. It was our last day and I used up the remaining air in my cylinder happily wandering around the reef a short distance from the anchor. When I eventually resurfaced lunch was ready. I had not been wearing a wetsuit yet I did not feel chilled in the slightest. Accustomed to clutching beakers of hot soup with hands violently shivering with the cold at the end of a dive, this was the life for me. Even the boat was rock steady. Those who only dive the Florida Keys 'don't know they're born' as they say in Yorkshire. Even when a thundercloud later appeared overhead we simply pulled up the anchor and moved out of the rain back into the sunshine.

Ten years after my dives in Pennekamp Park my son Ashley was in Florida evaluating the Florida Keys as a destination for package tours for the diving holiday specialists, Twickers World. Starting in Miami he travelled the full length of the Keys, sampling the diving en route to Key West where he discovered one of the best dive sites on that coastline. It was

called Ten Fathom Bar and consisted of a spectacular wall dive. The wall started at a depth of 25ft and dropped down to 130ft. For most of the year the water flowing along the wall was exceptionally clear. There were corals and sponges not found on the shallower reefs as well as Groupers, Snappers and possibly Rays.

But when I asked him to select his 'classic dive' he unhesitatingly said Pennekamp at Key Largo, (mainly because it was protected from spearfishing and coral collecting) and I had to agree with him.

Part of the huge anchor of the *San José* with a discarded salvage basket in the background. (Photo: Horace Dobbs.)

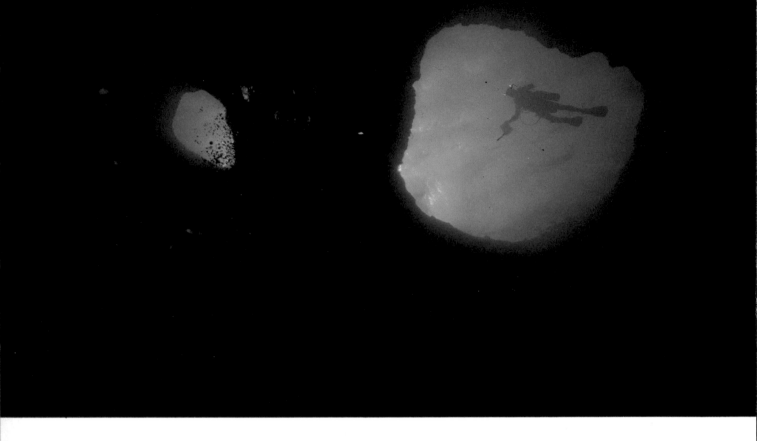

DIVE 5 ATLANTIC OCEAN: The Blue Holes of Andros Island by Martyn Farr

Diver near the surface in the blue hole in Mastic Sound – picture taken at a depth of 20m. (Photo: Martyn Farr.)

The word Bahamas is synonymous with sun, sea, sand, an image of luxury, beautiful bikini-clad females soaking up the sun, an ice-cold Bacardi within arm's reach and a cloudless blue sky resting upon an ocean of aquamarine; the tourist brochures appear before one's eyes.

It is without doubt one of the finest diving areas in the world. The islands abound in beautiful shallow water reefs while the shortest of boat rides will take the more experienced diver to some of the most spectacular 'drop offs' a diver could wish to explore. But there is more — the finest most exciting cave diving in

the world — the mysterious Blue Holes.

The Blue Holes are unique. They are water-filled caverns formed during the Pleistocene era, commonly referred to as the Ice Age. During this time much of the planet's water was trapped in the form of glaciers further north and the sea level fell to over 120m below its present level. The climate was also different and the Bahamas then lay high above the seas, and were subjected to all the processes of cave erosion and deposition that occur in any normal cave today. With the close of the Ice Age, some 14,000 to 15,000 years ago, the ice melted and the oceans rose. In the process the great cave systems in the Bahamas were flooded. Beautiful grottos of stalactites and stalagmites which had formed in the dry air of the caverns were lost beneath the water. Fish, sponges and all manner of crustaceans moved in to make these caves their home.

Blue Holes are found throughout the Bahamas, both offshore and inland. Native Bahamians refer to them as Blowing or Boiling Holes, reflecting the strong tidal currents that flush in and out of the marine entrances. As such, these caves are extremely dangerous to explore. Andros Island has a wealth of Blue Holes, in particular off the eastern coast of the island; deep and mysterious openings leading to extensive cave networks stretching for an unknown distance both seawards and/or inland. The pioneer of Blue Hole diving in this area was a Canadian, George Benjamin, who from the 1960s had devoted much of his life to the exploration of the marine openings off the east coast of Andros. Benjamin was a man ahead of his time and it was directly as a result of his work that a small group of British divers mounted two expeditions to this area in 1981 and 1982.

At this time the Blue Holes were very much a new frontier. None of the team had been there before and the prospect was long, continuous deep diving — possibly the most technically demanding and extreme cave diving in the world. Were we up to the challenge? Not only were there obvious dangers such as fierce currents and sharks but there were also mildy disturbing legends of sea monsters and the like which supposedly inhabited the entrances. On several occasions Benjamin had been confronted by Bahamian villagers determined to dissuade him from exploring these holes.

'You go down dere and Lusca, him of de hahnds get hold of you; you dead mahn!'

To the islanders the Lusca was a terrible creature, something like a huge octopus or squid, that could ensnare the unwary — be they swimmer or in a boat — and drag them down to the depths. Benjamin fortunately laid the majority of these rumours to rest.

Our first view of Andros, travelling by light plane from Florida, was not the scene that one might have imagined. The island seemed to be totally deserted, a level carpet of greenery with little indication of human activity; an island 100 miles long and 30 miles wide, forgotten or abandoned. It exuded an air of mystery. Gradually what appeared to be a mere cutting in the monotonous terrain transformed itself to an airstrip, and a few minutes later we bumped along the weed-infested runway of San Andros.

Barely had we arrived in August 1981 than our leader Rob Palmer, who had come out two weeks in advance to make the necessary arrangements, made an amazing disclosure. That very morning he had been for a reccc dive

A colony of hydroids on a cave ledge. (Photo: Martyn Farr.)

at an inland site, 'Uncle Charlie's Blue Hole' and had discovered a diver's body. This had to be a rather disturbing quirk of fate, especially as to everyone's knowledge there had only ever been one cave diving fatality on the island — that of a leading American diver Frank Martz in a Blue Hole off the southern part of the island in 1971.

In order to set matters straight with the authorities it was decided that our first operation would be to go to Uncle Charlie's, to try and make a better identification of the remains. Two days later we got the full flavour of diving down inland Blue Holes.

The still blue pool beckoned invitingly. It was a perfectly circular area of glassy water screened secretively by the canopy of jungle. Had Rob not been shown the site by our guides, who used it regularly as a swimming pool, we might never have found the place. Carefully lowering ourselves over the vertical one-metre drop into the water the relief from heat, exertion and surface hazards — such as tarantulas, scorpions and poisonwood — was unbelievable. It was such a contrast. One moment you felt it was all too much and you were going to flake out in the intense heat. The next you were floating, relaxed, in a warm bath of pure shimmering delight.

Rob led off, laying the line. At 13m we reached that sinister band of water found at all the inland sites, the 'sulphur layer'. The depth at which this localised layer is encountered varies from hole to hole but its essential characteristics are a brown or slightly purplish colour, an evil taste and an evil smell. It forms a sharp interface between the predominantly fresh water above and the salt water beneath — a halocline. From a diving point of view it presents atrocious visibility of just one metre and effectively cuts off all daylight to the deeper water.

At Uncle Charlie's Blue Hole the evil layer coincided with a dramatic narrowing of the shaft and at this point the steeply sloping walls were 'padded' to a depth of a foot by copious quantities of light-coloured organic debris. As one brushed or bumped into the side the visibility exploded, as flecks of what might have been mushy newspaper or decomposed human flesh blotched frighteningly around one's mask. I held the line fast, and thankful for the powerful 50-watt light, groped down into the world of total darkness.

Down, down, down and between the regular surge of expanding bubbles that raced towards me I could see that the grey walled shaft maintained a constant 2m diameter in the crystal water. At a depth of 40m we reached the bottom and intercepted a huge passage trending from right to left. Here we realised our error — Rob's discovery lay in a passage at about 20m depth.

We eventually found the small side passage and located the body. The tattered remains were quite lifelike as they floated or wedged in the crack in the ceiling. In the clear water the detail was gruesome. Around the wetsuited waist of the corpse diver were 3 or 4 weights, hanging away from the now empty suit on a grey webbing belt. A single black handtorch with a bulbous head was attached to an arm, while a single valve draped from a large grey, back-mounted cylinder.

It was all extremely tragic. Clearly the explorer was ill equipped for a cave dive and had been totally deceived by the initial clarity of the water. Basically he had broken more than one of the cardinal rules of cave diving. He appeared to have no reserve set of either lighting or air, but the most probable reason for his death was the fact that he had laid no line. Once the fine mud had been disturbed, finding his was out was virtually impossible.

The clouds of mud rolled in and obscured everything. For us it was just a matter of groping blindly 30m or so back along our guideline — just a few breaths back to safety. For the luckless diver in Uncle Charlie's the situation would have been one of pure horror — waiting for that moment when his air finally ran out.

There could have been no more ominous a way to start a major expedition. At the very least it was a blunt reminder of the inherent dangers of the environment. In this instance, fortunately, we were able to adopt an objective, detached attitude. Sadly, perhaps we had trained ourselves to suppress any emotions aroused by such encounters.

Just as the trip to Uncle Charlie's tuned us in to the nature of inland Blue Holes so our first dive at a Marine Cave, in Conch Sound, was to give us the full flavour of the offshore Blue Holes. The unusual hydrology of these oceanic Blue Holes, certainly the intensity of the currents (reaching three knots or more) would again seem to make them unique. For over 80% of each day the currents 'suck' or 'blow' from the openings and effectively preclude any safe underwater activity.

Why should such a hydrological pattern exist? Quite simply the few oceanic Blue Holes that line the shallow waters off the eastern side of Andros are linked with a large number of inland Blue Holes, via a maze of interconnecting passages. As the tide rises water flows into the oceanic Blue Holes and surges beneath the island. The inland Blue Holes then react to the tidal influx, but the actual variation in water level at these sites is dependent upon distance from the sea. Uncle Charlie's for example, only half a mile from the coast, might rise and fall by 30cm or more while another site several miles inland might only rise 3cm or so. When the flow is sucking in on a rising tide a vortex can often be seen to form and it has been known that a diver's exhausted bubbles will be pulled downwards. One could well imagine an unwary diver also being sucked in, like cork down a drain. And the older islanders would insist the Lusca had claimed one more victim.

As the tide falls the reverse action occurs and something of a 'mushroom effect' can be distinguished upon the surface of the sea where the water forces, or 'blows' its way out. At certain sites entry is utterly impossible. This cyclic effect is clearly dependent upon the rise or fall of the tide but there are further complications. The currents in the Blue Holes do not reverse at exactly the same time as the tides. Thus when the tide reaches its low point and starts to rise water continues to flow out of the Andros holes for two to three hours. Similarly, when the tide first starts to subside the water in the caves is still flowing inwards. The most plausible explanation is that during rising tide seawater is forced into the restricted Blue Holes and distributed underneath the island through the mazelike passages of the intertidal zone. During low tide the pressure is released and the direction of the flow reverses. In simple terms the island water table acts like a piston in a supersize cylinder.

Meticulous planning and observation of the current pattern at each individual site is essential for Blue Holes diving. Initially there appeared only one sensible way of tackling these holes, namely to dive in at slack water having established that there would be a 'blowing' current on the way out. These lessons were learned very quickly.

The line was tied off to a boat which had sunk in Conch Sound at one of the interconnecting entrances, and we swooped on down into a passage below. Conditions near the entrance gave no cause for concern despite the odd bits of weed and debris that were still moving inwards with the current. We presumed that the current was weakening and the visibility was well over 10 metres.

At 17m depth the gradient eased and a large dark tunnel loomed ahead. Glancing back towards the surface countless fish swarmed to and fro in an area suffused by a beautiful green glow, a mystical sight spelling safety and relief. A few more metres into the tunnel and all light was lost. We switched to the powerful 50-watt head lights. I still could not get over the temperature of the water; it was superbly

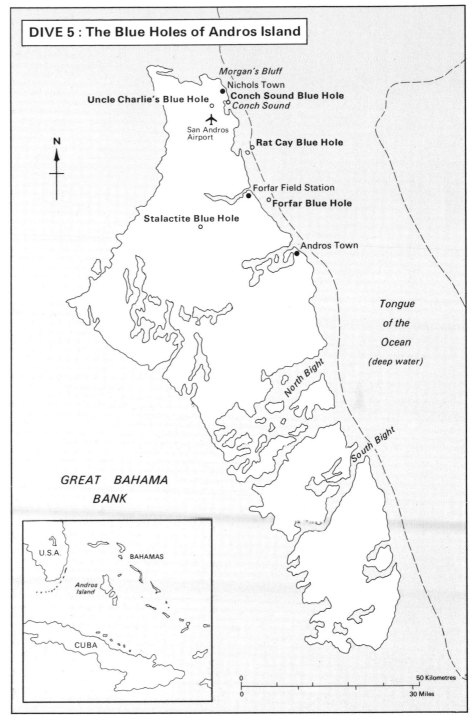

DIVE 5 : The Blue Holes of Andros Island

comfortable wearing our new 3-mm wet suits, with no need at all for the use of a hood. Before this trip I had never appreciated how restrictive, indeed claustrophobic, was the effect of a tight-fitting neoprene hood. Without it one felt so much more at ease. Breathing was much less of a strain and the water somehow felt more hospitable.

The current swept us on down the passage.

We stopped occasionally, to check that we could actually fin against the flow. We could—just! Without the reassurance of a heavy 5-mm line, which we could use if necessary to pull ourselves out, conditions would have been intimidating. A profusion of life was another striking aspect of this new environment. Near the entrance the most obvious form was that of the shoals of fish and hydroids. The latter looked like a type of fern and floated or wavered like long discoloured streamers with the current. Away from the entrance there seemed to be no fish at all but virtually every boulder or cleft concealed a lobster or crustacean. I'd never seen a lobster in its natural habitat before and here in the total darkness of the passage seemingly they had no fear; if anything I was far more worried than they were. Singularly, or in pairs, they just stood there, bigger than life, eyeing us up. It was the slow, deliberate movement of their amazingly long claws that appeared so menacing. One could almost imagine a swift whiplash action, with the lobster deftly removing one's mouthpiece, snipping through the air supply hose and just waving two claws at a horrified,

purple-faced diver. We left them undisturbed and cruised quietly on. By 100m the various life forms had thinned out appreciably but even so the roof, walls and floor displayed a heavy encrustation, the resultant build-up of countless years of marine organisms.

The second reel was tied on and it was my turn to take the lead and follow the current on its mysterious course. The 50-watt light was magnificent. At a glance characteristics of the huge tunnel could be noted and shortly stalagmites began to appear. In fact at about 125m they were commonplace. What a discovery, and on our first dive! George Benjamin had searched the South Island area for most of his life before making such a find. Eventually we ran out of line and it was time to tie off and exit. To our horror we found that the current was still flowing in, and strongly. Finning hard, progress was now desperately slow and it was two extremely chastened divers who eventually bobbed back to the surface low on air. We required no second warning. Nor did the other lads making their familiarisation dives that day.

A particularly harrowing time was experi-

Facing page: **Robert Palmer discovers a turtle shell in Rat Cay Blue Hole.** (Photo: Martyn Farr.)

Below: **Low tunnels abound in Rat Cay Blue Hole.** (Photo: Martyn Farr.)

enced by our biologist, Dr George Warner. Despite the fact that he'd never undertaken any real cave diving before, we had gained an immense respect for his all round ability and First Class British Sub-Aqua Club status. We believed that he would progress at his own pace, as he slowly gained experience in the new environment. After Rob and I had set off into the cave George thought that he would follow along our line, equipped with just a single 70 cubic feet bottle. Unknown to us he became totally absorbed with the marine life and was lured ever further along the passage. By the time he consulted his pressure gauge he was over 100 metres in and down to 55 atmospheres, compared to 130 when he had started out. A cave diver would have started on the exit when he had reached 87 atmospheres (one third of the air used en route in, two thirds for the journey out) but the conditions had deceived George as well.

Finning and pulling his way along against the current he remained cool but was soon aware of breathing heavily. Anger at being so stupid and concern as to how his family would fare without him, filled his thoughts. Fortunately George's lung capacity is quite astonishing; by remaining cool he made it — as the last of his air gave out. And it was just as well that he did not require decompression. Later he told us we should have been stricter with him, not been in awe of his First Class diver status, and should have insisted that he wore a twin set. We all learned a lot that day.

Progress was to be rapid at Conch Blue Hole and we were soon supplementing our side-mounted bottles with a third set. A distance of 410m was reached on the second dive, at an average depth of 22m. The third operation, using 4 bottles apiece (3 body mounted and one hand held 'stage unit') took us to 600m and a depth of 28m.

I was soon intrigued by my own attitude towards such diving. I had never enjoyed cave diving back in Britain; it was purely a means to an end — a way, albeit incorporating greater risks, of discovering new dry caves. Dive explorations for their own sake, e.g. those at Keld Head in the Yorkshire Dales, had never really appealed to me. In Britain the water was cold, 8° or 9 °C, visibility was generally a metre or so and the passages were small. We had come to Andros to try something different and I was amazed that this was thoroughly enjoyable.

Despite the novelty and apparent ease of Blue Hole diving it was extremely important to stick to the rules. In the context of changing mouthpieces, sticking to the 'third rule' is essential. There are so many things that can go wrong in a sump — failure of equipment, losing the line, entanglement or fatigue — the list is endless. Only by maintaining an adequate reserve in all cylinders can one stand any reasonable chance of averting a crisis; the diver with inadequate reserves is a liability not only to himself but especially to his companions.

One had always to be especially mindful of a valve failure. In the cold tense environment of British sumps one would have about 20 seconds to rectify the situation before things became critical. Here, feeling warm and at ease, that time could virtually be doubled. All things considered this diving was incomparably easier than the conditions under which we operated at home.

It was the marine life that ultimately rendered this diving so superb. Over the first 100m from the entrance for example, crustaceans, sponges of various colours and small corals were abundant. In the stalagmite chambers deposit-feeding sea cucumbers appeared to be common — chubby sausages crawling around on the floor. Amazingly, even 300m in there was marine life — crustaceans, eels, the odd anemone — all surviving in a delicate balance and dependent upon a food supply carried in the current. Just how the crabs and the like managed to catch their prey in the dark was anyone's guess but they certainly seemed to make the best of the situation.

One scene will remain with me always. At 250m a large boulder occupied the centre of the passage adorned with several stalagmites. On top of just one, was set a miniature colony of hydroids. In close-up it could have been a scene taken from a Christmas card: a beautiful little tree, covered in snow, set atop a rocky mound. Framed against the black of the cavern the hydroid wavered to and fro in the current — sifting essential nutrients from the passing water; making out a meagre existence. Marine life had thinned appreciably by this distance in to the tunnel and this setting was very much a wonder to behold. Tragically like many other spectacles of the natural world the stalagmite was to pay the price for our exploratory achievement. Sadly, on a subsequent dive later in the expedition, the stalagmite was to be broken off.

Beyond 400m life diminished significantly until by 555m even the sighting of a crab proved noteworthy. Occasionally in these deeper parts a Snake Eel might weave its way off to one side, or standing on its head excavate frantically downwards quickly disappearing in a small puff of cloud.

On the final solo dive in 1981 I reached a boulder obstruction at 700m. Five tanks of air were required to cover this distance (2 were hand held stage units) which were dropped off at 300m). Just after commencing the exit my first task was to try and capture an eel for George. This was achieved with difficulty and barely had I started moving again when I saw an amazing sight. A crab, about 15cm in diameter, was scuttling-cum-swimming directly in front of me. It was tightly clutching a squirming pink and white Coral Shrimp. This was certainly a ruthless environment where each had to survive as best he could. I felt quite guilty about removing the small eel. It was almost a crime. The Coral Shrimp was another matter — its death was demanded by nature.

By the time I'd regained the entrance I'd accumulated as much decompression time as the actual dive itself. But here even decompression was a relatively pleasant experience. There were so many things to absorb: a laser-like shaft of sunlight piercing some shadowy cleft, a shoal of silvery specks flitting to and fro, a myriad array of endless colour, fish, crustaceans, molluscs, sponges and plants. It was an experience like nothing else on earth.

It transpired that this dive had established a world record for a penetration into an undersea cave. Plans were quickly formulated for a return visit in 1982.

In August the following year we returned with a larger team and more ambitious aims. Evidently the cave extended further and we were certainly up to the challenge. Rob and I passed the boulder obstruction together on the first dive, then, each of us took it in turns to make longer dives supported by the others.

My final push, involving 4 support divers ferrying extra bottles for me, was to start from Rob's 1,050-m limit. It had taken us just 3 well planned dives to reach this point and psychologically I was now prepared to reach over 1,230m. However, as the big reel creaked and the line unwound I was not prepared for acceptance of the sheer vastness that shortly appeared. The passage proportions were almost unbelievable; I had entered a large chamber. Here the visibility was over 15m and I felt compelled to switch on a quartz iodine lamp to complement the main light. But it made no difference — there were no definite walls. This was a place utterly different to any other part of Conch. The cave between 400 and 460m was huge but in that instance one could at least sense the walls somewhere off to left and right. This was altogether of another scale, a vast room bigger than anything I had previously experienced below water.

I arrived at a stalagmite. But instantly I was aware that it was unlike any other stalagmite we had come across. It was visually free of any marine encrustation and to the touch it felt like glass. It was just like any stalagmite back home, a stalagmite in a cave that might conceivably have been flooded but a few weeks before. Waving a hand by it was like a quick dust off. It was strange sensation, as though I had entered some time vault where nothing had changed for over 14,000 years.

Swimming on, it soon became apparent that the place was totally devoid of life. There were no eels or small crabs, which were present up to and beyond 600m, no sponges, no anemones — nothing. I looked back and clouds rolled out across the floor and quietly dispersed. There were no apparent currents here. At 1,153 m murky water was noted ahead and an instant message came through — somehow I'd achieved a loop! I tied off, surveyed and back tracked. The final 50m had been in association with a wall and I now decided to follow this in the other direction. There was plenty of air left.

Where the line veered sharply from the wall I tied on once more and followed the chamber round. Shortly evidence of marine life began to appear. Droopy phallic sponges, or sea squirts, hung from undercuts in the wall. They were about 13cm long, and either white or grey in colour. On closer examination they seemed to have no substance at all, gossamer-like structures, the only life on the periphery of a barren desert. Exceptionally big holes characterised their bodies, working flat out to strain every bit of nutrient from the water. This suggested a possible current flow and indeed between the massive detached blocks lying on the cavern floor large openings were visible. These were at considerable depth, beyond the scope of this dive.

Then something moving caught my eye. It was a 12cm long Blind Cave Fish, a brochelid, *Licifuga speleotes*. We had encountered this rare species of cave fish at several sites, both inland and oceanic, but this was the first time it had been sighted here at Conch. This solitary creature swam eel-like about a metre or so above the floor, completely unperturbed either by me or the noisy rumbling of my exhausted air. It was almost a religious experience — meeting a survivor of a long lost age; a survivor making out a lonely existence at the very edge of life itself.

All too soon it was time to leave. Everything was going like clockwork. Eight bottles and 2 hours 46 minutes after entry I regained the first decompression stop.

As ever before, there was so much to see and absorb: glorious arrays of Tube Fans, Arrow Crabs, Pink and White-Banded Coral

Shrimps. There was always something new. Each had its niche, its territory, its home — bounded by invisible borders. Beautiful little Damsel Fish for example defended their patch of seabed even against something as monstrous as a diver. Prying too close inevitably stimulated little acts of aggression. With a thud a Hermit Crab, perhaps three or four times the size of the fish, would be knocked over and driven away. With a diver the brave little fish would resort to a head-on confrontation with the face mask; recurrent butts relating the clear message 'please leave me alone'. What an experience! Why explore lifeless tunnels deep underground when wonders such as these exist?

Six hours after entry I surfaced; the most enjoyable piece of teamwork that I had ever been involved in drew quietly to a conclusion. Conch Sound had yielded one of the finest cave diving sites in the world. It was undoubtedly a classic dive.

Above: **Stalagmite Grotto – 140m into Conch Blue Hole.** (Photo: Martyn Farr.)

Left: **Robert Palmer 500m in from the entrance to Conch Blue Hole.** (Photo: Martyn Farr.)

DIVE 6 CARIBBEAN SEA: The Cayman Islands
by Barbara Currie

Columbus may claim credit for first discovering the Cayman Islands in 1503. But it was Bob Soto who discovered their potential as a dive resort. And it was he who laid the foundations for what is now arguably the most popular dive destination in the world with divers currently logging an estimated 400,000 dives a year there.

It all began in 1957 when Bob Soto set up shop at the old Pageant Beach Hotel on Grand Cayman. He had an old Air Force compressor, three converted carbon dioxide bottles as tanks, gerry-rigged backpacks and a 19-ft Chris Craft boat 'assembled from a kit'. Over the next two decades he built his operation into the largest in the Caribbean and today 22 dive operations now serve a third of Cayman's 250,000 annual visitors.

The Cayman Islands (Grand Cayman, Cayman Brac and Little Cayman) are one of the few remaining British Crown Colonies in the world. Their combined population of 17,500 (1,750 on Cayman Brac and 40 on Little Cayman) forms a microcosm of primarily white English-speaking residents comprising expatriates from the British Isles and the West Indies, professionals, tradesmen and a sprinkling of retired people. It's a most unhomoge-

Grand Cayman is famous for its wall dives where giant sponges of different hues provide just one of many delights for the underwater photographer. (Photo: Paul Humann.)

nous mix of people, yet somehow they work and live together peacefully, enjoying one of the highest standards of living in the Caribbean. Grand Cayman has a distinctly North American flavour and appeal. It has an abundance of amenities decorating the west coast area around its famous Seven Mile Beach. Luxurious beachfront condominiums, a golf course, shopping centres, nightclubs and discos, a conference centre and a Hyatt Regency Hotel with 235 rooms — all add up to the island's polished, and often pricey appearance. With its ultra-modern airport terminal and daily jet service to and from Miami, Houston, Tampa and Atlanta, Grand Cayman can no longer claim to be the island time forgot.

Yet it is the reefs and drop-offs which provide the primary attraction for visitors. In 1986 a new Marine Parks Law was passed, ensuring the future of Cayman's underwater world. Despite the prodigious number of dives logged each year marine life around the island remains, for the most part, unspoiled. But while the undersea vistas remain a source of constant surprise, the support services Grand Cayman offers for its visiting divers are surprising too — in their professionalism and variety. Accommodation varies from luxury beachfront apartments, served by close-by operations offering first class pick-up and delivery services, to small informal hotels. You can charter a luxury 112-ft motorsailor, *Ports of Call,* with a complete dive shop onboard, and cruise the trio of islands for a week all by yourself. Or you can cruise around Grand Cayman with up to 16 other divers on the 90-ft liveaboards *Cayman Aggressor II* and *Cayman Aggressor III,* or the 80-ft *Little Cayman Diver* serving the sister islands.

The options do not stop there. You can cruise and reefs and drop off to a depth of 40ft in the *Atlantis* — a Jules Verne-style submarine that carries 28 passengers. You can also go down to depths off the wall, inaccessible to scuba divers, in a 4-person Research Submersible Submarine. You can learn underwater photography, video or modelling, or maybe even go for advanced scuba training, up to and including an instructor's rating. It is safe to say that there is nothing, except bottom time, that a diver or underwater photographer could run out of and couldn't find on Grand Cayman Island. There are well-filled dive shops in most hotels and speciality stores that stock every kind of underwater photography device imaginable. Most operations offer regulator equipment repairs, and rental replacements are always available. It's all there, if you can afford it.

The Cayman Islands boast an extremely high safety record. Their preoccupation with safety began in the early 1970s, when Cayman Island Divers (Branch 360 of the British Sub-Aqua Club) raised funds for the purchase of their own recompression chamber. By 1973 they had purchased a two-man double-lock recompression unit, which the BS-AC owns and operates today at the Cayman Clinic east of George Town. Trained chamber operators are on call 24 hours a day and the unit can be operational within five minutes of an emergency call.

Unlike its coastline which has now been tamed by 20th-century amenities, the fringing and patch reefs and dramatic coral drop-offs surrounding Grand Cayman offer diving that is predictable in only one sense — you can do it all year round, and it will be good.

Grand Cayman offers a great variety of diving. Dazzling patch reefs, bejewelled with coral and iridescent with tropical fish can easily be reached from the shore. Further out are the thriving fringing reefs where Elkhorn and Staghorn Corals form cathedral-like configurations penetrated only by throngs of fish and shafts of sunlight. And then there's the wall diving, from the gradual cascades of coral and sponge-encrusted slopes to the sheer vertical cliffs and stunning tunnels.

One of the most outstanding aspects of this underwater world is the prolific and varied sponge life. You'll see huge Barrel Sponges, big enough to hold two people, great tangles of multi-coloured Rope Sponges clinging like leftover party streamers to ledges and walls, opalescent azure Vase Sponges that grow in the depths like rare jewelled cups, and giant Tube Sponges that look like the whimsical creations of some pornographic underwater artist.

Such sights are all part of the varied seascape of Grand Cayman, where a diver can swim through the rivers of silver Tarpon along 'Tarpon Alley' on the North Wall. What may be the largest diveable Barrel Sponge in the Caribbean grows at a depth of 100ft on the wall, at Sand Chute. It measures 9ft high and 6ft in diameter. The site itself is exciting. It starts in 60ft of water, with a 300-ft 'ski slope' of white sand running between huge coral formations out over the drop-off.

There are 326 *recorded* wrecks in these waters, but the encrusted remains of fewer than a dozen can be seen by divers. One of the most popular west coast dive sites is the wreck of a 180-ft Panamanian cargo vessel, the *Oro Verde.* The ship went aground in North Sound in 1979. Later Bob Soto purchased the vessel and with the support of Cayman's dive industry, had it towed to a site off Seven Mile

Facing page
Top left: **Diver hovering over Yellow Tube sponges off the west coast of Grand Cayman.**

Top right: **Red Rope sponges on the North Wall.**

Bottom left: **Rare Red Cup sponges, one of Cayman's famous marine species on the North Wall.**

Bottom right: **Diver drifting above Tube sponges on the wall at Cayman Brac.**
(Photos: Paul Humann.)

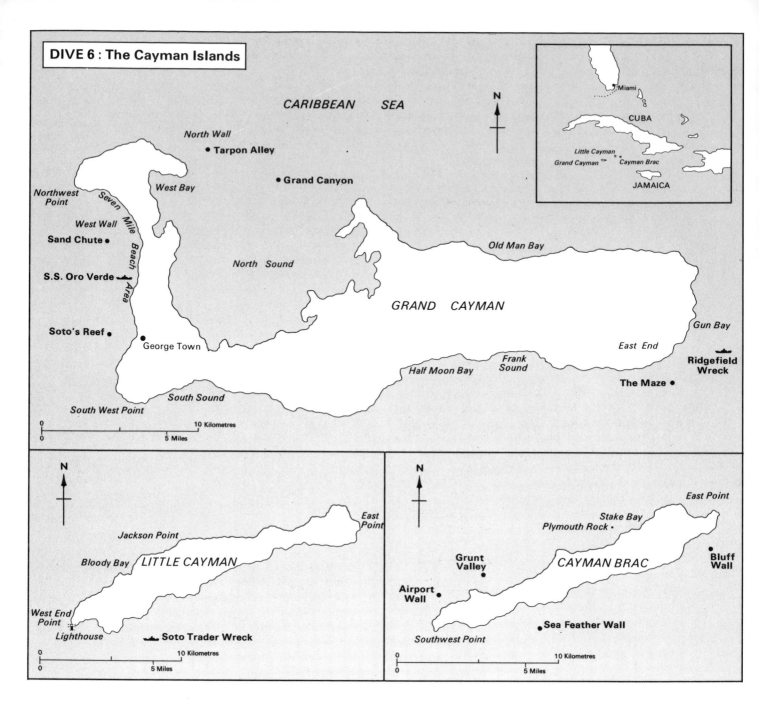

DIVE 6 : The Cayman Islands

CARIBBEAN SEA

N

North Wall
● **Tarpon Alley**

● **Grand Canyon**

West Bay

Northwest Point

Seven Mile Beach Area

West Wall

Sand Chute ●

S.S. Oro Verde ⊨

Soto's Reef ●

North Sound

Old Man Bay

GRAND CAYMAN

● George Town

Gun Bay

East End

Ridgefield Wreck

Frank Sound

Half Moon Bay

The Maze ●

South Sound

South West Point

0 ————— 10 Kilometres
0 ————— 5 Miles

Miami
CUBA
Little Cayman
Grand Cayman *Cayman Brac*
JAMAICA

N

Jackson Point

Bloody Bay **LITTLE CAYMAN**

East Point

West End Point

⚓ Lighthouse   ⊨ **Soto Trader Wreck**

0 ————— 10 Kilometres
0 ————— 5 Miles

N

East Point

Stake Bay
Plymouth Rock ●

Grunt Valley ●

CAYMAN BRAC

Bluff Wall ●

Airport Wall ●

● **Sea Feather Wall**

Southwest Point

0 ————— 10 Kilometres
0 ————— 5 Miles

Beach where it was sunk as a dive attraction. This site is popular with photographers who can enter many of the ship's chambers and from time to time encounter thick shoals of Silversides. Year round, however, this site is swarming with fish, including many tame Groupers, Green Morays and Yellowtails.

Bonnie's Arch is an excellent multiple dive spot near North West Point. Here coral gardens at a depth of 30 to 50ft shelter a healthy population of reef fish, near a small arch encrusted with corals and sponges, gorgonians and macro life. It is one of the most photogenic mid-range sites on the west coast.

In addition to such underwater scenic beauty several other features contribute to the meteoric rise of Grand Cayman to the top of diver popularity charts. One of the most important is the now legendary water clarity. The underwater visibility seldom drops below 100ft and is often between 150ft and 200ft in the summer. The water temperature of between 78 °F in the winter and 86 °F in the summer is equally inviting, and means the islands can be dived throughout the year.

When the wind blows on shore it can create

rough sea conditions. As diving in rough water is uncomfortable and can be hazardous, dive operators confine their trips to areas where the sea is flat and comfortable. This means that they do not routinely visit the North Wall on Grand Cayman during the winter when the winds blow from the north. As this is one of the island's best-known dives, visiting divers are often disappointed when they discover they can't dive what has come to be regarded as the classic dive in the Caymans. However, although at one time this claim to fame may have been justified subsequent exploration has revealed many better dive sites.

One such site can be found off the island's least developed district, East End. With 1,100 residents and two small resorts the coastline here still wears a thick cloak of coconut palms. The simple wooden houses, painted in pastels, present a West Indian vista of the kind that sadly, is gradually disappearing with development. But even if the East End is Grand Cayman's quietest community, the underwater world offshore is not, and it offers some of the island's best diving. The 26-mile stretch between Half Moon Bay, just east of Frank Sound on the central south coast, and Old Man Bay on the north coast, is an underwater frontier where the surrounding fringing reef shelters congeries of reef creatures that cruise through Elkhorn and Staghorn Coral formations.

Between 250 and 500yds offshore is the drop-off, a sheer coral cliff which begins as shallow as 70ft and plummets out of sight to 6,000ft. Here, Triton tempts photographers with a continual game of 'What next?' And that can include anything from Blacktip Reef Sharks and giant Green Turtles to static beauty, in the form of huge Basket Sponges and many varieties of Black Coral growing on the face of the wall — as shallow as 90ft.

This section of Grand Cayman supports some spectacular underwater architecture. Most famous is a 700-ft section called The Maze, an intricate series of crevasses, tunnels and coral chutes which make divers feel like they've just discovered Alice's legendary rabbit hole — beginning at five fathoms. Add to this the wrecks of the *Ridgefield* and *Vermonda,* freighters that went aground in the 1960s, plus an average of 125-200ft and you'll understand why I have selected this as my classic dive on Grand Cayman.

If Grand Cayman's topside amenities are tamed and governed by the maxim of 'no surprises', then the East End's maverick marine world comes as a surprising, and some might say welcome, contrast.

And referring to contrasts, none could be greater than that of the character of Grand Cayman and its sister island, Cayman Brac and the even smaller, Little Cayman. By comparison Grand Cayman is the flashy big sister of the trio, whose unspoiled siblings rest 85 miles east in distance and probably 50 years in the past in atmosphere.

Scenically the most beautiful of the Cayman trio is Cayman Brac with its limestone backbone rising to a sheer bluff 140ft high at the eastern tip. The ambience ashore on this rugged little island is wonderfully relaxed and completely free of expensive commercial distractions, cruise ship invasions and anything resembling 'man made' tourism. Except for the superior quality of its newest resorts and surrounding underwater world, the Brac's attraction is its captivating spirit and tranquillity.

Winston McDermot, who owns Cayman Brac's oldest dive operation, and has dived all three Cayman Islands for 20 years, admits even he can't accurately predict what passes through Brac's waters. Furthermore he has no idea how many outstanding sites remain undiscovered. Cayman Brac is untamed. The local fishermen attest to that. The profusion of reef fish that crowd the fringing reefs and edges of walls are subtle suggestions of the really big pelagic fishes that roam offshore. In 1986, for example, a local boat captain, Frankie Bodden, hooked several Blue Marlin estimated at well over 500lb right over the drop-off just a few hundred yards offshore.

The sense of mystery and the unexpected permeates this territory where tales of pirate treasure, centuries old, still lure hopeful hunters every year. The wall diving off the south coast of the Brac is outstanding — sheer vertical cliffs which drop into opaque blue seaspace, decorated with thick curtains of Red Gorgonians, Sponges and Black Coral. Crevasses, tunnels, sand chutes and large anchors from unknown wrecks are all part of its underwater attractions. On the north coast fine stands of Pillar Coral, towering above thriving communities of macro life on the sandy ocean floor, yield prime shallow diving that is especially rewarding for photographers. Cayman Brac is ready to be discovered by many more serious divers, and revisited by those who were turned off by the erratic air service during the past few years, when divers and gear were not guaranteed to arrive together, and sometimes not at all.

Little Cayman is the Crusoe's isle of the Cayman trio, with a permanent population of fewer than 40 and a grass airstrip which resembles the fairway on a good golf course. The two guest houses on this undeveloped 12-square-mile island both offer diving for

Top: **A Green Moray inspects a diver on the wreck of the *Oro Verde*.** (Photo: Bradley Graham.)

Bottom left: **A rare balling of Baitfish in a tunnel.** (Photo: Paul Humann.)

Bottom right: **You can dive Grand Cayman without getting wet on board this sight-seeing submarine.** (Photo: Rick Frehsee.)

small groups. Shark tales are common off the north coast where the legendary wall at Bloody Bay begins as shallow as 20ft. So you see, in spite of their popularity the Cayman Islands still have a lot of virgin diving and unknown depths to offer the more adventurous diver.

Dive 7 THE PACIFIC OCEAN: The Galapagos Islands by Horace Dobbs

The Galapagos Islands have several other names. For instance they were called the Enchanted Islands by the early sailors because in calm weather the islands would appear to drift past. We now know this was an illusion. It was the sailing ships that were drifting, carried by the silent currents that run between the islands.

To me, however, the islands are enchanted for another reason, and that is not an illusion. It is the abundance of wildlife and its complete lack of fear of humans. The animals exist in profusion above and below the water — many of them, such as the Sea Iguanas, Sally Lightfoot Crabs and numerous seabirds are dependent upon both the land and the sea for their survival. But there is one animal above all others that springs to mind whenever I think of the Galapagos. It passes much of its time lazing on the shore, often spending a considerable part of this time re-arranging its bulky body apparently attempting to find a comfortable position. However, it is more at home in the sea, where again it may idle hours away simply floating — sometimes with one fin raised like a small sail in the air. Once completely underwater however, the animal is transformed into the swiftest, most graceful,

The volcanic origin of the Galapagos Islands is apparent everywhere. The rock in the foreground is the plug of an ancient volcano. Behind it is a recent flow of black lava that runs right down to the edge of the sea. (Photo: Horace Dobbs.)

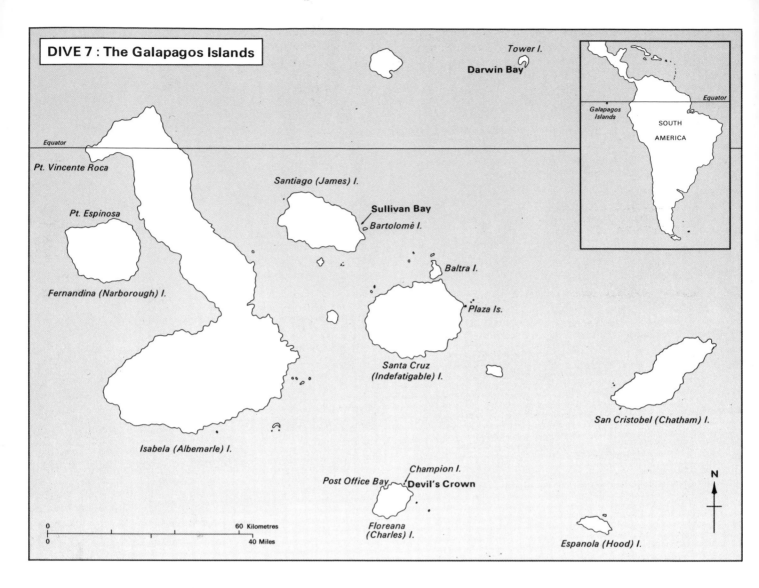

DIVE 7 : The Galapagos Islands

Tower I.
Darwin Bay

Equator

Pt. Vincente Roca

Pt. Espinosa

Santiago (James) I.

Sullivan Bay
Bartolomé I.

Baltra I.

Plaza Is.

Fernandina (Narborough) I.

Santa Cruz
(Indefatigable) I.

San Cristobel (Chatham) I.

Isabela (Albemarle) I.

Champion I.
Post Office Bay **Devil's Crown**

Floreana
(Charles) I.

Espanola (Hood) I.

N

Galapagos
Islands

Equator

SOUTH
AMERICA

0   60 Kilometres
0   40 Miles

most active, most acrobatic creature I know. It engages in the exciting game of tag, during which two or more of them will twist, turn and spiral in their three-dimensional playground in a manner that makes a Dervish look like a tortoise in comparison. On several occasions one from a group of such frolicking youngsters has plucked up courage and come right up to me — looking into my facemask with large, inquisitive, gentle eyes — before dashing away to rejoin the game. I refer to *Zalophus californianus wollebackii* the Galapagos Sea Lion which is endemic.

You meet Galapagos Sea Lions on every dive and see them on every shore-line, sometimes clearly visible on a strand of golden sand, at other times barely discernible on a rocky ledge just above the water line. When they are wet their coats appear sleek and black, but when they dry out their furs become a rich, dark, golden-brown colour, which to my eyes

is as attractive as that of the Fur Seals that also frequent the Galapagos Islands.

Everyone with an interest in wildlife cannot fail to dream of going to the Galapagos Islands, but, situated 500 miles off the coast of Ecuador, it is a far from cheap destination to reach from Britain. My dream of visiting the archipelago came true in 1977 as a result of the endeavours of Hedda Lyons, of Twickers World, a company which specialises in diving holidays. She managed to bring together a multi-national group of 10 to participate in an adventurous holiday expedition, under my leadership, to a destination that was new to all of us.

The flight to Ecuador was not without incident but I have to admit that when we completed the last leg of our journey and landed on Baltra I wondered just what the members of the group were going to get for their investment. The profound affection I now have for the Galapagos Islands and their native inhabitants certainly did not begin with love at first sight. For my first impression upon getting off the plane at Baltra was that we had landed on a hot, dusty, windy, flat, barren, featureless, uninteresting lump of brown rock.

We were ferried from the unsightly concrete airport buildings on a ramshackle bus to a jetty where we boarded small wooden dinghies, powered by ancient Seagull engines, that ferried us to our floating base for the next two weeks. Built in 1901 in Scandinavia the *Sulidae* had started life as a general cargo boat trading in the Baltic under the name *Sande*. She was 69 ft long and very solid, the hull being constructed of two layers of oak. The main cargo hold had been converted into a saloon and the remainder of the available space below decks was divided into tiny cabins in which the bunks took up most of the space. They were for the paying clients. My sleeping accommodation was a bench seat beside the table in the saloon.

Any misgivings about the cramped accommodation were dispelled as soon as we left the island of Baltra for we were joined by a school of Pacific Bottlenose Dolphins who crossed and re-crossed our bow with lazy strokes of their tails. Everyone rushed to the foredeck with Dr Bernhard Kempter, a paediatric cardiologist from East Germany, who specialised in fish photography as a hobby, taking the best position — in the net slung beneath the bowsprit.

Most of those onboard had been inspired to take up underwater exploration as a result of watching the films and reading the books of the Austrian Hans Hass. He had sailed his magnificent yacht, the *Xarifa* to the Galapagos and a picture of it appeared on the front cover of Eibl-Eibesfeldt's book *Galápagos – Die Arche Noah in Pazifik*. We moored in the self-same spot where that picture was taken for our first 'try-out' dive.

A small shoal of Concentric Puffer Fish, which are endemic to the Galapagos, milled about under the boat as soon as we moored. They were one of several different species of Puffer Fish we were to meet on our dives. They are not strong swimmers and do not have the false eyes that many tropical fish have near their tails and which ichthyologists say are present to deceive would-be predators into thinking that their potential prey is much bigger than it is. The Puffer Fish doesn't need this anyway as it achieves this illusion much more convincingly by engulfing water and swelling up to a much larger size. When fully blown-up they become almost spherical, and the spines, which normally lie flat against the body, stick out. And were I a hungry, but knowing fish, I would certainly think twice before attempting to consume such an obviously uncomfortable mouthful. Because they are slow swimmers it is often possible for a diver to catch a Puffer Fish with his hands. Indeed one of the diver guides I met on a later trip was an addicted Puffer Fish puffer-upper. He could not resist catching the poor fellows and gently massaging them, which was his method of fish inflation. He did however, always wear gloves which was a wise precaution, because skin punctures from the spines often turn septic.

On our first dive into Galapagos waters we occupied ourselves with just looking at the fishes and the undersea life. Having seen the remainder of the group safely into the water I jumped into the sea with my diving partner Dr Luciano Manara, a long-standing friend, who had flown out from Milan to join the group. We headed towards the huge rock that stuck out of the water like a giant knife blade. The underwater visibility was about eight metres and we were escorted for the first part of our journey by Concentric Puffer Fish some of which seemed to mistake the tiny bubbles from our exhausts as prey. They chased the scintillating spheres as they oscillated upwards, and ate them, burping them out when they discovered their lack of nutritional value.

There was a swell around the base of the rock, where we were greeted by more fish. These included White-Banded Angel Fish and Hieroglyphic Hawkfish. Life was much more prolific close to the rocks, and shoals of fish swam past like billowing sheets of chiffon. Most of the shoals were made up of the same species with a few foreigners following the same flow of movement. During our dive we all re-accustomed ourselves to the joys of being back in the sea again. We adjusted our equipment and started taking pictures.

A comparison of the notes made in the expedition log by the various diving pairs after the dive made interesting reading and reflected their different interests. Martin Kaufman was obviously interested in invertebrates. Apart from seeing a Sea Lion underwater the highlight of his dive was the five different species of starfish he recorded. Everyone was pleased with their first dive. That evening it was hard to believe that a few hours before we had been sitting tightly packed in a plane miles high in the sky eating plastic food. Now after our first sea dive we watched the sun set over a calm sea and ate a sumptuous meal in a gently rocking boat, in seas that had been frequented by pirates two hundred years before.

As a policy I always organise an official diary of my expeditions in the form of 'The Expedition Log' in which all of the dives are

Top: **A yellow Puffer fish doubles its size to that of a football when it takes in water.** (Photo: Horace Dobbs.)

Above: **The bright colour of Sally Lightfoot crabs makes them very easy to spot as they skitter across the rocks.** (Photo: Horace Dobbs.)

recorded. Each day I ask a different person to recount the events of the day — giving them total editorial freedom. In the log I list the names and addresses of all of the participants, together with details of boats etc. At the end of the expedition I retain the log but make it available to any members who wish to borrow it.

Here is part of Martin Kaufman's record of our first full day in the Galapagos Islands, 13th April 1977:

'That this is the first day of the expedition proper we find difficult to believe. The civilisation of Quito seems a long way away in time as well as distance.

The quarters are of necessity cramped, but it is for our equipment rather than ourselves that we would like more space. Already we feel the lack of fresh water for washing. Gonzalo, our cook is doing a wonderful job and much of the food is fresh and well prepared. Any discomfort is immediately offset by the wonderful spirit of comradeship shown by all onboard. Even those not onboard — Sea Lions, Dolphins, Pelicans etc, are very friendly — especially the Sea Lions whose sense of humour is almost as childish as our own.

Two dives and two land sorties is an ambitious programme, but we did it all today and I enjoyed every minute. After this can there be more to come? 'Lucky Luciano' was so overwhelmed by his luck at finding so much to photograph that he spent most of his first dive preparing focus and exposure without taking a single shot! Fortunately he recovered from his bewilderment on his second dive and may have got some good shots of a Sea Lion suckling.'

I was with Luciano when we spotted the huge cow Sea Lion gently resting on the surface of the sea in a cove. Knowing how fiercely protective animals can be if they think their young are threatened we watched from afar as the calf nuzzled its mother suckling her rich milk. The mother saw us, looked at us, but she did not move. She must have weighed 200kg or more. She showed no signs of nervousness at our presence so we finned very, very gently towards her. Still she continued to suckle her pup. We approached closer and closer and stopped when we were about two metres from her. I remember her looking at me with her large eyes as if she was pleased with herself. A happy Sea Lion enjoying the closeness of her offspring. Then she rolled over withdrawing her nipple from the mouth of her babe and the two of them swam gently past us — the young pup tucked securely alongside his mother. There was no haste in their movements. Mum had just decided it was time to move on. We stayed where we were, watching them sliding under the surface of the sea with slow movements of their flippers — until they disappeared from view. We both felt privileged to have been allowed to witness the tender love of the mother and baby. We were also sensitive to the fact that our presence caused mild interest — certainly no fear or concern. It was this aspect of the behaviour of virtually all of the animals that we encountered in the Galapagos Islands that had the most profound effect upon me — and all other members of the expedition.

However, it was during our excursions onto the islands that the complete lack of fear on the part of the residents struck us most forcibly. We all discovered for ourselves that the Galapagos Islands are a wildlife photographer's paradise. We had planned in advance a tour of the archipelago which involved two dives and two land excursions each day.

The two land expeditions we made on the first day of our visit gave us a good insight into the ecological origins of the archipelago. Our first major shore visit was made onto James Island which is dominated by the cone of a volcano that rises to a height of 2,974ft. Looking up from our landing point we saw stretching up the hillside before us a river of solidified black lava that was over two miles wide where it came to an abrupt stop at the edge of the sea. It was less than 100 years old and had not eroded. Even at the water's edge its exact shape before it congealed was visible. In some places the rock had the ruffled appearance of shiny black freshly whipped cream. In others the rock was pock-marked with circular blisters that were obviously created by bubbles of gas rising to the surface as the mass solidified. At the water's edge Sally Lightfoot Crabs scuttled to and fro, their bright red hues standing out vividly against the jet-coloured background. They appeared to be easy subjects to photograph until you actually tried. Then, just as you had got close enough and started to focus they would whiz away sideways as if on elastic.

Away from the water's edge the lava flow appeared to be utterly barren. That was until your eyes detected the fleeting image of a Lava Lizard running across the rocks. Unlike the Sally Lightfoot Crabs the Lizards blended with the background and it wasn't until they moved that they could be spotted.

By the late afternoon we had cruised right round James Island and moored again in Sullivan Bay. Then we all climbed into the little wooden pangas (dinghies) and were ferried to a natural landing stage on Bartlomé Island, which like most ledges near sea level provided a resting place for Sea Lions, who were reluctant to move aside even when we stepped ashore. We climbed steadily to the 359-ft high summit, stopping frequently to listen to the guide who pointed out the fragile nature of the ecosystem and asked us to keep to the well defined path.

He indicated the simple plants that had managed to gain a foothold, or should it be roothold, in the powdery lava dust that rose in tiny clouds as we tramped upwards. The ability of plants to survive in such hostile circumstances amazed me. They were the pioneer plants that would prepare the way for the more diverse and exotic vegetation that would follow. I was looking at a newly created living space on earth and I could well understand how it stimulated Charles Darwin to ponder on the origins of the multitudinous life forms he encountered on his travels.

The higher we climbed the more spectacular became the view. We reached the summit just before the sun set and looked down. The *Sulidae* was quietly anchored in the bay and was dwarfed by Pinnacle Rock, the plug of a long-extinct volcano that had been sculptured by nature over the centuries. On a nearby neck of land dark green mangroves were bordered by coral sand strandthe colour of Jersey cream. In the distance the volcanic peaks of James Island turned from grey to black as the sun sank behind them. The silence was immense. It was almost dark by the time we returned to our base which was floating on a blood-red sea.

Dusty, sun-burned, tired yet still exhilarated by the events of the day we sat on the deck letting our emotions slowly uncoil as we sipped drinks before being summoned into the saloon for a splendid feast prepared by hard-working chef Gonzalo. After dinner some people took their bedding on deck and slept under the stars.

They barely wakened when the engines started at midnight and the boat set sail northwards in time to anchor for breakfast. At 9.30 am we jumped into the water for the first dive of the day in Darwin Bay.

The bay, formed by the rim of a partly-eroded volcanic crater, provides a good anchorage. However its partially land-locked nature creates its own undersea character, as we soon discovered. The water was green, due I suspect to the large amount of phytoplankton flourishing on the nutrients dropped into the semi-static water by the birds that were nesting on the island in huge numbers. The underwater visibility appeared to be even poorer because the cliffs cast a shadow on the zone in which we were diving. The fish seemed to be more timid than on our previous dives. But the abundance of Sea Lions made up for that, and an inspection of one member of our group by a Hammerhead Shark was noted in the log as the highlight of his dive. However, from a photographic standpoint the dive was disappointing.

The same could definitely not be said for the land excursions where we were able to get within a few inches of the birds. Amongst those we photographed were Blue-footed Boobies, who pointed their beaks skywards and produced an enchanting flute-like call. They nested on the ground and their vivid pale blue webbed feet made them easy to identify. Their close cousins, the Red-footed Boobies, nested nearby in the bushes. They have prehensile feet with which they can grip branches and therefore perch in trees, and I amused myself with the thought that if a Blue-footed Booby tried to do likewise it would fall off — making a real booby of itself.

But of all the birds I saw it was the Frigates that I enjoyed most of all. It was courting time and the males were doing their utmost to attract females. To do this they put on a marvellous display — inflating a throat sack with air until it swelled up like a small brilliant red balloon. With their heads held back and beaks open they chortled their love messages towards any bird, be it Frigate or non-Frigate, male or female, that flew overhead. They were so caught up in the mate-procuring process that they ignored the camera-clicking crowd from the *Sulidae* completely. I was able to focus on a fly on one inflated throat sac. It was much easier than attempting to take a picture of a sparrow in London.

Only the male Frigate Bird has the extraordinary red display pouch and when it takes off to fly away the sac gradually deflates until it has the appearance of a shrivelled and rather unattractive scrotum. Once airborne they are masterly in flight and soar above the cliffs with a superior grace waiting for other seabirds to return from fishing trips. When a suitable victim is spotted the Frigate swoops down and harasses its victim to such an extent that it regurgitates the catch it has been storing in its crop. The flying hustler then pounces on his prize — a sort of airborne mugger.

A further lesson in animal behaviour awaited us when we returned to the boat. Along the beach we encountered several female Sea Lions, frolicking in a pool like a group of nubile maidens. Entrance to their aquatic pleasure-garden was via a channel between the rocks. At the sea-end of the channel a large bull Sea Lion, identified as such by both his size and his heavy brow, swam back and forth, occasionally barking and making his presence felt by one and all. This was quite intentional and was only partly for our benefit to inform us he was aware that we were wandering through his harem. However, most of his display was directed at the group of younger male Sea Lions who were swimming further offshore. They were waiting their chance to rush up the channel to the tantalising females the minute the old bull went out to catch himself a spot of lunch. The poor old fellow was in a predicament — go hungry or be cuckolded.

Our affection for Sea Lions increased with every encounter. The following day I dived with Luciano at Punta Vincenta Roca where we explored an underwater cliff face where the layered rock had been eroded to form a series of shelves and a large cave. They acted as display cabinets for static marine life with colourful Sea Squirts and other encrusting species decorating every nook and cranny. The cuttings in the rock also provided a safe refuge for multitudinous fishes — amongst them the Golden Hogfish which is endemic to the Galapagos Islands. It is very unusual in that every fish has a different patchwork colouration, ranging from white and gold to black. Thus it was possible to identify every individual fish. What benefit, if any, the Golden Hogfish derives from this we could not fathom — and we put it down to being yet another of the sea's unanswered mysteries.

It was an enchanting dive with my mind unable to assimilate the great variety of new species of fish I had seen. At the end it was briefly tainted with annoyance when I discovered I had lost a detachable close-up lens. However my irritation was short-lived when it was produced by Luciano. He had seen a Sea Lion swimming around with it in its mouth. Realising that the cheeky devil had probably pulled it off the front of my camera

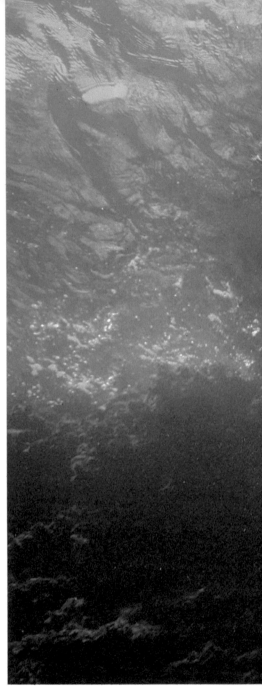

This magnificent male Frigate bird posed for me whilst I focussed on a fly on the pouch he had puffed-up to attract a mate. (Photo: Horace Dobbs.)

and swum away with it, he attempted to recover it for me by shouting at the Sea Lion and waving his arms. His ruse worked. Startled by the manic behaviour of the strange intruder the Sea Lion dropped the lens in fright and departed with the speed of a rocket. Whereupon Luciano swam forward and caught the lens as it zig-zagged down into the depths.

Nowhere did we encounter Sea Lions in greater abundance and fearlessness than off the small island of South Plaza. We moored the *Sulidae* in the channel between North Plaza and South Plaza and joined the Sea Lions that

Cow sealion with cub. (Photo: Horace Dobbs.)

crowded around the small stone jetty. The sea alongside the jetty was a Sea Lion nursery and swimming there was like being in a three-dimensional underwater playground seething with the twisting and turning bodies of young Sea Lions. They behaved just like children at playtime, continuously on the move. There was lots of physical contact as they jostled with one another. The arrival of a couple of skindivers, Luciano and me, in their midst was a new source of interest for their lively young minds. They were wary at first. But their intense curiosity was stronger than their fear, and they egged one another to come closer and closer to us. When they felt reasonably sure we posed no threat they came right up to us. One of them, seeing his reflection in the dome port of my wide-angle lens, came right up to my camera and touched it with his nose whilst another Sea Lion gripped one of my fins in his mouth and gently tugged at it. I turned round to see what was happening. In doing so, I startled them so much they exploded away from me. In two seconds the sea was empty. Five seconds later faces started to peer inquisitively at me from a distance through the

67

milky water. Within half a minute confidence was restored and I was once again in the middle of a maelstrom of Sea Lion cubs.

When I returned to the same site several years later we moored our tender alongside the jetty whilst we went ashore to inspect, amongst other things, one of the rocks on the low island of South Plaza. It is the throne upon which the biggest bull Sea Lion in the colony sits, or more accurately, lolls. Over the centuries the volcanic rock has become polished as smooth as marble. Upon returning to the jetty we discovered that a facemask had disappeared from the back seat of our tender. One of the crew, who was waiting on the shore nearby, said he saw a young Sea Lion jump into the small boat, pick up the mask, and then jump back overboard to show his newly-acquired toy to his playmates frolicking nearby.

When we eventually returned and were ferried back to the big boat in the channel the entire group of young Sea Lions came along too, swimming excitedly around us and sometimes leaping like dolphins. This was their normal pattern of behaviour but they usually turned back to the security of their playground before reaching the centre of the channel. On this occasion, however, they stayed with us all the way and then milled around the big boat as we climbed back onboard for lunch. When we were all back somebody noticed a Sea Lion wearing a facemask playing alongside. The man dived into the sea and returned a few moments later triumphantly carrying his stolen facemask.

In addition to the large colony of Sea Lions the island of South Plaza is also home for a sub-species of Galapagos Land Iguana, which is endemic, but has relatives in Central and South America. No two animals, living side by side, could contrast more vividly than Iguanas and Sea Lions. Iguanas look like prehistoric dragons, with long tails, scaly skin and a ridge of spines along their backs. If all one saw were pictures of them appropriately enlarged one could well imagine them spitting fire and clawing at St George as he valiantly tried to rescue a distraught maiden held hostage in a cave. On meeting them in real life, however, they are not at all fearsome. Indeed, the opposite applies. They are rather lovable creatures. Iguanas are vegetarian and those that live on Plaza chomp the pads of the Opuntia Cactuses with apparent relish. They do so as if eating ripe plums, despite the fact that this food supply, which is a type of Prickly Pear, is covered with needle-sharp spines. I watched fascinated as one used its back legs and tail to form a tripod, thereby enabling it to stretch up and reach a fleshy cactus pad out of

which it took a semi-circular chunk with a single, shark-like bite.

Even more remarkable than the Land Iguanas are the Marine Iguanas that spend most of their time on the land but feed mainly on seaweed. Their short blunt noses allow these animals to crop the close-growing seaweed from the rocks at low tide. They also dive to feed on algae and can stay underwater for over an hour. This is a truly remarkable evolutionary adaptation and once again I can envisage how Darwin must have pondered on the driving forces that caused it to come about.

Marine Iguanas, like all reptiles, are cold-blooded, their temperature varying with that of the environment. However, the enzymes that liberate the energy necessary for movement work best at about 98 °F, or 38 °C i.e. the body temperature of mammals. Thus after spending a relatively cold night they need to warm themselves up in the morning before venturing into the sea to feed. There is one place in the Galapagos Islands where they congregate in great numbers each morning to do this. It is at Punta Espinosa on Fernandina Island.

They crowd together on the rocks soaking up the sun's rays and a human intruder walking amongst them may well be sprayed with a jet of saturated salt solution ejected from their nostrils. 'Water, water everywhere, nor any drop to drink' is a line from the *Ancient Mariner* which reflects the toxicity of salt water to humans. The ability to ingest sea water and then eliminate the salt via 'salt-glands' that open into their nostrils is yet another example of the remarkable changes that Marine Iguanas have undergone during their evolutionary transition from land reptiles to sea reptiles.

The Marine Iguanas totally ignored us on the land and we could film them easily. But they were much more elusive underwater. This was partly because they fed in shallow water where the sea surging over the rocks made it uncomfortable for the diver. The Iguanas could cling to the rocks with their sharp powerful claws. This I discovered when I eventually found one which continued to browse on the seaweed like a sheep on a mountainside whilst I was swept back and forth by each successive wave.

The Marine Iguanas are smaller than the Land Iguanas, reaching a maximum length of one metre. They are also distinguishable by their colouration which is sooty, although some of the seven sub-species are suffused with red or green. We occasionally spotted them well offshore, usually with their heads above water. When approached they would submerge

Facing page: **Sealion cubs are natural acrobats and zoom about at great speed.** (Photo: Horace Dobbs.)

69

Above left: **Sea iguanas warm up on the land before diving to feed on shallow seaweeds.** (Photo: Horace Dobbs.)

Above right: **A Land iguana uses its tail and back legs to form a tripod when reaching up to take a bite out of a prickly Opuntia cactus pad.** (Photo: Horace Dobbs.)

and swim away with alternate sideways sweeps of their laterally compressed tails, their fore-limbs hanging like arms by their sides in a slightly comical posture. I saw several, with distinctive orange-red markings, in open water off Hood Island which has a spectacular blow hole at Punta Suarez.

At different intervals, according to the wave pattern, the sea rushes into gaps at the base of the cliffs. Then with a gurgle, followed by a deep hiss, a jet of water gushes into the air, sometimes to a height of 10 metres. When the sun is out the spray creates a short-lived rainbow with each blow.

Marine Iguanas are sometimes seen at the top of the highest cliffs on the island which rise to about 100m. They are most numerous in the region of the blowhole where they often remain immobile on the rocks enjoying, one assumes, being drenched with water at regular intervals. One day however, I was aghast to see in the water jet, the black silhouette of an Iguana propelled skywards like a cannonball. The unfortunate creature must have been caught unawares and swept into the blowhole by the inrushing water. I watched the Iguana twist as it flew through the air. Then it thumped down onto the rocks when the water jet switched off. I ran forward expecting to find a corpse, but the Iguana scuttled away, apparently none the worse for its aerobatics.

Thus I can say, with a modicum of truth, that I have seen a flying Marine Iguana on the Galapagos Islands. I wonder what Darwin would have made of that.

The Galapagos Islands have been described as an anvil of evolution and one cannot help feeling that the process is still forging ahead as strongly as ever. The islands lie at the confluence of three major ocean currents, each of which is subject to variation. Thus the underwater environment is influenced by changes that may have taken place a thousand or more miles away. This in turn gives rise to unpredictable visibility and currents. It also gives rise to a veritable galaxy of underwater life with the greatest diversity I have seen anywhere in the world. Each island also has a unique character both above and below water and that makes it virtually impossible to select a single island or dive as typical of the entire archipelago. However the island of Floreana is as much of a 'must' for all those visiting the Galapagos as is the Tower of London for visitors to London.

Firstly, the island is famous for its mail box in Post Office Bay. The first box, in the form of a wooden barrel was erected in the late 18th century and it has served as an unofficial mail box ever since. It is the only public post box in the world where no stamps are required. In the past outward-bound sailors would leave letters in the box and homeward-bound travellers would collect them and deliver them by hand. Buccaneers would leave messages for one another in the box. Nowadays the tradition has been carried on, but in a different way. Visitors rifle through the letters and postcards, selecting those of greatest interest to post once they get back home. They also leave cards for the next batch of tourists to rummage through, read and hopefully post, with appropriate stamps, at a later date.

The island of Floreana is also famous for its human inhabitants. In 1932 Heinz Wittmer left Germany and arrived with his wife Margret and son Harry. Two months later the self-styled Baroness Eloisa Bosquet von Wagner, brandishing a riding crop, arrived with a retinue of lovers. The extraordinary behaviour of the sex-mad Baroness, her disappearance and the discovery of the mummified body of one of her companions coupled with tales of a tropical paradise set tongues wagging and

To the delight of everyone aboard we were often escorted by Bottlenose dolphins who loved riding the bow wave. (Photo: Horace Dobbs.)

newspaper reporters tapping the keys of their typewriters. John Treherne picked his way through the plethora of facts and fantasy generated by these events to produce a book of compelling fascination which was published by Jonathan Cape in 1983, entitled *The Galapagos Affair*. I had the benefit of the contents of the book when I revisited Frau Margret Wittmer in November 1985. Grey-haired and spritely, she still ran the official Post Office on Floreana. I could detect no difference from when I first visited her in April 1977 when she was already 86 years old. With the aid of her 79 year-old sister on that occasion she had cooked and served an evening meal for our entire party during one of our few nights ashore.

It was immediately prior to my visit to Frau Wittmer's in 1977 that I made my first dive off Champion Island which lies a short distance off the north-east coast of Floreana. The island was small and we jumped into the sea from the deck of the *Sulidae* which the captain took close inshore. Once we were all safely in the water the captain moved away from the rocks and left the two wooden dinghies, expertly manned by his crewmen, to cover us on the surface. There was a current running and my partner Jan and I let it carry us along as we descended. The layered rock of the island was well eroded and this gave rise to a very interesting stepped undersea topography. As we swam down and were moved along by the current it was like going down an escalator in the London Underground, but instead of advertisements we had a living exhibition of corals, algae and hosts of fishes to look at. At a depth of 10m we discovered a cave with two entrances. As we arrived at one entrance a 2-m shark swam out of the other. We hovered outside the opening, holding on to the rock to prevent ourselves being pushed along by the gentle current. Inside we could see another shark resting quietly on the floor of the cave. It was about 1¹/₂m long and appeared to be a Galapagos White-tipped Reef Shark.

I went to take a picture but could not do so because my supplementary wide angle lens had come adrift from the camera and the string, attached to it to prevent it getting lost, was tangled with my regulator hose. I tried to unravel it without success. So I signalled to Jan to stay put, to keep an eye on the shark, whilst I surfaced. I also wanted to know exactly where I was — because it's not every day you find a cave with sharks in it. Within a few seconds of my arrival on the surface one of the Ecuadorian boatmen was alongside me. I partially inflated my lifejacket and he quickly untangled the mess. I re-attached the lens to the front of the camera and sank down again

using Jan's rising bubbles to lead me back to her. But not before I had made a careful mental note that the shark cave was about 50m off a small white beach on the south-eastern side of the tiny island.

After taking a photograph of the shark, which had its head pointing into the cave, I gently stroked its tail. It felt like fine sandpaper and I could understand why shark skin was once used to polish wood. The shark edged forwards a few inches and settled again. Sharks have no swim bladders with which to regulate their buoyancy and in open water must swim forward all of the time using their pectoral fins as hydrofoils to regulate the depth. When I was a schoolboy I was told that sharks needed to move forward constantly to maintain a flow of water over their gills and that they therefore never rested. Well my dive off Champion Island proved that I had been misinformed on both of those counts. The shark in the cave was taking a nap and using its negative buoyancy to rest firmly on the bottom. There was no current in the back of the cave and we could see the gill slits opening and closing as the shark used a regular muscular action to pump oxygenating water over its gills.

When we left the cave we were once again picked up in the current and propelled effortlessly on our journey, barely using our fins at all and changing our buoyancy to regulate the depth. At one stage I dropped well below Jan and looked up to see her black silhouette above my head. Around her was a disc of clear blue water that was rimmed with a shoal of Amberjacks, each about 1m long. They circled round her at high speed moving with the controlled power of a gang of leather-clad motorcyclists on powerful machines. Capable of tremendous acceleration they were, I felt, far more menacing to any small fry than the sharks that we saw cruising lazily past in the hazy distance, often amidst shoals of fish.

The undersea ledges and caves we passed on our drift dive around Champion Island provided places for turtles to settle and rest in peace. That was until the human visitors arrived. To the knowing diver a resting turtle is like a stationary bumper car at a fairground. Most find the offer of a free ride irresistible. I have to admit it was with some amusement I watched a diver towed past whilst clinging to the carapace of a turtle. The look on the turtle's face was more one of resignation than fear or annoyance.

In many ways the Galapagos Islands are a giant amusement park for the undersea naturalist, with new and colourful experiences enticing the visitor from one location to the next. In this Darwinian Undersea Disneyland

the drift dive along the southern coast of Champion Island could be likened to a fast roundabout ride. With good surface cover it is safe and exciting, even for novice divers. However, for the experienced diver with strong nerves looking for thrills it is just a warm-up for the roller-coaster ride round an even smaller island close by that is aptly called 'The Devil's Crown.' It is the top of the cone of a volcano and consists of a roughly circular crown of viciously jagged rocks that stick above the surface of the sea like a ring of misshapen black teeth.

There is so much to see in the Galapagos Islands that we invariably moved to a new site for each dive. However, on my last visit in November 1985, such was the reaction to our dive at The Devil's Crown that it was unanimously decided to go through the whole experience again the following day as a pre-breakfast dive. Our Galapagos naturalist guide, Jimmy Iglesias, had never experienced anything like it before and in the diving log he noted it as a six-star dive! I would have to put it in my list of the top three dives in the world.

It was listed as dive number seven in the log

— which meant that the little difficulties that always arise at the beginning of an expedition had been resolved, and we had established a routine for diving. There were six divers in all, and we started off as three pairs, rolling in backwards over the gunwales of the pangas when the boatmen yelled 'go'. The current was running like a train. Falling through the water was like dropping through a huge flock of starlings. There were fish in every direction. Underneath us the seabed of dark broken volcanic rock rushed past. When a rocky upthrust in the seabed appeared I swam as fast as I could towards it and grabbed at it with my gloved hand. The current ran even stronger over the top of the outcrop. The piece of rock I was trying to cling to snapped off and I was whisked away by the current before I could get a second hand-hold. My partner had disappeared. We were all very experienced divers, however, and I knew he would try to drop down behind a rock out of the current, as soon as he could. If not he would surface and be picked up by one of the dinghies. I swam down to the seabed, but the loose rocks were totally encrusted with barnacles which were jagged

A shark dormitory? I found sharks sleeping in the same cave on several occasions. (Photo: Horace Dobbs.)

and sharp. So I let the current carry me to the next outcrop, behind which I immediately swam. There I encountered two other divers, a husband and wife, who had managed to stay as a pair. I signalled the OK sign to them and started peering into the crannies. One of the rocks opened into a small cave decorated like a miniature shopping arcade at Christmas time with colourful corals and sponges. The far end of the cave was open to the sea, the aperture providing a pale blue backlight on the occupants which were both static and mobile. On the floor of the cave a Sea Turtle had planted itself. So had a Sting Ray with a one-metre wing span. They decided to evacuate when I poked my head in the front door of their home, but two huge groupers also in residence moved slowly backwards into the darker recesses. Then they too decided it was safer outside than in, and exited sharp right as they left the far end of the cave. I entered swimming very gently so as not to damage any of the delicate coral during my transit.

After I had swum through I turned back on myself and peered in again. My eyes were adapted to the darkness and I saw that the two groupers were back in residence again having swum round the rock and re-entered the cave by the front door.

I was aware of a presence behind me and turned round with a start. I found myself looking into the lens of a camera wielded by my partner who had found me. Behind him a curtain of yellow and black Surgeon Fish passed; they were so densely packed they completely obscured the view beyond.

When we entered the sea we all knew that the small island of The Devil's Crown was on our left-hand side when we went with the current. As water never flows in a continuous circuit around an island I knew if I kept the rocky mass on my left-hand side and went with the current I would eventually come into slack water. Well that was the theory anyway. And it worked out in practice too. I surfaced on the remote side of the island from where I had entered the sea. I was in shallow water over a tumbled mass of large boulders in the company of a troupe of inquisitive Sea Lions. I sat quietly on the seabed and looked up. One very curious Sea Lion came slowly down. I stopped breathing and remained perfectly still whilst he put his nose on the glass plate of my facemask and felt around it with his whiskers. Knowing that blind Sea Lions can use their whiskers as sensitive fingers to find crustaceans, I wondered what he made of us. It was doubtless a new experience for both of us.

I deliberately ended my dive in the centre of The Devil's Crown because I knew from previous experience that the Sea Lions would provide a fitting finale. I wasn't disappointed. A small group came in and whirled excitedly round the enclosed space as if it were a stage. I always thought of their performance, with its graceful acrobatic whirls and twirls as a spontaneous ballet performed by natural artistes for the sheer love of it. There was no set choreography. Every performance was different and more enjoyable from my point of view because of its unpredictability. I was happy to be on my own. Indeed, without the distraction of fellow humans I felt closer and more intimate with the surroundings and my Sea Lion playmates.

As all members of the party were photographers, as well as experienced divers, I knew they too would be safely and happily engaged in pursuing their pictures. We all had roughly the same underwater endurance on a single cylinder of air — about an hour. So once the boatman picked up one diver he knew it wouldn't be long before the others would surface holding one arm vertically above the water which was the signal we used for 'I want to be picked up'.

When I had sucked the last of my air from my bottle I snorkelled out to the boat. After the boatman had relieved me of my camera first, weight-belt second and air cylinder third, I hauled myself over the gunwale to join the

Sometimes the underwater visibility was limited by the density of fish such as this shoal of Surgeon fish. (Photo: Horace Dobbs.)

husband and wife team, who unlike everyone else were still together.

As always after such a dive there was an immediate exchange of information. They reported they had seen a shark, which I hadn't, and two Moray Eels, whereas I had seen only one. They also said they were aware of considerable temperature differences in the current, varying from very cold to comfortably warm. This suggests that two major currents come together in this region, which could account for the exceptionally prolific life.

When returning to England after my first visit to the Galapagos Islands I was acutely aware that virtually all of the scenery in Britain has been influenced and changed by the hand of man. Even the heather-covered North York Moors were once forested. In the Galapagos Islands I couldn't help feeling that I had had just a peep at the dawn of creation — before man with his ingenious mind. his manipulative fingers and his machines started irrevocably to change our planet.

Luciano with a playful sealion who blew out a stream of bubbles as he whizzed past. (Photo: Horace Dobbs.)

DIVE 8 THE PACIFIC OCEAN: The Poor Knights Islands by Wade Doak

Above left: **A dive boat emerges from Rikoriko Cave.** (Photo: Horace Dobbs.)

Above right: **The Poor Knights Islands, twelve miles off the Northland coast, New Zealand.** (Photo Wade Doak.)

Standing near the edge of the continental shelf The Poor Knights Islands are remnants of an ancient string of volcanoes that once erupted along the fault line off New Zealand's eastern coast. When Ice Ages froze so much of the world's water that sea level changed, the surf pounded rocky beaches (now 50m down), creating vast sea caves, tunnels and archways in the softer portions of the rock.

The Poor Knights cliff faces soar hundreds of feet up in a vertical forest and plunge sheer through the surface to depths as great as 100m, broken by ledges, fissures and underhangs. At 50m there is often a sandy plain, shelving away gently before a second slope carries on to greater depths beyond scuba range. Such submarine topography offers the diver a wide range of depths within a short horizontal distance.

I have found that other offshore islands around New Zealand do not generally rise from deep water like the Poor Knights. Above, their cliffs may be just as lofty but below there are few dramatic drop-offs, the islands being based on a shallow subtidal plateau. At the Poor Knights I can glide gently down a giant staircase to an Ice-Age beach, fifteen storeys below. This is a vertical city. As if a section of the world were tipped on edge, facing the open ocean, it is blanketed with living creatures, a wall of hungry mouths.

The encrusting inhabitants of the deep-sea cliff depend on imported food supplies. Day and night the ocean currents bring them rich streams of plankton. With their stinging tentacles the polyps of Anemones, Gorgonians and Black Coral Trees seize the tiny ocean drifters and thrust them into their central maws. Sponges draw them into their filtration systems as a dilute plankton soup. Barnacles, Bryozoans and Tubeworms ensnare them with bristles and tentacles. Bivalve Molluscs and Sea Squirts suck them into their siphons; Feather Stars entrap them in delicate plumes. Almost every animal which competes for standing room on the sea cliff filters and digests the tiny plankton creatures passing by on the ocean wind — an endless energy flow from afar.

The giant staircase is the best starting point for an understanding of this complex community. In the course of a single descent the changing life patterns of huge zones on the conshelf unfold before my mask.

Suppose you now join me on a scuba dive down the cliff face we have surveyed on Landing Bay at the Poor Knights. We don our equipment, check our air supply and decide upon the general direction of the dive. We are going to make a steady descent to 55m, compensating with our buoyancy vests en route.

As we fin from the dive boat to the cliffs above the giant staircase a concrete frame becomes visible, cemented to the rocks among the Limpets and Periwinkles of the splash zone. The rock face at water level is fringed with seaweeds: the large brown *Carpophyllum* and the small reds, their tresses alternatively hanging from their hold-fasts dripping and shiny, or floating out in the incoming surge.

Directly beneath them the *Ecklonia* forest begins. Sparse at first because of heavy wave action, it burgeons into a dense canopy at between 10 and 20m, and suddenly thins to scattered clumps and dwarfed individuals as

the staircase steps down past the 25m level through the sombre blue depths.

In the initial 10m between the stalks of kelp, and especially within the many curving cham-

A light is useful for peering into the nooks and crannies when drifting down a wall in the Poor Knights Islands. (Photo: Horace Dobbs.)

bers or recesses in the rock, a multi-coloured Sea Anemone, *Corynactis haddoni* is the dominant encrusting form. If the diver peers into these small, wave-sculpted grottoes, he will see a kaleidoscope of colour. Little seaweed can grow in these dark spaces but the surge sweeping the fronds aside allows a brief glimpse of the vivid carpet of anemones, a random splatter of red *Lithothamnion* 'paint', orange *Tedania* Sponge encrustation and delicate Bryozoan floss. Beneath the *Ecklonia* such Bryozoans form a very dense zone down to 15m interspersed with Thecate Hydroids like fragile trees or ferns. Red Algae wave in the gentle rocking of the sea-swells, and from every crevice and hollow weed-dwelling, Butterfish, Kelp Fish, and Black Angels dart or mould themselves into the walls.

The upper 25m is a zone of dizzying profusion. Beneath the *Ecklonia,* life forms encrust each other and use every inch of space threefold to secure a position on the staircase. This intense competition for space has resulted in an astonishing variety of fauna: these organisms can only live where other life forms permit.

Close to the diver's mask a fantasy of tiny marine organisms, several inches thick, smothers the rock walls. The sessile, filter feeders are among the first animals in the food chain. On them the mobile feeders, such as Crabs, Starfish and Whelks, rely for food and shelter. Many filter feeders strain microscopic plant life, *phytoplankton,* from the upper regions. Others are carnivores on a small scale, catching tiny animal plankton. Where light intensity is low carnivorous animals such as the anemones cannot colonise unless an ample food supply is created by vigorous water movement. Hence the enigma of their presence in dark recesses in shallow water, but their absence beyond 10m. Water movement rather than light intensity appears to be the limiting factor in their case.

It is the interplaying factors of water movement and light intensity, brought about by increasing depth, and variations in the rock slope, that produce micro-environmental changes. These in turn create favourable opportunities or limits for the inhabitants of this vertical garden and together with biological disturbances, account for the crazy quilt-patchiness of each form.

However, as the divers glide beyond the 25-m level a marked change is apparent. Wave action no longer has any real part in the distribution of species. From now on it is all a matter of light intensity, as determined by the degree of slope or the increasing depth, for the sea is a great light filter.

This lower region is the supreme realm of the sponges. Most seem to prefer a light intensity below one per cent of normal sunlight, and in the shallow regions they must seek dark underhangs or fissures in the underworld of the *Ecklonia* forest. At the upper levels heavy wave action often inhibits development, but in the quiet, dim depths, as competing life forms diminish, sponges gradually dominate the rock slope with encrusting varieties — lemon-yellow, violet, or bright orange-red. Farther along the wall at 60m stand graceful erect sponges like candelabra, salmon-pink funnel shapes, organ pipes, yellow golf balls, and where Scorpion Fish lie camouflaged, massive dark-blue crenellated cups like eroded battlements. At these depths the Hydroids too have developed from the stunted one-inch growth at 6m to dainty filamentous Plumularians up to 4 ins long. They festoon the slope, along with the fragile lolly-pink *Reteporan Bryozoan* known as 'Lace Coral' and the pink, delicately beaded Gorgonian fans of the Primnoides family; the gilled Cup Corals and fleshy, pliant Alcyonacean Corals in pastel hues.

The divers, falling gently down through skeins of friendly Demoiselle Fish, land on a shining white beach. From the cliff foot they gaze up the fantasy staircase, its multitudinous life forms in silver-rimmed silhouette, to where the *Ecklonia* forest looms in dark knots, merging in the haze of distance just beneath the living quicksilver of the surface. A poetry of drowned colours, frozen sound and sublime weightlessness invades the mind at these depths. The divers are endangered by the hazards of nitrogen narcosis and the bends, and must ascend the staircase to the sun.

No single descent could possibly take in the seething life of these sea cliffs any more than one could become acquainted with all the inhabitants of a skyscraper in a single elevator ride.

For me the most distinctive quality about the Poor Knights Islands is that I dive *in* them, not at them. So many caves, archways, domes and tunnels give an architectural dimension to the underwater experience. Sometimes it seems like a dream as I fly through the galleries, halls and corridors of a gravity-free metropolis. One of my favourite dives is Airbubble Cave.

Like a lake of mercury suspended overhead, the bubble shimmers and bellies with our scuba exhausts. We surface through the mirror. Not much clearance overhead in this low dome, but a glance back down the way we entered offers a rare sight for the skindiver: a turquoise blue light filters up through the water and dances on the cave roof. It has come bouncing down from the sea surface to the cave floor and then up into the air-bubble.

Around the cave entrance schools of fishes moving to and fro cause the blue radiance to shimmer and pulse. Further back into the cave our torches pencil through the clear cave waters picking up schools of Bigeyes, like copper sculptures. The water in sea caves can be very, very clear as no plant plankton can live in these sunless, secret places. We head right to the back of the cave and then upwards. Our heads burst through into the second air bubble.

This one has a much higher dome structure so that there is plenty of clearance overhead. On the far side the water shallows over the cave floor, forming a handy seat where we can rest waist deep in the water. A muted blue light filters in from below. We remove our mouth pieces and start talking in the echoing chamber. Our breath forms vapour clouds which vanish and reappear like ghosts before our eyes.

Each time a surge meets the cliff face outside the cave we feel our ears click with the changes in air pressure. This is the cloud chamber effect which meteorologists can only study under expensive laboratory situations. We are 8m down in a natural undersea habitat. To stop and think about it for a few minutes produces a lasting impression in the mind.

Airbubble Cave is one of the deepest such structures at the Poor Knights Islands. The air in it does not come from diver's exhausts. My theory is that it gets there naturally. The eastern side of Tawhiti Rahi is the most exposed to heavy weather. Powerful wave action in the rocky basin along the southern side of Hope Point produces tremendous surges and the whole area becomes one seething mass of white water. For days the cave is filled with tiny bubbles and these gradually percolate upwards and collect in the domed roof of the cave, forming an air bubble.

The air is sweet to breathe (until a boat load of divers drop in) and each storm replenishes it. Under pressure it is constantly dissolving into the water — like the bubbles in beer.

On one occasion an expert snorkeller accompanied us into the cave and each time he needed a breath, he just pinched one from the air bubble. In sea lab experiments seals and dolphins used to do this. But this is high-pressure air. When the snorkeller came to leave for the surface he had to remember to breathe out on the way up or the compressed air in his lungs could have caused a fatal embolism.

Outside in the strong sunlight the *Ecklonia* kelp forest dominates the scene and encrusting animals come off second best in the scramble for living space. But with the reduction of light

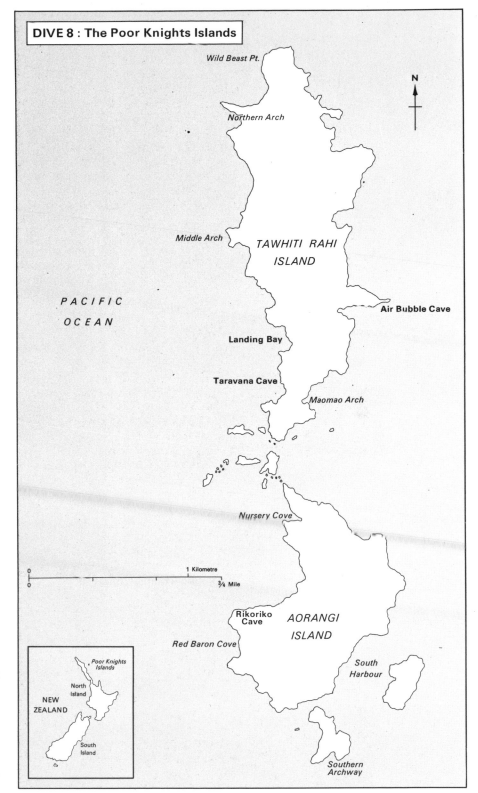

DIVE 8 : The Poor Knights Islands

Wild Beast Pt.

Northern Arch

Middle Arch

TAWHITI RAHI ISLAND

PACIFIC OCEAN

Air Bubble Cave

Landing Bay

Taravana Cave

Maomao Arch

Nursery Cove

0   1 Kilometre
0   ¾ Mile

Rikoriko Cave

AORANGI ISLAND

Red Baron Cove

South Harbour

Poor Knights Islands

North Island

NEW ZEALAND

South Island

Southern Archway

intensity inside the caves the plant life diminishes and the filter feeding animals get the upper hand.

Rikoriko Cave is one of the largest sea caves in the world. As we swim towards the back of Rikoriko at a depth of ten metres, the light

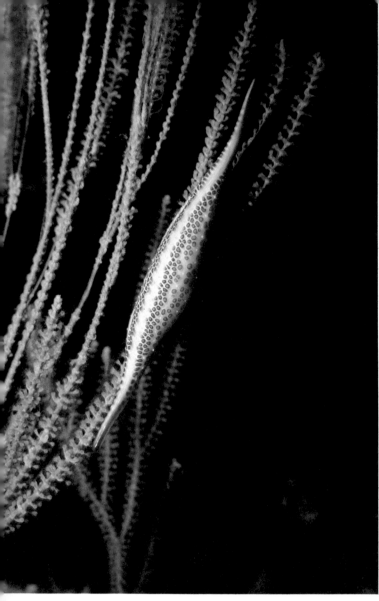

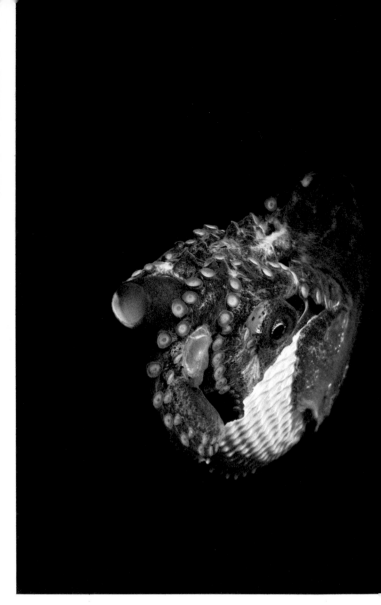

level drops dramatically until it is equivalent to an ocean depth of 100m. The next few metres further in represent 200m and then 400m. Thus, in this sea cave, as our eyes adjust to the twilight we find light conditions which are relevant to our entire continental shelf. In the furthest recess of this cave there lives a tiny salad green coral polyp *Paracyathus conceptus*, at a depth of only 10m. Previous records were from sunless regions 2,000m down.

On the shaded walls plant life can no longer convert nutrients into organic compounds using the sun's energy. For the inhabitants of the sea cave, water movement is their sole source of food.

The sea cave acts as a large shock absorber and the moving energy of food-bearing waves is quickly dissipated. This accounts for the density of filter feeders near the entrance zones, even on the ceiling. These encrusting animals shun light but they are dependent on suspended food particles reaching them. Deeper within single entrance caves like Riko-riko, as water movement is reduced the number of sedentary animals falls to zero. The back of such caves is called the 'empty quarter'. Mobile animals, crustaceans and fishes often abound there, but there just isn't enough food for encrusting life.

In submerged caves below 30m this empty quarter extends almost to the cave entrance. Whenever there are two entrances, as in archways or submerged tunnels, water movement will be vigorous all the way through, promoting dense growth. If the archway is at water level the violence of water movement may inhibit the more outstanding filter feeders, while in submerged tunnels these can flourish without hindrance.

The rate at which the water within a sea cave is being processed by the filter feeders is quite astonishing. The German biologist Rupert Riedl has calculated that if a large sea cave were sealed off with all currents ceasing abruptly, the filter feeders encrusting its walls would exhaust the cave's entire plankton content within one hour.

Scientists have classified sea caves into four basic types, each variant providing a unique combination of light penetration and water movement, factors which determine the patterns of encrusting marine life. At water level there is the sea cave and the archway. Below tide level, these are matched by the blind alley and the tunnel. The diver who familiarises himself with the dynamics of sea caves will find it much easier to understand and enjoy them.

The most unusual sea cave system I have explored is the Taravana cave system at the Poor Knights.

On the west side of Tawhitirahi Island is a bay called Landing Bay which runs south to Maomao Arch. In the huge vertical cliff face adjacent to this archway 20m below the surface is the main entrance to Taravana Cave, with its vaulting walls curving down to white sand 40m below. This part of the cave is like a vast cathedral swarming with fish life — splendid Perch, Red Pigfish, sleeping Pink Maomao, Golden Snapper, Roughies and Bigeyes. It is possible to continue along the right-hand wall of the cave where there is a passageway that curves around and leads back out into the smaller entrance of Taravana, further along the cliff. However, there are several blind alleys and the distances involved are considerable. Such a dive should only be tackled by experienced divers, suitably equipped with guide ropes etc. But for me the most rewarding areas to explore are near the entrance where the diver will find a living museum of natural history to admire.

Facing page
Top left: **The Volva shell spends its entire life on the same Gorgonian coral, nipping off polyps no faster than they can regenerate.** (Photo: Wade Doak.)

Top right: **A Paper Nautilus, a small pelagic octopus, carries its eggs in a fragile shell.** (Photo: Wade Doak.)

Bottom left: **The feathery protrusions on this nudibranch are its gills.** (Photo: Horace Dobbs.)

Bottom right: **A Starfish illustrates the diversity of colour, shapes, sizes and textures that Nature has splashed across the rocks in the Poor Knights Islands.** (Photo: Horace Dobbs.)

DIVE 9 THE CORAL SEA: Lizard Island by Gilbert Dinesen

Lizard Island from the air. (Photo: Edward Childs.)

Fate has been kind to me, as a diver. Opportunities have arisen for me to dive in all oceans but one (the Antarctic), so that when I, without hesitation, consider Australia's Great Barrier Reef my favourite diving region, there must be good reasons. But in my conscious mind I find it difficult to pinpoint them. Because of the warm tropical waters teeming with brightly coloured fish and other life? Perhaps — but not necessarily so. Some of my most memorable dives have been in the Arctic Ocean with its rich marine-biological flora and fauna. On mature reflection I believe that my predilection for the Great Barrier Reef must be rooted in one single word: AWE. For if there ever were Seven Wonders of the World, the Great Barrier Reef must surely be one of them.

Some of the seven wonders of ancient times, nominated as such by our worthy forefathers, have proved rather ephemeral in their existence. Others still survive fairly intact — like the pyramids of Egypt. The biggest of these (Cheops) contains a mind-boggling 2,300,000 limestone blocks, each weighing more than one ton. They were hewn, transported and put into place by a vast multitude of thinking human beings supervised by intelligent, highly skilled engineers and architects.

But this immense construction fades into utter insignificance in comparison with the work performed by the tiny coral polyp. This is a very lowly animal on the evolutionary ladder — it has not even developed a proper digestive system, but encloses in its middle a multipurpose hollow sac (coelenteron). But whereas the Egyptians could only hew their blocks from ready-made limestone rocks, the simple coral polyp is able to create the stone itself by extracting calcium from the ambient water. And what is the Cheops Pyramid beside the building works created by the coral polyps in a reef, which runs along the north-east coast of Australia for a length of about 2,000km, with a width of nearly 250km (at the widest) and with a depth (since the last Ice Age) of about 100m? The Great Pyramid of Cheops covers 13.1 acres — the Great Barrier Reef over 80,000 square miles!

The platform base of the reef was there — presumably due to the sinking or tilting of the Australian mainland. At the height of the last Ice Age the water level in the oceans was about 100m below the present level. However, as the ice slowly melted and the ensuing water flowed into the sea, the coral polyps were able to keep pace with the increasing water level and to build up this gigantic structure, which is known today as the Great Barrier Reef.

Scientifically, the name is a misnomer, because it is not really a barrier reef. It is not like a huge breakwater, or an unbroken chain. In the south, where it attains its greatest width, it is more like a series of reefs grown up from a submarine platform. This will explain how it was possible for Captain Cook to sail inside the reef for more than 600 miles before he realised the situation when his ship hit a reef to the south of what is now Cooktown. Admittedly he was hugging the shore at the time, preoccupied with the task of charting the coastline. But when Cook then climbed a local hill, and shortly afterwards climbed to the top of the rock on Lizard Island, he could clearly see that he was trapped inside a gargantuan barrier reef. The Great Barrier Reef tapers from south to north. Starting with a width of about 150 miles near Rockhampton it narrows to 50 miles opposite Townsville, and to 20 miles at Cairns. It is only 7 miles wide north of Cooktown, before it starts widening again. From Cairns northwards the reef assumes the character of a true barrier reef, with a series of outer reefs separated by narrow channels, through which strong tidal currents flow.

Against this barrier the true powers of the ocean come into play. Whipped up by, and driven before the South East Trade Wind, the huge breakers have had an unimpeded passage for a thousand miles or more. Then suddenly

Exploring a cave off Lizard Island.
(Photo: Edward Childs.)

they hit the rampart of the outer barrier. Almost out of sheer resentment they tower up to a considerable height, showing their white teeth when beginning to curl over. They appear to hang poised in consternation for a moment of time and then, with a thunderous crash, they come tumbling down, spewing out their watery contents over the reef, amidst turbulent cascades of swirling foam.

A similar regular pounding of such force would in the course of time destroy even granite rocks, so how can a calcareous reef stand up to such punishment? Nature has seen to that! The rampart is covered with coralline algae, consolidating and cementing the reef together; the more water is poured over them, the more nourishment they can extract, and the more luxuriantly they grow!

Inside the Great Barrier Reef you find a veritable maze of islands and reefs, intertwined by lanes and channels. The islands are of two different kinds: the rocky ones are the relics (and sometimes only the mountain pinnacles) of the sunken and now submerged part of the Australian continent; and the low, sandy ones (called cays) are more recent creations, starting with an accumulation of coral rubble left high on a reef after a tempest, and then built up by the addition of sand and silt, with bird droppings fertilizing the soil for subsequent vegetation. Some of the rocky islands may have their own fringing reefs, but not the cays.

I have already mentioned the prodigious building activities of the lowly coral polyp, but it also shows amazing versatility. It admits into its body some tiny plants (called Zooxanthellae) and maintains with them a symbiotic relationship. They supply, amongst other things, additional oxygen to the coral polyp, and remove certain waste products. As a result, the reefbuilding corals grow much faster. But such corals must not be more than about 15m from the surface because the Zooxanthellae, being plants, require light. These plants are absent in deepwater corals, which live too far down for the penetration of light.

Another aspect of the surprising versatility of the coral polyp is its ability to adjust its shape to suit local conditions. The same coral which appears as a beautiful branching bush on the leeside of the reef, or in the lagoon, can be found on the weather side as a squat or stunted growth, or even forming an encrusting layer. A nightmare for the coral taxonomist!

In no other reef have I found corals of so many hues and tints as here. The corals which you find on the beach or see in the shops are dead and therefore white; the living coral can have all kinds of lovely colours, mainly at the tips. Occasionally you come across an outcrop of Heliopora, which is always blue. The Tubipora is generally covered with greenish polyp flesh, but when touched the polyps withdraw and expose their brilliant red tubes. Add to this the many colours of the soft corals, the colours of sponges, and the magnificent colours of the numerous fish weaving in and out of the corals, and you perceive a colour picture of kaleidoscopic multiplicity.

There are of course diving opportunities all along the Great Barrier Reef, but of the principal islands renowned for diving (Heron Island in the south, Green Island off Cairns, and Lizard Island north of Cooktown) I have a special predilection for Lizard Island. It is a small rocky island, but admits of an airstrip. There is a resort, and a marine-biological station. The peak of the rock is nearly 400m high, and there is even on the island a patch of tropical rainforest near a small brook. The eponymous lizards are quite large, about 2m long, and abound. One great attraction of Lizard Island is that it is situated almost where the tapering Great Barrier Reef is at its narrowest. As the island is near the middle of the reef the distance to the chain of outer barrier reefs is merely a question of a few miles. Weather permitting, it is possible to sail through one of the apertures and dive on the seaward side of the reef.

Such a dive is fantastic. The outer rim of the reef is not exactly a straight line; there are occasionally indentations. Some of these have doubtless been created by forces difficult to imagine. When a raging cyclone whips waves to stupendous heights, they sometimes manage to wrench off a huge chunk of the outer rim, and throw it bodily on to the reef. The notch thus created serves as a 'run-off' for the water regularly poured over the reef by the crashing breakers, and it is a good place to dive. You can meet some big fish and sharks here, and what cannot help affecting your mind is the knowledge that you are literally on 'the very edge', and that just a mile or two further out the depth to the ocean floor will exceed 2km! Another good place to dive is in the openings between two outer reefs, where the richness of water supply ensures a prolific marine-biological life; but caution is required as these gaps are indeed tideswept.

It was during one of these dives that I witnessed a peculiar spectacle. At some depth I noticed a large grotto with a comparatively small opening. I shone my torch into it and saw a huge Grouper. Having once in the muddy waters of the Niger River near Port Harcourt in Nigeria caught on a hook a Grouper weighing 534lb, I could see by comparison that

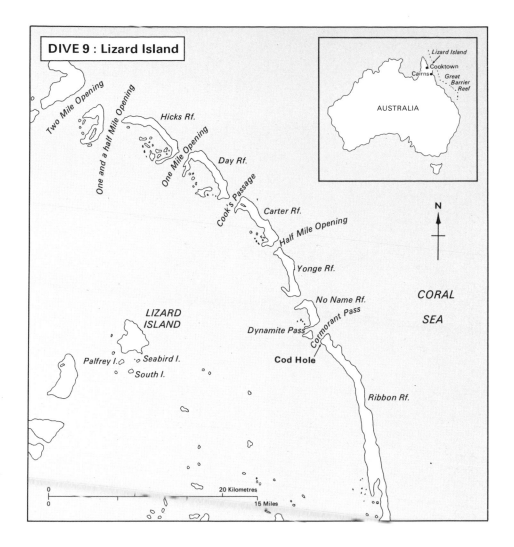

this one was even larger. It had just caught in its mouth a sizable Moray Eel, the head and tail of which were still writhing furiously outside the mouth. I doubt whether the Grouper had ever before seen an air-bubbling human diver equipped with a torch; it was obvious that after a short reflection it decided that discretion was the better part of valour. It rushed past me, with its wriggling prey still in its mouth, at such a speed that the displacement of water almost caused me to rotate!

My daughter, who was my diving companion at Lizard Island, was at the time collecting material for her Ph.D. thesis. It was mainly a question of studying in situ certain corals living in the penumbra of a grotto or under an overhang. So the only thing I saw of my daughter was her yellow fins jutting out. My task was to ensure that no errant shark took advantage of my daughter's preoccupation. This gave me ample opportunity (moving about in a slow, air-preserving manner) to look into every nook and cranny of the coral reef. It was amazing what you could notice and find. I am not a highly qualified scientist, who at short notice can identify specimens to generic or even to specific level, but my marine-biological knowledge is sufficient to ensure that most things I come across fall into some kind of place. I thoroughly enjoyed these long, leisurely dives. I really began to appreciate the complexity of the reef ecology, and to marvel at all its aspects. As I was moving so slowly I caused no disturbance and blended in with the reef. Around and above me the Parrot Fish with their fused teeth, used for scraping off corals, emptied their stomach contents of crushed, inorganic coral sand, which came down like fine rain. Digging down on sandy spots amidst coral rubble revealed a microcosm of teeming life, anxiously snapped up by little fish showing no fear of me. Every spot on the reef is used somehow — a temporary exception may be the white wastes left behind through the ravages of the rapacious Crown of Thorns Starfish. One can never get tired of watching the antics of the

Clown Fish weaving in and out of the tentacles of a Sea Anemone, without being harmed by its stinging cells, or of admiring the organisation of a nearby 'cleaner-station', frequented by all kinds of fish to get rid of their embarrassing parasites.

A nightdive in these waters is especially fascinating. I recall one dive in particular. We left the boat and slipped into the water exactly as the last golden rays of the setting sun disappeared from the horizon. With a few exceptions the stony corals are nocturnal, and in the torchlight you could see the web of their twisting tentacles. We swam past a huge sleeping Turtle, which had wedged itself under a coral block; I noticed that perhaps years ago a shark had bitten off one of its hind legs. A Squid became mesmerized by our torchlight and permitted us to play with it. All the creatures which during the day hide themselves in crevasses and hollows in the coral reef were now on the rampage. Contrariwise, most fish were now asleep; the Parrot Fish neatly enveloped in a transparent cocoon, like a plastic balloon. This is discarded in the morning and remade every night, and the purpose of this expenditure of energy is apparently to thwart the olfactory sense of its deadliest enemy, the Moray Eel, which hunts by its highly developed sense of smell.

Suddenly I was startled. In front of me was something eerie, which at first I could not comprehend. It turned out to be a huge crab poised on a ledge. Its carapace was ridiculously small compared with its long 'arms' equipped with powerful pincers at the ends. But the crab was apparently so old that it had ceased its regular moulting. So seaweeds had attached themselves all over the body and long strands of algae hung down from its arms and claws, which the crab furiously waved against us, in resentment at our intrusion. No horror movie could have produced a more terrifying effect!

When we returned to the surface we were greeted by a lovely moon and the twinkling constellation of the Southern Cross. The sea was full of phosphorescence. When I took a mouthful of water and spat it out, it produced a glorious luminescent cascade. These scintillating nocturnal pinpoints of light are mostly caused by a planktonic dinoflagellate called *Noctiluca Scintillans*. What a felicitous choice of name!

Whilst on the subject of nocturnal activities, nothing is more awe-inspiring than watching the great Turtles, forced by their reptilian origin to lay their eggs ashore, emerge from the sea at night, and laboriously clamber across the beach to a suitable place above high-water mark. Here the Turtles, so agile in the sea but

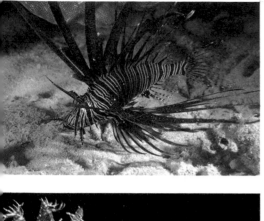

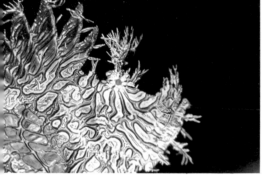

so cumbersome on land, will scoop out a hole in the sand, lay their eggs, cover them again with sand by filling in the hole, and use their last strength to regain the water the same night. You may think that sufficient punishment has thus been meted out to the turtle family, to expiate their audacity in adopting an aquatic existence, but no! The eggs themselves are subject to heavy predation; after incubation the young ones have to dig themselves out of the sand and make a quick dash for the sea, whilst running the gauntlet between birds, shore crabs and other predators. Even those which are fortunate enough to reach the sea are not safe. These adorable little creatures have to come to the surface to breathe, where waiting sea-birds pick them out. They have to swim across the long reef flat where an estimated further 50% are eaten by numerous predators before they reach deeper waters. Sexual maturity is only reached after many years, and merely a tiny fraction attain such age. It is amazing that they have survived at all!

So life can be harsh for the inhabitants of this Garden of Eden, and for the diver there

Facing page
Top: **A Moray eel emerges cautiously from its lair in the reef.**

Middle: **Cod Hole was so named by divers because of the huge friendly Potato cod that live there and now expect to be fed by their visitors.**

Bottom: **Some of the inhabitants of Cod Hole can become too friendly when looking for handouts.**
(Photos: Edward Childs.)

Above left: **A Lion fish on the prowl.** (Photo: Edward Childs.)

Below left: **One of the inhabitants of the Great Barrier Reef—a Scorpion fish with dermal appendages which constitute a mastery of camouflage.** (Photo: W. Nash.)

Below: **A member of the Operation Raleigh Expedition to Lizard Island looks in wonder at the corals.** (Photo: Edward Childs.)

are dangers too. I personally prefer to wear a full rubber suit as a protection against the Fire Coral and the mainly seasonal but rather poisonous Jellyfish ('sea wasps'). The magnificent Lion Fish with their long, poisonous fins are slow-moving and can easily be avoided; and the thoughtless tourist, who goes 'reef-fossicking' and puts live Cone Shells into the breast pocket of his shirt has really only got himself to thank when the highly poisonous foot of one of these shells, with a spearlike motion, penetrates his shirt and his skin, and deposits its venom at the worse possible place — near the heart. The risk of a diver getting his foot caught between the valves of a Giant Clam (so often shown in old films) is very much exaggerated; the adductor muscle closing the valves does not work so fast. After all, the Giant Clam is a filter feeder, and does not live on prey caught by an instantaneous closure of the valves. More insidious is the extremely well camouflaged Stone Fish which can be an ugly customer. It may be possible to tackle a Blue Ringed Octopus, but my advice is: 'Don't' — unless you have got an unshakable faith in your fellow diver to give you artificial respiration for several hours to tide you over the pulmonary collapse.

But the main danger is, of course, the sharks. An Australian diver once told me that without doubt the worst sharks were to be found amongst second-hand car dealers; but the aquatic ones must not be taken lightly either. Generally speaking, the sharks inside the reef are well fed, and consequently, if you leave them alone, they will leave you alone. Admittedly, if you dive at a more distant reef, the local sharks may never have seen a diver before, and will approach you out of sheer curiosity. Otherwise, the advice given is simple and sensible: 'No jump entries into the water, unless you can see your way clear, sharkwise. If a shark does join you, try not to tense up, keep up a leisurely stroke (no violent finning), and if you do get bumped, try to relax and in any event do not overreact.'

This peculiar habit, whereby sharks bump intended victims, has been described at some length in shark literature. It is believed to have its origin in the fact that the shark possesses certain sensory ducts around its head; when it bumps, the shark gets an advance taste of the anticipated meal, a kind of appetizer. A disturbing habit, anyway, and one which I was unfortunately to witness towards the end of my first visit to the Great Barrier Reef.

Setting out from an island in the northern part of the Barrier Reef, the boatman Chris eventually anchored his boat a considerable distance away from the shore, over an underwater coral pinnacle, surrounded on all sides by deep water. The small plateau lay at a depth of 5 – 10m.

Chris professed to be an ardent spearfisher, but his 'sportive' proclivities also constituted a regular source of revenue to him, as he sold his catch to the local hotel on the island. In the boat were a number of tourists who went snorkelling; I happened to be the only one equipped with scuba gear.

Scarcely had I got into the water with my aqualung when three sharks made their appearance — two about 2m long and one measuring about 3m. The two smaller ones were White Tipped Reef Sharks; the larger one, some distance away, I could not identify. Yet, they seemed inoffensive enough; as a matter of fact I swam after one of them in order to get some close-up photos. It started circling around the pinnacle, and I was full of admiration for the effortless way in which it glided majestically through the water. Aeons of evolutionary time had pushed the streamlined shape and propelling technique of this ancient fish to a pitch of perfection! We must have swum nearly round the pinnacle when, at a depth of 15m, it began to descend at a fairly steep angle. I had no intention of following it and went back to the plateau, which was extremely beautiful. Fascinated, I stayed in as long as I could, and when I had finished the air in my bottle, I returned to the clearly visible boat, got into it and took my gear off. A number of speared fish were lying at the bottom, and I was told that Chris was still spearfishing. Just at that moment he appeared, adjusted his mask and shouted: 'I have been attacked by a shark, knocking off my mask. It hit me on the side of my head. I saw stars everywhere. Am I bleeding?'

'Come into the boat, quickly', cried one of the passengers, but Chris replied: 'I would rather Gilbert came into the water with me.'

I guessed at once what had happened. The suddenness and violence of the attack had given him a fright and he knew that, unless he overcame that fear at once by retrieving the spear gun, he would never be able to go spearfishing again in these shark-infested waters. Other people in the boat protested vehemently, but they just did not understand this.

Grabbing the remaining spear gun, and adjusting my snorkel and mask, I slid gently into the water and swam over to Chris. He had speared the biggest fish of the day at a depth of about 20m, and about 12m down we could see the spear gun and the speared fish amongst some coral; the line was now badly entangled. Chris borrowed my knife so that he had some kind of defensive weapon, loaded the speargun, handed it back to me and asked me whether I would dive down with him. I was to cover him whilst he retrieved the speargun and the fish, and continue to cover him on the way to the boat.

Years of training and underwater snorkel swimming now served me in good stead. We descended to 12m. While Chris was disentangling the line, extricating the fish and retrieving the gear, I carefully scanned the blue depths, from where a shark might emerge. I was preserving oxygen by keeping fairly still, and although the whole operation did not last more than $1^1/2$ minutes or so, I began to feel that I was running short of breath. Presumably the tenseness of the situation caused a greater consumption of oxygen. So I was glad when Chris gave the signal that he was going up. I followed, keeping my eyes on the deep all the time. Fortunately, no shark appeared. We got quickly into the boat and hurried back to the island. Chris's fear that he had broken the upper part of his jawbone proved groundless, but he certainly had a serious concussion. He was put to bed and slept for a solid 14 hours.

Cousteau and others have pointed out that there appears to be no rigid code of behaviour by sharks, and you can never really tell how one of these fish is going to react. But it is known that blood does attract sharks and may arouse their appetite; it can even whip them into some state of frenzy. Obviously, the spearing of the large fish by Chris proved too much of a temptation for the shark, which, until then, had been satisfied with watching us from the deep. My own, and rather convenient, theory is simply that sharks do not do any harm to good people. At least in my case, it still has to be disproved!

DIVE 10 THE PACIFIC OCEAN: Truk Lagoon by Horace Dobbs

The sunken ships in Truk Lagoon have become a war museum that can only be visited by divers who arrive from many parts of the world. (Photo: Horace Dobbs.)

In the limited visibility and gloom of the underwater world shipwrecks are mysterious and invite exploration. The diver drifting into the metal labyrinth is ever hopeful that he will come across at least one relic that will convey some of the romance and mystery that all shipwrecks have.

Of the many wrecked ships I have swum around on the seabed I have no hesitation in selecting one as the ultimate wreck dive. It is the *Fujikawa Maru* in Truk Lagoon in the Eastern Caroline Islands that are situated in an area of the Pacific Ocean indicated on some maps as Micronesia.

There are many reasons why the *Fujikawa Maru* has come to the top of my wreck list. Many shipwrecks are no more than a mass of twisted and broken metal spars which, if transferred to the land, would look like ugly scrap heaps. The *Fujikawa Maru* doesn't come into this category because it is fully intact, and furthermore, it is still loaded with cargo. For the historian interested in the ironmongery of warfare the *Fujikawa Maru* is as fascinating as a World War II museum.

The exact date that the ill-fated ship sank to the seabed is known exactly and during the years that have since passed she has become encrusted with coral. Marine biologists who are interested in coral growth rates thus have a clearly defined datum from which to work.

Finally, especially from my point of view, the *Fujikawa Maru* is photogenic. She is just what most of the non-diving public think of as a wreck in which all of the bits can be clearly identified. And as the visibility is usually good it is possible to convey on film some idea of what the vessel was like before she sank, as well as showing the transformations that have taken place since. Indeed, it was on an expedition to Truk Lagoon to make a TV film that I made my first dive on her, on 6th May 1979.

It always takes a couple of dives in a new area to get into the rhythm of diving. Equipment has to be sorted out, and weights adjusted etc. These are routines that divers learn and practise during training and come as second nature to experienced divers on expeditions. However in Truk Lagoon we had the added task of becoming familiar with some new filming and photographic equipment. Divers can't talk to one another underwater and any instructions must take place via sign language. So when making a film it is vitally important to establish a sympathetic rapport between the various members of the film unit as quickly as possible. This is especially true when working on a documentary film at a new location with little or no prior knowledge of what will unfold during a dive. The Bolex camera my filming partner Chris Goosen took into the water with him was loaded with 30m of film which would give him a running time of about two and half minutes. Changing the film was a tricky and tedious job that involved opening the underwater housing. So he couldn't just pop up, change the film and go down again.

Our lighting man, Mike Stevens, carried a single powerful battery-operated lamp that also had a limited duration. His job was to use the lamp creatively to illuminate subjects which we wanted to film in close-up. He also had to act as my diving buddy whilst Chris filmed the two of us exploring the wreck together with me taking still pictures and pointing out any interesting subjects that presented themselves as we went along. My job was also to anticipate what would make a nice sequence, signal to Chris and Mike what I wanted them to do, and then swim off into

Cameraman Chris Goosen and lighting man Mike Stephens emerge from the hold of a sunken ship. (Photo: Horace Dobbs.)

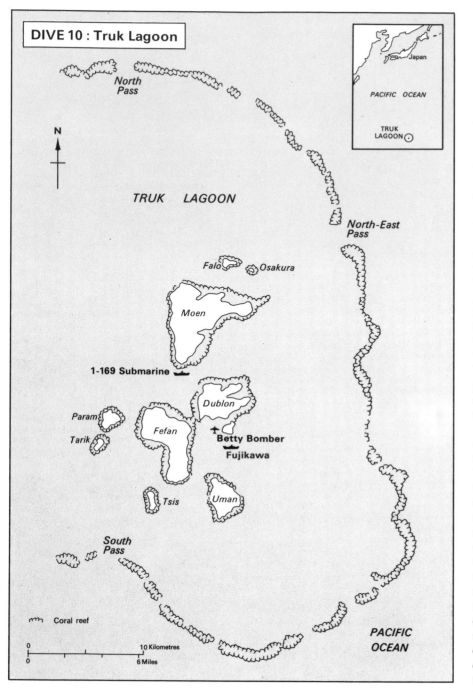

DIVE 10 : Truk Lagoon

North Pass

N

TRUK LAGOON

North-East Pass

Falo · Osakura

Moen

1-169 Submarine

Dublon

Param

Fefan

Tarik

Betty Bomber

Fujikawa

Tsis

Uman

South Pass

PACIFIC OCEAN

Japan

PACIFIC OCEAN

TRUK LAGOON ⊙

Coral reef

0 — 10 Kilometres
0 — 6 Miles

very stout steel posts and we tied up to one of them.

Once in the water the heavy camera and lights were lowered over the side on ropes. Immersed in sea water they weighed very little. We exhaled and drifted slowly down. The water was beautifully transparent and we could clearly see the deck of the wreck about 20m beneath us. It always takes a long time for me to clear my ears. Having burst one of my eardrums a couple of times as a result of diving too quickly I have to resign myself to a slow descent, no matter how enticing the view below. The critical region is close to the surface where the relative pressure change is greatest. It is very difficult to judge a rate of descent in open water. So I prefer to have something which doesn't move in my view all of the time to give me some idea of how quickly I am going down. The anchor rope, which is what I normally use, was attached to one of the posts. So I swam to the post as a reference point whilst my two companions, who were not troubled with 'slow ears', plummeted down. They knew I would join them eventually. The post was totally encrusted with hard and soft corals, further embellishments being added in the form of sponges and shell fish.

To find a pillar of intensive, compact colonial life in the vast and apparently empty sea was like coming across a bustling New York skyscraper in the middle of the desert. Close to the surface it was vibrant with colour, especially red. As I descended in my imaginary outside elevator, the colour filtering effects of the water above me muted the decor of the coral-coated building until it was a subtle mixture of soft greens, greys and blue. Once I reached a depth of about 10m I could descend more rapidly and I turned my attention away from the post. Through the clear blue water I could see a curtain of glistening bubbles streaming upwards. Beneath it my two companions were foraging amongst the coral encrusted winches and other structures on the upper deck. I swam down and joined them just as they reached one of the huge holds. The hatch cover was missing. We drifted down through the large rectangular opening of hold number two into the dim recesses of the vessel.

As our eyes became accustomed to the darkness the shadowy shapes took a more definite form. I recognised the fuselage of a small aircraft. It was a Zero Fighter — of the type used by the famed Kamikaze pilots who flew only one mission — piloting their aircraft loaded with explosive directly onto the target and blowing themselves to oblivion when they made contact. When Mike turned on his light everything became bright, sharp and solid. I

action hoping my messages had got through.

It was precisely ten minutes past eleven on the morning of the 6th May when Chris, Mike and I jumped into the sea for our first dive on the *Fujikawa Maru*. We launched ourselves from the deck of the ancient boat that had chugged out from our base at the Truk Continental Hotel on the island of Moen. The six-mile journey had taken over an hour but the skipper had no difficulty finding the exact spot because two of the masts of the wreck broke the surface of the lagoon. They were eased myself, fins first, down into the tiny cockpit allowing the joystick to project upwards between my legs. I held the top of it with my hand and discovered that it was free. The controls were still intact and as I rocked the joystick from side to side the tail fin behind me moved. I really did feel as if I had stepped back into history, into the far-off times of the Second World War.

Whilst we had been looking at the Zero Fighter the other sixteen members of the expedition had been roaming about the vessel peering into crevices and prodding the darkest recesses of the holds with pencil beams of light from their underwater torches. As we slowly rose out of hold number two a small posse of divers passed us — going the other way. We mingled briefly with them before crossing the deck and drifting down into another hold in which the previous visitors had discovered a box of gasmasks. A diver put one of the masks over his face and came up behind me. I jumped when he touched me on the shoulder and was even more startled when I suddenly found myself looking at the rubber mask — the eye pieces of which looked like the eye sockets in a ghostly skull.

I was still suffering from tachycardia when we swam into a hold loaded with torpedoes and unexploded shells. Minutes passed as if they were seconds, and it seemed that no sooner was I really getting into the wreck of the *Fujikawa Maru* than it was time to return to the surface. As we drifted slowly upwards I looked down and saw one pair of divers leaving the wreck via a hole ripped in her side by the torpedo that had sent the ill-fated ship to her doom. Thirty-five minutes after jumping into the sea I was climbing out again, up the diving ladder, still reeling from all I had seen and filmed. Although there were many other wrecks in the lagoon we had to visit and investigate I felt it would be hard to beat the *Fujikawa Maru*. It was a wreck we would surely have to come back to.

Part and parcel of wreck diving is piecing together the history of the ship and the circumstances under which it was sunk. I gleaned the story of the *Fujikawa Maru,* and the other wrecks in Truk Lagoon, from many sources.

Their story started when the Japanese were preparing for World War II. They secretly moved 40,000 troops and civilians into this remote, but strategically important natural harbour which was about 40 miles wide and covered an area of 820 square miles. An airfield was built, so too were submarine pens. The passes into the lagoon were either mined or defended by guns that could blast into

kingdom come any enemy ships attempting to enter the lagoon. Having dubbed Truk Lagoon as 'The Gibraltar of the Pacific' the Japanese were convinced it was impregnable. Impregnable, that is, from a sea attack. But the concept that Truk was an 'invincible bastion' was totally shattered in one mighty 36-hour naval air raid that began at dawn on the 17th February 1944 and caught the Japanese totally by surprise. Storming over Truk in 30 waves from elements of the U.S. Navy's Fast Carrier Force 90 miles away came hundreds of American fighters and bombers, unleashing devastation and destruction on the lagoon

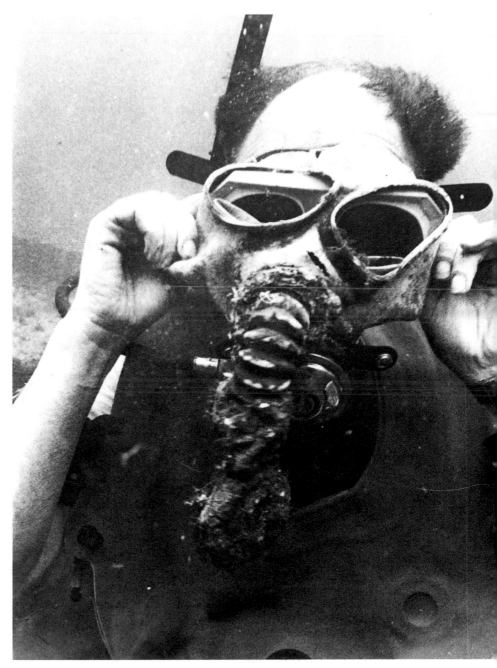

I jumped when I turned round and found myself looking at a rubber mask – the eye pieces of which looked like the eye sockets in a ghostly skull. (Photo: Horace Dobbs.)

before returning to the safety of their aircraft carrier bases. When the din had ceased and the smoke had cleared the Japanese counted their losses. More than 60 ships, including 15 naval vessels, 17 cargo ships and 6 tankers had been sunk or permanently damaged. 250 aircraft had been destroyed. The Japanese attack on Pearl Harbour, which had brought the USA into Second World War in 1940, had been avenged.

So surprising was the Truk raid that most of the ships, many of them loaded at the time, sank at their anchorages. Collectively they represented the largest fleet of ships sunk at one time in the history of the world.

Now they lie on the seabed, coral-quilted memorials to those for whom the clock stopped in February 1944.

Whilst we were diving and filming in Truk Lagoon we met an American pilot who flew 747 Jumbo Jets for a living. He was over fifty years of age. During his youth, however, whilst his compatriots were screaming across the skies of the Pacific he was flying Spitfires and other aircraft over Europe. Nonetheless he was fascinated by the fall of the Truk Lagoon and always wanted to see the wrecked aircraft for himself. But it was not until 1979, just prior to our visit, that he had learned to dive.

The water in Truk Lagoon is tepid and most divers do not wear any thermal insulation. Most, however, wear some covering, usually old clothes, to protect themselves from the sharp corals, or being cut by wreckage. Not wishing to sacrifice his best clothes for this purpose the airline pilot purchased some clothes from a shop on the island of Moen, which is one of the most depressingly poor places I have ever visited. The quality of clothes sold reflected the quality of life of most of the islanders. The socks he bought were no exception. The dye bonded more strongly to his skin then it did to fibres of his footwear, dying his feet a vivid green. So if you ever come across a 747 pilot with green feet you will know he has been to Truk Lagoon!

One of the aircraft he was most interested in was built by Mitsubishi and was given the name of Betty Bomber by the Americans. The Jumbo pilot spoke quite lyrically when he talked about the Japanese place in an interview, part of which we eventually used as voice-over in our film. It was obvious that he held the bomber, which had the long range of 3,700 miles, in very high regard, and would have loved to have flown one himself. But he had to content himself with visiting the remains of an aircraft, that was obviously a delightful (from a pilot's point of view), 28m down on the seabed off the island of Eten.

Facing page
Top: **One of our guides brandishing a gun he found in a sunken aeroplane.**

The Betty Bomber rested on the sea bed like a giant stranded whale. (Photos: Horace Dobbs.)

Below: **Bicycles still hung in the hold – exactly as they did when the ship sank in 1944.** (Photo: Horace Dobbs.)

The Betty Bomber in question was shot down after take off and nose dived into the sea. The engines were ripped off when she hit the water and the cockpit area was caved in. The rest of the aircraft remained intact and when we looked down on her from above she looked like a Whale with huge flippers stranded on the seabed. We easily entered the fuselage and swam inside through the entire 20m length of the aircraft. Halfway along was a circular hole which was originally covered with a clear plastic dome which could be used by a side-gunner. Evidence of this function was apparent from a machine gun and rounds of ammunition we found inside the opening. We raised the heavy gun to the surface using a lifting bag. Having filmed and examined the gun in detail we returned it to exactly where we found it. Continuing our journey we gently fingered the cables and piping attached to the inside of the fuselage before swimming gently into the large cockpit where we found a radio transmitter complete with dials and legible inscription. The Perspex windscreen had gone but the twisted framework in which it was once mounted was still there and formed an open cage which was home for a small shoal of Butterfly Fish. They flitted gracefully out through the ever open portals when we invaded their territory. The outside of the cockpit frame was partially encrusted with corals. Most of the body of the aircraft, however, was uncolonised. It was just covered with a layer of dirty silt.

For a brief time the Betty Bomber was a scene of scurrying human activity as the divers inspected it, inside and out. The swirling action of their fins caused the silt on the aircraft and the surrounding seabed to swirl up in clouds. When we came to leave I looked down from the surface before I climbed back into the boat. Beneath me I could see the entire aircraft resting on the seabed as if it was sitting on a runway. Even as I watched the last of the divers leaving the scene the clouds of silt were settling. The Butterfly Fish had already returned to their unusual house under the sea — provided by the providence of war.

At a depth of 28m the Betty Bomber was completely unaffected by surface conditions. So even when the sea was rough she would remain quietly at rest until the next group of divers came finning down just as we had done — like visitors to an undersea war museum — which is exactly what Truk Lagoon is. There are many exhibits in this unusual museum which is open only to those who can dive and are prepared to travel to this remote location. During the course of our two-week stay the party of 19 divers who made up the expedition completed a total of 433 dives.

The most demanding from a diving standpoint was that onto a sunken submarine which lay at a depth in excess of 40m. The submarine has become a classic dive since it was filmed by the American diver Al Giddings. Indeed it was his film 'The Silent Warrior' that made me aware of the existence of Truk Lagoon and inspired me to go there in the first place. The story of the sinking of the submarine, the I-169, is a bizarre and tragic one. The huge vessel, which was one of the prides of the Japanese submarine fleet, was powered by twin 4,500hp engines, and had a range of 16,000 miles, a surface speed of 20 knots, and a submerged speed of 9 knots. But she was not sunk during Operation Hailstone. The I-169 foundered 6 weeks later during a relatively minor U.S. air strike.

When the alarms were sounded she crash dived. Unfortunately for those onboard somebody neglected to close the valve in the storm ventilation tube. As a result the control room was flooded and the submarine could not surface when the raid was over. A diver was sent down to investigate. He reported that there were responses to his hammer signals from all hatches except the conning tower. It was assumed that only a little water had entered the sub. A 30-ton crane was dispatched to raise her bow to the surface, but the cable snapped. Soon all signals within the submarine ceased and lifting the vessel was abandoned. Japanese divers recovered 32 out of the estimated total of 87 crewmen onboard before depth-charging the ship to render it useless to the invading U.S. forces. When Al Giddings entered the submarine in the late 1960s he discovered and filmed the skeletons of the Japanese submariners who remained inside the vessel that became their sunken tomb. The submarine claimed some more victims a few years later when another group of American divers visited the wreck. They got lost inside and ran out of air before they could find their way out.

Our dive on their submarine of ill omen was not without incidents — one of which could have added my filming partner Chris Goosen to the I-169's list of victims. It was a grey, sullen day and the choppy sea was unfriendly. We anchored over the submarine and Chris and Mike descended at their usual speed leaving me to follow at a slower pace down the anchor rope. I quickly lost sight of my companions. I was alone in the blue — surrounded by open waters in every direction — with no sight of the surface or the seabed. The rope I was following down went slack. I took little notice assuming the wind and/or current had changed the position of the boat. Holding the rope very gently in one hand I allowed my excess weight to pull me slowly down. In the other hand I clutched our stand-by Bolex camera in its heavy pressure-resistant housing. I watched my depth gauge that told me I was steadily getting deeper. At a depth of about 35m the end of the anchor rope slipped through my fingers. The rope had parted. Decision time. Should I do the sensible thing, abandon the dive, swim back to the rope and go back to the surface? If I did that I knew I would never dive on the I-169. Or should I try and find my companions who hopefully had found the wreck? I quickly looked about me. At the extreme limit of my visibility I thought I could just see the occasional hint of glinting silver which indicated bubbles rising to the surface. I swam as hard as I could in the that direction knowing that I would be safer if I could join them. The bubbles became clearer. I looked down and there below me was the cigar-shaped hull of a submarine. I stopped. I had a reference point. I wound-up the mechanical motor of my camera and could hear it whirring as I swam towards an open hatch — filming as I went.

Mike was hovering above the aft engine room hatch beaming his lamp down into the bowels of the submarine in which Chris had disappeared. An eerie yellow glow spilled out of the opening. This came from the lights on Chris's camera. They illuminated the silt he had stirred up inside. Knowing how we were always exceptionally careful not to disturb the sediment because it could reduce the visibility to zero in seconds I wondered what Chris was doing. He appeared to be struggling. I was about to give my camera to Mike to investigate when the camera with its attached lights still blazing emerged from the opening, thrust forward by Chris who was holding the two handles on the camera housing. His legs had got caught up in some cables inside the sub and he had had to struggle to extricate himself. When I had filmed his exit we closed the hatch. It slammed shut with a resounding boom that still echoes round my head when I think about it.

We were all short on air when we headed towards the surface. Fortunately my companions didn't know that there might not be a boat to pick us up, for it is very easy to drift when an anchor rope parts, and for the crew to be unaware of what's happening.

Fortunately my fears were unfounded. Although our diving guides were a touch laid back in their general demeanour they were very alert and efficient when it came to boat handling and diving. I later discovered that they soon realised they were drifting offsite and having returned to station dispatched a diver to locate the anchor and reconnect the diving vessel to it. Being super efficient he also made sure that the anchor was well and truly bedded in. This was fine until we came to leave when all of the group had completed their dives. When we tried to haul in the anchor it wouldn't budge. Fortunately we had the aquatic equivalent to Superman in our party. We dubbed him 'Aquaman'. He relished the title and all that it implied. Here is what he wrote in the expedition log:

Chris Goosen filming the superstructure of a wreck that had become colonised by delicate soft corals. (Photo: Horace Dobbs.)

The outside of some of the wrecks, which could have been hideous eyesores if left above water, had been converted into exquisite gardens under the sea in Truk Lagoon. (Photo: Horace Dobbs.)

'After the dive the anchor became fouled, so Bruce and I re-dived and freed it. ANOTHER JOB FOR AQUA-MAN!'

Although some people might argue that the submarine I-169 is the classic dive of Truk Lagoon the opinion of virtually all of my party, myself included, is that the best dive in Truk is the *Fujikawa Maru*. It was to this wreck that we returned to celebrate our last dive on the expedition. We could have spent our entire time exploring and documenting this extraordinary exhibit in our undersea museum. As an example of a Japanese armed cargo vessel of the Second World War the *Fujikawa Maru* is probably the best preserved one still in existence. The six cargo holds are still filled with a great variety of equipment ranging from large engines to tyres and mess kits, in addition to the Zero fighters already mentioned. Inside the bridge area are two large tiled bathrooms. The triggers, handles and sighting mechanisms

of the guns on the rear and aft sections are still intact. In the holds beneath them are considerable quantities of ammunition, some in boxes. Unused shells, pointing upwards, are packed like jars of jam on supermarket shelves. Inside the wreck where there is little light and no current to carry the nutrients essential for coral growth, everything is covered in a thin layer of silt. Much of the outside of the wreck however has been transformed into an exotic coral garden. Passageways have become tunnels from which soft corals hang like clusters of flower blossoms. Delicate exquisitely coloured fish, always on the move, add their own contribution to the extraordinary kaleidoscope. By decorating the tombs of the dead in this way, nature is surely demonstrating the beauty and resilience of life, and in doing so makes us even more aware of the brutality and futility of war.

DIVE 11: THE INDIAN OCEAN: The Great Basses Reef by Arthur C. Clarke

If you look at a map of the world, you will see that the island of Sri Lanka (formerly Ceylon) hangs like a teardrop off the southern tip of India. Running parallel to the south coast of Sri Lanka, at a distance of about 6 miles off shore, is a wave-swept line of submerged rocks bearing the curious title *Great Basses* which comes from the Portuguese *Baxios* and means a reef or shoal. A glance at the map shows that the Great Basses — and its sister reef the Little Basses, a few miles to the east — might have been especially designed to snare ships rounding the southern coast of Sri Lanka. This double trap lies directly across one of the main trade routes of the oriental world; every ship

of any size passing the longitude of India has to contend with it. (The narrow passage to the north of Sri Lanka, full of shifting sandbanks and almost blocked by the submerged land ridge known as Adam's Bridge, is not navigable except by very small craft at certain seasons.) For at least 3,000 years the twin reefs must have taken their toll of shipping; it is conceivable that there has been a greater concentration of wrecks here than anywhere in the world outside the Mediterranean or the Aegean.

Even in daylight, during perfectly calm weather, ships have come to grief on the Basses. At night, the two reefs must have

Launching the lighthouse relief vessel *Pharos* into the surf at Kirinda. (Photo: Arthur C. Clarke.)

99

presented an appalling hazard to ships, especially when they were being driven landwards by the winds of the south-west monsoon. Not until the middle of the nineteenth century could anything be done about this danger. By then, however, progress in engineering had made it practical to construct lighthouses on such remote, wave-swept rocks, and the government of Sri Lanka, alarmed by the continual losses in this area, gave orders for work to proceed.

The first attempt to erect a lighthouse on the Great Basses was a total failure; after the British Board of Trade had sunk £40,000 into the project all it had to show for its money and three years of work was a solitary flag pole on the rock. Though a lighthouse made of cast-iron had been built in England and shipped out to Sri Lanka, no one could manage to get it across the remaining ten miles of sea to the reef.

A new approach was obviously needed, and it was provided by Trinity House, the London corporation responsible for matters affecting the safety of shipping. The cast-iron lighthouse was shipped off in disgrace to the Bahamas (where, as far as I know, it may still be doing a good job), and an all-granite version was designed in 1867 by Sir. J.N. Douglass, the engineer of Trinity House and builder of the famous Eddystone Light. For advice on the construction of the lantern itself, one of the greatest scientists of the nineteenth century was called in — Michael Faraday, whose discoveries made possible the age of electricity.

The thousands of tons of granite were carved and assembled in Scotland, then the blocks were carefully numbered and shipped to Sri Lanka. Only one of the more than a thousand blocks was damaged in its transit halfway round the world, and even that caused no delay, for the engineers had thoughtfully provided spares.

The actual job of erection on the reef was supervised by William Douglass, brother of the designer, and having seen what he was up against, I have an enormous respect for him. The huge blocks of granite (two or three tons in weight) were carried out to the site from the port of Galle, 60 miles to the west, in two small steamers specially built for the job. In the first year, a crane was set up on the reef, and with its aid the blocks were slung ashore. In the second year, most of the tower was built, and in the third, it was completed. The ruby beams began their circling on March 10th 1873, and have flashed every night from sunset to sunrise ever since.

There can be few men who have left a better monument than the Douglass brothers; think of them, if you ever round Sri Lanka on a stormy night.

In the late 1950s I and two diving companions, Mike Wilson and Rodney Jonklaas, were attracted to this out-of-the-way spot for a very simple reason. As underwater photographers, we were always on the look-out for clear water — which was not as easy to find as you might think. A rock 6 miles from the nearest land should be an ideal place, for it would be far enough out to avoid the wind and silt which the great rivers were constantly sweeping into the sea. Equally important, it would be virgin territory. No one had ever dived there before — indeed, everybody said it was impossible because of the dangerous breakers — and all of the marine creatures we would meet should be unafraid of us and our cameras.

Though there are plenty of isolated rocks in the sea there are very few upon which men can live. That was why the Great Basses Reef, with its 110-ft high lighthouse, was so attractive. The lighthouse was not exactly a luxury hotel, but it would make a splendid base for our operations. Lighthouses, are not, of course, normally open to visitors, but we had been offered hospitality by the Imperial Lighthouse Service in return for a small salvage job we had done on one of its relief boats.

Mike and Rodney made reconnaissance visits to the reef in 1958, taking their equipment out each day in a small fibre glass dinghy. The 20-mile trip across dangerous waters in a light open boat was a hair-raising performance I was glad to have missed.

We chose the time of our 1959 expedition — April — with care, for it is only possible to dive on Great Basses for a short period every year. For almost ten months out of the twelve, the weather is so rough that it is difficult even to approach the lighthouse, and quite impossible to land. The rock on which the tower is built is not much larger than a tennis court, and is nowhere more than three feet above the waterline. Even in calm weather, waves are liable to break over it at any moment.

Fortunately, the good season can be predicted with a fair degree of accuracy. This is because the Indian Ocean has a mysteriously regular system of winds — the famous monsoons — which come and go almost according to the calendar. Between October and March the winds blow from the northeast; then it slackens, and there are about two months of calm weather. But between April and May the wind switches to the other direction; the south-west monsoon sets in, with heavy rain and violent storms. The only time that operations on the reef are possible, therefore, is through March and April; and we could not always count on this, for the monsoon is not absolutely reliable. But in 1959 we were lucky; we had almost perfect weather.

Both the Great and Little Basses lighthouses were serviced by a relief boat based at a little fishing village with the lovely name of Kirinda. At Kirinda, the Imperial Lighthouse Service maintained a stoutly built powerboat, the *Pharos*, with a crew of skilled seamen who knew how to get her out to the reef, unload a couple of tons of stores, and bring her safely back.

Because the *Pharos* sailed before dawn, when the sea was at its calmest, we had to be on Kirinda Beach at the hideous hour of 4 am and our aqualungs, underwater cameras, compressed-air tanks, drums of gas, canned food, weight belts, air compressor, and other gear were loaded in the dark, being carried out on the heads of husky Kirindans wading through the surf. It was a clear, starry night, and above us the constellations of the equator hung at angles I had never seen before, being too addicted to sleep to be a good astronomer.

Out on the horizon, 10 miles away, the bright ruby flash of the lighthouse flickered every forty-five seconds. As we drew away from land, I could not help wondering when we would get back to civilization. The relief boat was due to pick us up again in 5 days, but there had been times when it was delayed for weeks by bad weather. If this happened, we would certainly not starve, but we might get rather tired of eating fish.

We were several miles out to sea when dawn broke, not as quickly as it usually does in the tropics, but almost slowly through low banks of clouds. A few minutes before the sun finally appeared, its beams fanned out across the sky in great luminous spokes, like those of a slowly turning wheel. It was a spectacle I had seen on such a scale only once before, when I was sailing back to the mainland of Australia from the Great Barrier Reef. Then it had been a symbol of farewell, but now it heralded a new adventure. And I thought how perfectly Homer had described the sight 3,000 years ago, when he wrote of the 'rosy-fingered dawn'.

An hour later, the coast of Sri Lanka was only a low, misty band far behind, dimpled blue here and there by the inland mountains. It no longer seemed to have any connection with us; all that mattered now was the white column of stone rearing starkly from the waters ahead. Around the base of the lighthouse the waves were breaking continuously at the end of their long march from Antarctica, the nearest land to the south. Every few seconds the exposed reef would be completely hidden by foam, so

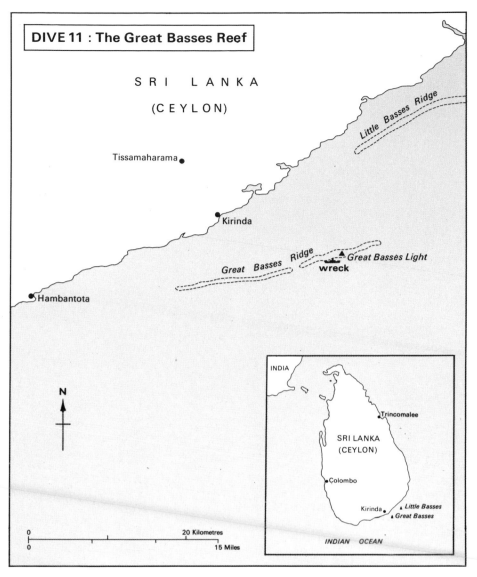

DIVE 11 : The Great Basses Reef

that only the lower platform of the lighthouse was visible. It was difficult to imagine how we could land — or, having landed, get off again.

For the next ten minutes we watched with anxious interest while the crew manoeuvred to get us and our equipment onto those wetly gleaming rocks. The *Pharos* had been towing a large surf-boat, in which we travelled with our stores, and while she stood by at a respectful distance this was rowed through the bucking waves until it came to within fifty feet of the reef. Then two anchors were let out, spaced well apart to keep the boat from being dragged onto the rocks.

The men on the lighthouse had been waiting, and as soon as our boat had come close enough they threw us a rope. The other end of this passed over the pulley of a sturdy crane bolted to the stone platform at the foot of the

lighthouse. Now the surfboat was secured at three points; by pulling on one or more of the ropes, the crew could hold it at a fixed distance from the reef. There was nothing they could do, however, to prevent it from rising and falling in the swell. At one moment we would be several feet above the level of the lighthouse platform; a second later, in the trough of a wave, we would be several feet below.

So that we could travel along the aerial ropeway now linking us to the rock, wooden bars had been lashed beneath it to act as seats. Perched on these, we were hauled up to the lighthouse, swinging back and forth with our feet just above the waves. And up that same rope, during the next two hours, went all our equipment, carefully packed in watertight containers.

Then followed the hardest work I have ever done (or ever will do) in my life. Merely living in the lighthouse was a strange and often exhausting experience. The temperature was always in the nineties, and we had to keep climbing up and down a spiral stairway a hundred feet high as we moved from one room to another. After a while I began to develop a fellow feeling for such creatures as snails and the chambered nautilus. Everything was curved; it was impossible to walk more than a few paces in a straight line, and I had to learn to sleep in the arc of a circle, for the bunks were neatly tucked into the yard-thick walls.

We had arrived at the lighthouse at midmorning, and as soon as we had unpacked our equipment and had a meal, we prepared to dive. And this involved problems, for the Great Basses is certainly no place for beginners. Indeed, we had been told that it was utterly impossible to swim around the reef, and at first sight this seemed to be perfectly true.

For though the sea was now quite calm, the water was never still for a second; the level could rise or fall a couple of yards almost instantly over the jagged, barnacled rocks. Getting in and out of the water — especially when wearing an aqualung and carrying one or often two heavy cameras — therefore required good timing and strong nerves. You had to wait for the crest of a wave, and then literally throw yourself and your gear into the sea. If you missed, you were liable to be cut to ribbons on the barnacles.

It was impossible to do any exploring really close to the reef, because the surge of the water made it far too dangerous and also stirred up such clouds of bubbles that visibility was reduced to zero. We had to aim for deeper, calmer water a couple of hundred feet away, and getting there involved fighting strong currents which always seemed to be against us, whether we were coming or going. To serve as a mobile base while we were working over the reef, we had brought along an inflatable rubber dinghy which we could anchor whenever we pleased. Our circular raft was scarcely well streamlined, and to make matters worse, the aqualung cylinders dangling beneath it caused additional drag. It usually took about twenty minutes of steady flippering to reach the spot we had aimed at, less than a hundred yards from the lighthouse.

But the struggle was worth it. Beneath us was a fantastic fairyland of caves, grottoes, coral-encrusted valleys — and fish in such numbers as I have never met anywhere else in the world. Sometimes they crowded round us so closely that we could see nothing but a solid wall of scales, and had literally to push our way through it. They were inquisitive and completely unafraid; during our visit we met, in addition to the usual menagerie of small multicoloured reef dwellers, Eaglerays, Turtles, Anglefish, Jacks, Tuna (up to 300lb), Groupers, and Sharks. Especially the latter.

One of our chief objects in coming to the reef was to get some good shark pictures; though we had encountered sharks scores of times in the past, we had never taken any really good photographs of them — they were always too shy. We had hoped that the ocean-going sharks out here on the reef would be a little less nervous than the inshore ones; this proved to be the case, and we were able to get near them without difficulty. Though the sharks were the most dramatic — and dangerous — of the reef's inhabitants, they were not the most interesting.

On our very first dive we discovered a family of three Black Groupers (species *Epinephelus Fuscoguttàttus*) each of a different size and with a distinct personality. They came solemnly out of their caves to inspect us, but kept their distance until Rodney had speared a fish. Then hunger got the better of caution; the largest of the Groupers darted at the struggling fish, and tried to wrench it off the spear. But as the barbs on the harpoon had now opened, it could not do so, and Rodney was quickly involved in an underwater tug-of-war. With considerable difficulty, as he was being jerked back and forth on the seabed, he managed to unscrew the barbed head of his spear, slip off the harpooned fish, and hand it to the surprised Grouper — who now accepted it quite gently. This was the beginning of a touching though somewhat boisterous friendship.

The biggest Grouper, which weighed about 100lb we named Ali Baba; the next, at 75lb, was Sinbad, and the smallest — only about 40lb — was Aladdin. I have already remarked that they had different personalities, and this statement often surprises people who cannot

imagine that fish, like human beings, are individuals. The middle-sized Sinbad was by far the boldest and most aggressive, and often made a nuisance of himself by trying to steal fish we had shot for our own meals. (We had to eat, too.) The most striking personality, however, was little Aladdin; he was astonishingly intelligent, and never ceased to amuse us by his display of almost human emotions — especially impatience and jealousy.

It took the Groupers only a few demonstrations to learn that Rodney's speargun was much better at catching fish than they were and that if they behaved themselves, they would be rewarded by a free meal. Once we had got this lesson across — and very few land animals would have learned so quickly — we were able to get down to the serious business of taking still and movie photos of our three actors. During the course of about a dozen visits, we were able to record some extraordinary examples of Grouper intelligence; indeed,we would have hardly believed our own eyes, if we did not have films to confirm what we saw.

Since Rodney had to do all the work of training — and feeding — our three unusual actors, I cannot do better than quote his own words on the subject:

'As soon as we arrived on the "set", which was the seaward end of the Great Basses Reef adjoining a beautiful cave, at least two of our stars would be there to greet us. Usually Ali Baba swam up from the cave, which he regarded as his own private castle,

Mike Wilson looking down on Great Basses Reef from the top of the lighthouse. (Photo: Arthur C. Clarke.)

while Sinbad had already joined us from his own territory a few yards to the lee. Aladdin was last on the scene, and usually performed his actions after the larger two had had their fill. It was because of this that he displayed such amusing actions of haste, jealousy and peevishness.

My job was to shoot a fish with a speargun and start the action. Long before I had loaded the gun underwater, one of the Groupers would stand by expectantly, a few feet from me and literally "point" for me. As the gun was discharged it would alert itself, and make a wild dash for the struggling fish. If I missed (which was fairly often), the expression of bewilderment displayed by the disappointed Grouper was remarkable.

If the bait-fish was hit by the harpoon, it was rushed by one or two of the Groupers close by, and I had to be very watchful and active to retrieve it. Most often I failed, and one or other of the Groupers grabbed the bait, harpoon and all, and made straight for a cave. That would start a tussle between either Ali Baba or Sinbad or myself. Playing tug-of-war with a 100-lb Grouper underwater, even with an aqualung on, is a little one-sided. But thanks to the strong line, I eventually got hold of the harpoon and jerked it free, together with the mangled fish, from the cavernous mouth. This took place three or four times per bait-fish, until the Grouper decided that the harpoon was not intended for his digestion. Once, in the excitement, Ali Baba took harpoon, bait, and my hand in one quick gulp, and thanks to a tough cloth glove, my wrist was not badly bruised by his numerous small teeth.

Another time Sinbad was so desperate that he opened his mouth extra wide and took in too generous a section of the harpoon which had impaled a small Rudder Fish. This resulted in the harpoon head piercing his lower jaw, bending at right angles, and causing him considerable pain. He changed colour with distress, spat out everything in great disgust, and sulked in the cavern for at least twenty minutes while Mike and I wasted precious air trying to reassure him. Eventually he calmed down and even took the bait by swimming slowly, ever so slowly, through a red hula hoop held in my hand.

After removing a fish from the harpoon (a process which was always a little ticklish with one or more hungry Groupers waiting to pounce on it), the next step was to feed them, and do it slowly and ostentatiously enough for the still and movie cameras. With one Grouper I could always manage, but with two it was impossible; as I hid the fish behind my back after flaunting it before a Grouper's face and luring him close, the other would rush in from behind and steal it. Once Sinbad did this with such vigour that he strained my right hand and gulped part of my aqualung harness down with the fish. In shark-infested waters, and with all my attention concentrated on Ali Baba in front of me, this was quite a nerve-shattering experience. After the lung harness had been released, I found that the attack had left a small bruise on my right side.

Petting the Groupers could always be done as soon as they had taken a fish from my hand and soon they actually stayed still to be stroked once their appetites had been satisfied. Ali Baba liked being petted most of all. Sinbad did not quite mind, but Aladdin was too nippy and impatient for this sort of treatment.

If anyone had told me, before I visited the Great Basses, that Groupers could express indignation, disappointment, jealousy and impatience, I would have laughed it off. But I was soon to observe unmistakable emotions such as these, displayed by all three of them, but mainly Aladdin. Once, when I was unduly slow in loading the gun and shooting a passing fish for them, Aladdin sidled up to me, looked me in the face, then made a half rush to a passing Blue Caranx and actually nodded at it. I obliged by transfixing it and all the while Mike was an incredulous spectator with his Rolleimarine. Then again both Sinbad and Ali Baba had been fed and only Aladdin was hungry. He gave vent to his disappointment by swimming straight up to my speargun while it lay on the bottom and giving the reel an impatient bite!

The culmination of our fraternizing with Groupers was the hula hoop act. The idea was to make each Grouper in turn swim through a hula hoop with a bait in front of it. We soon found that when they were very hungry the action was far too frantic for any camera, still or movie. But with a *hors d'oeuvre* already inside, Ali Baba or Sinbad would oblige with ponderous grace while Mike joyfully filmed the action.

Matador-like, I had to perform all the motions of the bull ring to prevent the bait from being gulped down, yet keep the Grouper swimming through the ring and close enough to me for the camera. Ali Baba turned out to be our best hula hoop exponent, but after a particularly trying sequence, when Mike never seemed to get enough footage, he got quite sulky and retired into the cave. I pleaded with Mike underwater and at last, when his film was exhausted he gave me the nod. Ali Baba had to be followed deep into his cavern and cajoled into taking his lunch, a Caranx all of 15lb. At last he did, but could not swallow it all at once — and he lumbered away into the gloom with the tail protruding grotesquely through his jaws.

The behaviour of the three Groupers, and the shark attacks, Mike was able to record on colour film which he later cut into a remarkable little movie for the Ceylon Tea Propaganda Board, *Beneath the Seas of Ceylon*. This was screened and shown on TV in many countries, and its production — though we certainly never dreamed so at the time — was an important stepping stone to much bigger things.

We had been so busily photographing the Groupers, Sharks and other local inhabitants of the reef that we had done practically no sightseeing, and had certainly not gone looking for wrecks — although we knew that many must exist in so dangerous an area. As we sailed back to the mainland with the storm clouds of the south-west monsoon already gathering on the horizon, we would have

The Grouper we named Ali Baba
performing his hoola hoop act.
(Photo: Mike Wilson.)

laughed had anyone told us that all the time we had been diving within half a mile of treasure.

Just before we left, I snapped Mike on the gallery of the lighthouse a hundred feet above the sea, looking out thoughtfully across the reef. The result was a good portrait of the reef, though a poor one of Mike; and by a strange coincidence he was looking almost directly at the site of the treasure wreck — two years ahead in his future, and four years in mine.

We bypassed the reef in 1960, but Mike returned in 1961 with two young Americans who were first class swimmers and divers. And when I say young I mean it. Bobby Kriegel was fourteen; Mark Smith only thirteen. The three explorers set off from Columbo in our Volks-

wagen Microbus and that was the last we heard of them for almost two weeks, except for a brief 'All Well' message flashed one night by morse from the lighthouse.

It was a great relief to everybody when late one afternoon Mike and the boys arrived back safely and started unloading the bus. When I asked them eagerly 'Well, how did it go?' They avoided a straight answer but mumbled something like 'Oh, not so badly' as they staggered to my office carrying a battered tin trunk.

Mike locked the office door and said mysteriously, 'Look at this.'

He threw open the lid — and there were two beautiful little brass cannons, badly worn but

genuine, honest-to-goodness treasure. These unimpressive-looking lumps were masses of coins — hundreds of them, cemented together. When I bent down to pick one up, I could hardly lift it. It was not (alas!) heavy enough for gold, but it could only be the next best thing — silver.

Besides these big lumps, there were hundreds of loose coins. Many were badly corroded, but most of them seemed to be in remarkably good condition. They were covered with Persian lettering, and the total weight of silver came to about 115lb. 'But,' said Mike 'there's a lot more where we found this.'

That evening, we asked the boys' parents round to our house; at our request, Mark and Bobby had not breathed a word about the discovery, though this must have been something of a strain. Then we had the pleasure of watching the Smiths and the Kriegels do a double take, exactly as I had done, when they looked into the treasure box and realised just what it held. During the next few days, we were to grow accustomed to watching perplexity, wonder, disbelief, and finally excitement spread across the faces of the few trusted friends we introduced to the finds, which now rested safely in a massive wooden chest with a big brass padlock.

For two years that chest stood in the corner of my office. At first there was an aura of unreality about it; I could not quite believe that all this had actually occurred. I am not an unimaginative person, but I would never have imagined that anything so improbable could have happened to us. From time to time, to reassure myself, I would open the lid, and look at the evidence with my own eyes. But even with my eyes shut, a reminder was always there. Out of the chest welled a curious metallic tang as of iodine and seaweed — not at all unpleasant. It was one of the most evocative smells I knew; it brought back vivid memories of the sea, and of spray-drenched rocks glistening beneath the equatorial sun. It was the scent of treasure.

How the treasure was found and the wreck site was subsequently mapped by the underwater archaeologist Peter Throckmorton, was told in my book *The Treasure of the Great Reef* which was first published in 1964 in the U.S.A. by Ballantine Books Inc. In the revised printing in 1974 I was able to include Peter Throckmorton's description of the site together with his plan of the wreck site which showed the position of anchors, iron canon and bronze swivel guns as well as concreted silver coins. The identity of the vessel is still completely unknown.

gleaming brilliantly where the sea had polished them, and obviously very old. I cried out in excitement 'You've found an old wreck.'

Then, without saying a word, Mike lifted the guns and showed me what lay underneath them. At first, I thought I was looking at dirty lumps of coral, about the size of coconuts. Then I realised just what those lumps were! I was too astonished to say anything.

It was one of the unforgettable moments of a lifetime, for I knew then that I was staring at something that very few men have ever seen —

DIVE 12 THE INDIAN OCEAN: Shark Alley — Chagos Islands by David Bellamy

In November 1972 I was privileged to stand with one foot in paradise along with the eleven other members of the First Joint Services Underwater Expedition. Our particular patch of paradise was the Egmont group of islands forming an atoll which lies on the south-west edge of the great Chagos Bank in the centre of the Indian Ocean. It's odds on that your map doesn't even show it, and if it does then it's certain that the Egmont Group is shown in the wrong place, to be inexact at Latitude 6°39' south and Longitude 71°22' east, as surveyed by Commander Moresby, I.N. (Indian Navy) in 1837.

The Chagos Archipelago is a gauntlet of coral atolls and islands each appliquéd by the actions of coral colonies onto pillars of basalt rock which rise up from the ocean floor. The Bank itself lies deep below the poorly-charted turbulence of white water like some lost Atlantis.

Atolls come in a range of shapes and sizes and their lagoons in a range of open-ness and enclosed-ness. Ecologically a lagoon is best regarded as a lake, an area of more or less sheltered water set in the middle of what can be a very rough sea. 'An ideal place in which to live,' unquote.

In 1972 I stood with one foot in paradise on an island in the middle of the Indian Ocean. (Photo: 'Dickie' Bird.)

107

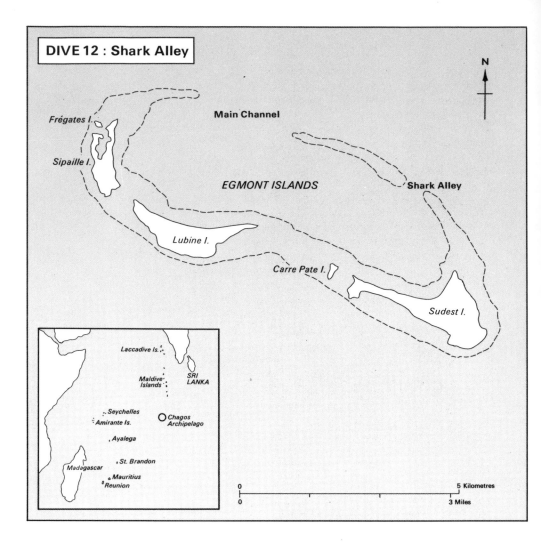

If a lagoon became completely encircled by dry land, and cut off from the sea, it would soon become stagnant and unfit as a life support system. The life blood of any lagoon pulses through its channels, the ebb carrying away the staler waters and the flood replenishing the basin with cooler oxygen-rich water from beyond the reef.

It is interesting that the one form of life that does not do at all well within the confines of the lagoon is the reef-forming coral. The environmental factors which weigh against their success are complex, a mixture of too much fine sediment in the water, temperatures which could rise above 37°C, which is lethal to most corals, too little oxygen during periods of stagnation and, under certain circumstances, too little salt during periods of maximum dilution by heavy rain. Fastidious creatures, corals, aren't they? The strange fact is that if they were not like this then atolls could not exist, for they would soon get filled in with coral growth. If lagoonal conditions are not too extreme, the whole basin will be pock marked with coral heads, many of which break the surface at extreme low tides. Between the coral heads the lagoon floor is covered with deposits which range from coarse ground coral talus to the finest of white clay, and it is these deposits which cause the cloudiness of the lagoon's water.

According to the survey carried out by Captain Moresby in 1837 the rim of reef rock forming the lagoon at Egmont was crowned with six islands. An aerial photographic survey made by the RAF, however, showed only five islands with two deep channels giving access to the central lagoon which boasted a total of 362 coral heads. The mouth of each channel appeared to be guarded by a rim of hidden rock.

There were many questions to be answered about the formation and ecology of the Chagos Archipelago — my job was to co-ordinate the research of a team (immediately christened *The Scientificos*) who could adequately cover the major range of plants, animals and ecology found on the 419 hectares of dry land and 15 miles of reef which surround the lagoon and give Egmont its very existence.

We were the first scientists to set foot on Egmont since the Percy Sladen expedition in 1915 and they spent only a few hours onshore. One of our first tasks was to survey the reef along a series of transects. Each dive brought up a bewildering array of corals and a preliminary look made us feel that Egmont was as rich, if not richer in corals than any other Indian Ocean reef area surveyed to that date. Yet among all that diversity there was a certain uniformity; a basic pattern could be recognised again and again. The reef was in fact zoned.

Having cut our teeth on the easier dives we turned our attention to the channels. Without doubt the most exciting intra-lagoonal dives are always around the mouths of the channels, or along their ravine-like banks, which snake back into the lagoon giving off blind branches at various intervals. Transect 8A went right through the entrance of the main channel and it promised to be an exciting one to study from the start.

The first echo sounder run showed a drop away from just inside the mouth of the channel down to a depth of about 20m then up came the bottom again, ridging at about 3m below low water mark before it plunged away into the black abyss. We retraced our echo sounder footsteps, there it was again, the sharp knife-edged ridge, and the drop away on the reef front.

The dive was to take the same form as usual but, as weather conditions were beginning to deteriorate and the water in the channel was in a rough mood, we took extra precautions: two boats were covering each dive team.

The visibility was down to a milk-white 30ft, the anchor rope, taut as a bowstring in the current, disappeared down out of sight. In we went, bunching up below the boat before following the line down to the anchor weight. We were at the base of the ridge on the seaward side where it was fretworked with a sparse growth of living coral. The big fish were there with a vengeance and, perhaps worried by the low visibility, were swimming fast in straight businesslike lines. Eight feet of White Tip Shark shot over my head to disappear in the milk; the acceleration really was fabulous, his whole body quivered, strength shooting him forward in effortless motion. Sharks have very special tails called *heterocercal*, which signifies that the bulk of the fin is situated on top of the tail section; this is in marked contrast to the tails of the bony fish, which consist of two

David Bellamy looking appropriately apprehensive before jumping overboard to meet the sharks. (Photo: Mike Ballentyne.)

more or less equal halves and are called *gephyrocercal*. Whatever they are called they are very efficient organs of propulsion and a shark can make light work of the problems of channel life.

Within the confines of the channel the strict zonation of the reef front breaks down, at least in part. Perhaps it is because all the material in suspension reduces light penetration in such a way that the zoned light environment is missing. Or perhaps it is because at least some of that particulate matter is organic and some of it will be food for the corals. Plenty of food could mean less competition and hence the possibility of a whole range of deep and shallow water forms living together in affluent harmony.

Finning down through the top 10m it was easy to understand the breakdown of the zoned light environment, but a real surprise came when we broke through the surface layer of milk down into gin-clear water still with plenty of light left for photography. Our destination was the 30-m mark just over the lip of the main drop-off, where the reef front at this point shot down almost vertically. There are two main problems in working on these cliff-face situations. The first is how to hang on while chipping off the coral. The second is that there are much more interesting things to do than make long lists of the things which grow there. It is in these situations that you can have the real thrill of free diving, proof that you are master of the three-dimensional world. A gentle push off from the cliff and then you can hover in your own free space, adjusting your vertical station simply by breathing out for down and in for up. Great fun, but the sharks do it much better, so Paddy, my shark guard, amused himself by shouting at them in broad Irish bubbles. Having finished the work, we started back up the cliff as the whole world of fishes seemed to move in to work over the ground we had deserted, searching out the food we had disturbed. What a spectacle — a maelstrom of darting fish set against a deep black-blue background and a living lace curtain of Sea Fans and Whips.

The surface milk had by now churned into a thick cream and the anchor lines were jerking as the boats rode the now choppy channel. Conditions were deteriorating; time to end the dive. Four sharp revs on the motor signalled the other team that it was time for up.

The main channel had yielded some of her secrets, including this peculiar ridge-like structure, an outer lip almost like a coffer dam enclosing a cup of sheltered water. Subsequent survey and inspection of the air photographs confirmed that this ridge did go right across the mouth of the channels. Here was another first for the annals of coralology. All we could do at this stage was to wonder why it ever formed. Our primary surveys had sketched out the bare bones of the Egmont Atoll, which was growing at what was theoretically the wrong end, with the most active growth taking place along the most sheltered north-west shore. Here the reef fell away to a depth of 8m then dropped in an almost vertical cliff down to depths of more than 50m at which point the reef-building communities came to an abrupt end.

Sitting perched on the edge of that undersea cliff you cannot get away from the feeling that you are part of an actively living thing. Everywhere you look there is something going on, coral with the polyps out actually feeding, fish darting in and out of the coral heads, Sea Whips are whipping and gorgeous coloured Parrot Fish and assorted Sea Cucumbers are chomping their way through the sections of dead coral. The whole cliff is so seething with life that you begin to feel that it is moving its ponderous way forward, a feeling which produces instant vertigo. This is an up and down world of weird shapes and truncated vistas.

The other end of the atoll was a very different kettle of fish. The reef cliff was almost a mile from the reef ridge; between these two

the reef was planed almost flat by the action of the waves. Diving here was like diving on the open range, a predominantly white world of sand with scattered patches of coral. There was no cover, so we found very few fish of any size except for sharks, and they were there often in ultra abundance, so much so that the area was promptly named 'Shark Alley'.

All stories about diving, whether fact or fiction, are well laced with sharks. The great fish are always there lurking in the murky waters just beyond the intrepid diver's vision, always hungry, especially for 'Steak bon homme'. And ours was no exception.

However, if you think long and carefully, you will soon find that some of the oft-stated facts about divers and sharks just do not fit. For a start, the average diver is nearly 2m long and the average shark is between 2 and 5m. Even for the big ones which swell up in size when dramatised to 8m, an average diver would make a large mouthful. Secondly, the average diver is festooned with neoprene, plastic fins, rubber hoses, a lead weight belt, a metal cylinder or two and sundry bits of harness. Even their most delectable and readily noshable extremities are adorned wth glass face plates, depth gauges, wrist watches, knives and collecting bags. Add to this the fact that the average shark has never seen a diver before, and at irregular intervals this strange two-legged creature spews out great masses of bubbles and makes muffled noises that sound something like 'come 'ere and look at this'. Certainly it doesn't look much like an enticing meal! Finally, on most reefs where there are a lot of sharks about, there are usually a lot of fish, fish of the right shape, sort and size, and, unless we are dealing with very polluted waters, containing little or nothing in the way of a toxic metal burden.

So the basic hard facts make it odds on that the diver won't get his foot chopped off the first time he dives on the reef and it is consoling to reflect that, if he does, the shark will probably spit the rest of him out.

Nevertheless, working on the assumption that not all sharks are conversant with our hypothesis and since, like all good divers, we had seen the film *Blue Water White Death*, we took the necessary precautions. Armament consisted of a bang stick, which is a 2-m metal pole with a muzzle containing a shellacked .303 cartridge. Safety-catch off, and one sharp prod should spell doom for the largest shark. The next line of defence was a cunning device like a 1-m hypodermic syringe filled with compressed air. A sharp prod from the 'Shark Inflator' should mainline the shark into a trip to the surface, on a one-way ticket. Apart from these

The islands abounded with a great variety of reef fish. (Photo: 'Dickie' Bird.)

main items of field artillery, small arms varied from pickaxe handles, through broom-sticks, to collecting hammers, all known as 'shark billies'.

Every diving party thus bristled with armaments and each was accompanied by a shark guard whose official task was to ward off inquisitive sharks, but whose job often became guarding the sharks from interfering photographers. Each dive was accompanied by sharks, the record score being Art and Jeff's 60 at one go. The peculiar thing was that very often the sharks appeared to take little or no notice of the team working away on the bottom, except that they kept close, circling the shark guard who hovered just above the team like some neoprene angel with a rocket back pack. So it went on day by day, the sharks maintaining some interest in the new component of their scene and the diving party maintaining a higher than usual level of adrenalin coursing through their tubes.

Sharks are members of the great group of cartilaginous fish, that is, they have soft bones. The group includes rays and skates, and the gastronomically much maligned Rock Salmon (Dogfish, Huss, or whatever you call it in your part of the fish and chip shop world) is in fact one of the smallest sharks. The cartilaginous fish are in the evolutionary sense more primitive than their bony cousins. Once underwater with sharks and rays you really begin to understand what perfection is when it comes to riding the currents of the three-dimensional underwater world.

Every man did his allotted job, but every man also took his fair share of shark guarding and each had his own particular habits when on guard which made him easily identifiable even in full diving rig from 30m away. Some nervously fingered the safety-catch on the bang stick, others practised with the Hawaian sling (the rubber bit on the end). Chuggles slow marched through the water at the 'present arms' position and Paddy perched on a rock holding the long stick like some emaciated sitar and played revolutionary songs on it. The leading shark guard was without doubt Commander Alan Baldwin, R.N., thought for a long time to be the first coloured officer in the service. This mistake came about simply because when exposed to more than 10 kilo

A shark fits naturally into the underwater environment of a coral reef. (Photo: David Bellamy.)

111

Each diver was accompanied by a shark guard whose official job was to ward off inquisitive sharks, but whose job often became guarding the sharks from interfering photographers. (Photo: Mike Ballentyne.)

calories of the sun's energy he turns an instant chocolate brown. Done to a turn, ready for eating, he had the exalted rank of Chief Shark Guard added to his post of Diving Officer. The motto of the shark guards soon became 'they don't like it up 'em, sir!'

Immediately the stake boat was on station at *Shark Alley* the sharks were there, big ones, medium-sized ones and a very few small ones, boiling about in a great funnel between the boat and the bottom, as if waiting for the divers.

Imagine, first planning to dive in such a place and secondly sitting on the gunwale of an inflatable boat waiting to drop into this maelstrom of predatory fish. Yet it had to be done, and in achieving it we had the seven most exciting dives of the expedition. The plan of campaign was to photograph strips of the reef front each 10m long at the following depths: 5, 20, 25, 30, 40 and 50m. Once photographed,

pieces of all the different corals, seaweeds, etc found in consecutive metre squares along the line would be collected for identification.

The first dive was to 50m. Down went the anchor weight and up came the sharks, curious about the black shape floating above. Two shark guards joined them, somersaulting backwards through their own bubbles with the dappled sun glinting on the long polished bang sticks. The three divers followed and the whole party set off along the anchor line through the clear upper water down towards the outer reef cliff. The shark guards were on full alert facing outwards towards their pack, their lances at the ready. Soon the divers were lost from sight, their presence only evidenced by the plume of silver bubbles like ephemeral Jellyfish rising to burst at the surface. Was it our imagination, or were the divers breathing faster than normal? The sharks were certainly still there because two small ones, probably attracted by the glint

of light on the ring of face masks peering down from the boat, left the pack and rose quickly to the surface.

On the bottom, all hell was let loose, not because of the sharks but because of the current. The whole team was finning flat out just to maintain station and the precious eight minutes were ticking away. The line was eventually laid, one end fixed to the anchor and the other to the only coral present, a large piece of black Dendrophyllia. The photography complete, collection was easy as there was nothing to collect apart from a few scattered Sea Whips among which the sharks motored, accelerating as they turned with the current. When they had finished collecting, the divers gathered on the line and the sign for going up was given; one decompression stop at 6m and one at 3m were required. Jim Barnes, who in making the photographic record had probably finned the equivalent of 3 miles, came slowly up, the Rolleimarine camera trailing on about 3m of line. This was too much for the shark pack, a flashing bait of silver and glass just about bitesized, an ideal mid-morning snack, so in they came.

Unfortunately, long-distance underwater photography is out, but there it was, the original underwater mobile, dangling below us. Boat at top with three masks peering down, 6m below the knot of 5 divers, complete with bubble plumes, bags, hammers, chisels and bang sticks, and some 3m below this a small glinting object surrounded by between 30 and 40 large sharks. Jim didn't know what to do, reel it in and with it the shark pack, or leave it there and hope that the sharks didn't like the taste. Fortunately they didn't, so once the decompression stops were over — and by all accounts it seemed more like 30 than 5 minutes — a team of jubilant divers emerged from the sea and once all the team was clear they reeled in an intact camera, probably the most expensive spinner ever used. Talk over the supper table that night revolved around one topic, and having watched the action from above, we knew there was no exaggeration of size. Those sharks were big, very big, no need for fisherman-type stories. To top it all Alan had landed a barracuda, and fresh barracuda steaks are out of this world, even if you are a diver in paradise.

When watching sharks you really begin to understand what perfection is when it comes to riding the currents of the three-dimensional underwater world. (Photo: Mike Ballentyne.)

DIVE 13 THE RED SEA: Ras Muhammed by Horace Dobbs

Above: **Sunset off Tiran Island near Ras Muhammed. To dive the Red Sea from a specially equipped luxury yacht such as** *The Lady Jenny V* **is the ultimate diving holiday experience.** (Photo: Horace Dobbs.)

Facing page: **The richness and profusion of the undersea life is in dramatic contrast with the adjacent barren land mass at Ras Muhammed.** (Photo: Horace Dobbs.)

The Sinai is one of the most inhospitable places on earth. It sticks out like a dagger into the northern end of the Red Sea. It is bounded on one side by the Gulf of Suez, and on the other by the Gulf of Aquaba. It is where Moses came down from the mountains with the tablets of stone.

Historically it is a region of human conflict. Close to Eilat, in bordering Israel, lies the island of Jezirat Fara'un which is more commonly known as Coral Island. It is crowned with the ruins of a castle which was built in the twelfth century by the Moslem leader Saladin to ward off the Crusaders, who came from all over Europe to pillage the towns of the Red Sea and plunder the pilgrim ships bound for Mecca. Because of its geographical location the Sinai is still an area of considerable strategic importance. In 1967 it was overrun by the Israelis in the Six Day War. In 1982 it was handed back to the Egyptians as part of the Camp David Agreement signed by President Carter.

The two great pioneers of undersea exploration Hans Hass and Jacques Cousteau both discovered the beauty of the Red Sea early on in their diving careers. However, most of their activities were confined to regions well clear of

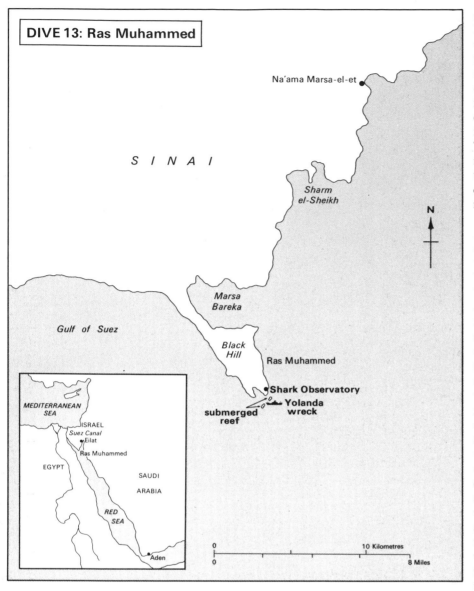

result of the Six Day War, the Sinai became Israeli territory. The Israelis realised that one way to keep hold of their new acquisition was to encourage investment in the area. It was unsuitable as a place for industrial development but with sunshine throughout the year it had potential as a tourist attraction — especially for holiday-makers seeking escape from the rigours of the European winter. Those pressing this idea had a truly exceptional selling point — superb diving. Furthermore many diving sites could be reached directly from the shore — thus eliminating the need for boats.

The reason for this was because the Gulf of Aquaba was created by a huge crack in the earth's surface — the Syrian-East African Rift that separates Africa from Asia. Just south of Tiran Island, in the throat of the Gulf, the V-shaped trench reaches a depth of 1,800m. As these prodigious depths are reached in relatively narrow straits geometry requires steep descents. The fact that the water is very deep close to the shore has many effects which influence the diving. Firstly, heating and cooling such a vast quantity of water cannot take place quickly. Thus the water temperature ranges between 21–26 °C throughout the year and is little affected by daily, or seasonal atmosphere temperatures. Secondly, although the wind can be quite severe and the sea is often covered with white horses, the turbulence created does not stir up sediment on the seabed and thereby reduce the underwater visibility with a mass of suspended particles. The all-important underwater visibility does not therefore change dramatically with the weather. It is influenced mainly by changes in the concentration of plankton which varies unpredictably, throughout the seasons and from year to year.

Those who dive the region regularly would regard a visibility of 10m as exceptionally low. A visibility of over 50m is not unknown. For professional creative photographers, such as Mike Portelly who uses the sea as a studio, such reliable good visibility is a very important feature when considering a location for an underwater assignment.

But I am getting ahead of myself — he did not appear on the scene until Ras Muhammed had become established as one of the great classic dives of the world. Some of the credit for its rise to that elevated status must go to Shlomo Cohen, who wrote a book called *Red Sea Diver's Guide*. It was a brilliant concept that was superbly executed. In addition to cataloguing many of the fish and corals in the region the book contained aerial photographs of selected dive sites. The clear water enabled

the Gulf of Aquaba. One of the reasons was the simmering conflict between the Israelis, who occupied the seaport of Eilat, and the Arabs who occupied the neighbouring port of Aquaba. Shell fire exchanges were frequent and any foreign boats in the area were at risk — from both sides. Thus the coastal waters adjacent to the Sinai were unexploited, apart from a tiny catch by local Bedouin fishermen who waded out from the shore to cast their nets on the shallow reef table. One of the positive results of the conflict between the Arabs and the Jews was that whilst other less troubled waters were being ruined by over exploitation this undersea paradise along the shores of the Sinai remained virtually untouched and unvisited.

However, things changed in 1967 when, as a

underwater aspects of the seascapes to be seen alongside the adjacent surface of the shore. Each of these photographs was covered with a translucent overlay on which essential features were shown. Suggested routes to take on a dive were also indicated. With such a guide the diver could plan his dives from the comfort of his armchair at home. Once there he could move from one location to the next if he had suitable overland transport.

I was fortunate to obtain a copy of the *Red Sea Divers Guide* just after it was first published in 1975. At the time Bruce and Hedda Lyons, who now run the travel organisation Twickers World, were looking for new destinations to send pale Brits seeking sunshine in the winter months. Israel was high on their list.

With memories of Hans and the delectable Lotte Hass cruising amidst the corals (not to mention the sharks) in the Red Sea, I didn't need too much persuasion to join Bruce on a reconnaisance expedition to Eilat. We had only a couple of days to see what the area had to offer would-be holidaymakers with an interest in diving. After hiring a VW Beetle we called in at Aquasport, right on the shore at Coral Beach. It was run by Willy Halpert who had contributed the section on diving in the *Red Sea Divers Guide*. He provided us with aqualung cylinders and the other heavy diving equipment we needed to complete our mission. He also provided us with some first-hand knowledge of what we might expect in the way of diving. I have to admit that going into the

When a diver takes a bag of food down she is likely to be surrounded by voracious Sergeant Major fish. (Photo: Horace Dobbs.)

Above: **To get pictures like this you just rest quietly on the reef and wait for the fish to appear.**

Facing page
Top: **A Grouper eyes the photographer warily. Flash reveals the hidden colours.**

Middle: **A Clown fish nestles safely in the stinging tentacles of an anemone.**

Bottom: **Lion fish have poisonous tips on their fins and display them as a warning – which makes them easy subjects for photography.**
(Photos: Horace Dobbs.)

sea just outside the dive centre itself looked as if it would have yielded an excellent dive. But both Willy and the dive guide promised even better things further south. Indeed, the guide indicated that if we went to the very southern-most tip of the Sinai — to a place called Ras Muhammed — we could experience the best dive the region had to offer.

And so it was, we set out on our quest. We thought we would stop on the way. Several times we parked the car and looked down into clear blue water. But Ras Muhammed lured me like the peak of Everest. So we pressed on, through the mountains of Sinai and along the shores of the Red Sea. At times, especially towards the end of the journey along unmade roads with corrugated surfaces, we felt as if we were riding inside a pneumatic drill. Eventually we made it to the beach at Ras Muhammed, with our precious cargo of air cylinders, still fully charged, but minus most of their paint. But if ever a long, hot, dusty and uncomforta-ble journey was worth it — that one was. We climbed up the cliffs to a place called the Shark Observatory to work out what direction to swim once we were in the sea. From that

vantage point we made our plans having read the following paragraph in the guide:

'Taking the northern track at the fork after the black hill you will arrive at what is unquestionably the most exciting diving site in this volume.
(Follow the directions below faithfully for an uneventful arrival.)
The reef table is very narrow and its sheer seaward wall vanishes into a deep blue where it stops at 70 m (231 ft).
It is a veritable treasure trove of coral species guaranteed to drive a marine biologist 'Up the wall'. A word of caution, however, for divers. The fish, the caves, the crevices, and the colour tend to so exhilarate . . . they push the explorer deeper and deeper. The fine visibility may also lend a false note of security. Check your air, your depth, your decompression requirements and your distance periodically. This is no ordinary dive.'

It was no ordinary dive. As we snorkelled out over the shallow reef towards the deep water Surgeon Fish and Parrot Fish glided though the maze of channels beneath us. Suddenly before us was a huge expanse of water so clear and blue we felt we were looking into the sky. We had reached the drop-off.

Hanging in the azure sea were immense shoals of fish such as Barracuda. We drifted slowly down the near vertical coral wall and roamed through an underwater wonderland of such beauty it was breathtaking. Although we were sometimes enveloped in clouds of small fish most of the large fish were shy. The Bumphead Wrasse, or Napoleon Fish, for instance, always remained 10m away no matter how carefully I tried to approach them.

Conscious of how far we were from assistance, and with the warnings in the guide still fresh in our minds we were careful not to become so carried away by the beauty of our surroundings that we risked the bends or running out of air. Nonetheless, there was very little air left in our cylinders when we drove back to Eilat.

By running charter flights to Eilat, Bruce reckoned he could take British divers to the Red Sea at a price that was affordable by many and would compete favourably with less exotic destinations. But Ras Muhammed was virtually unknown and divers would need to be convinced before they parted with their hard-earned cash that what was on offer wasn't a tour operator's hype.

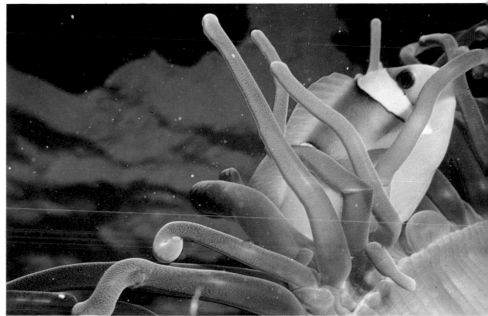

We proposed that our would-be adventurers should travel from Eilat to Ras Muhammed by overland safaris, camping en-route. However, Bruce had to be sure that such a new type of diving holiday could be made to work in theory and in practice. To establish this new diving market he offered places on the very first safari at knock-down prices and invited the press to join us.

On the 5th November 1976 a group of 22 divers, with ages ranging from twenties to sixties and diving experience to match, gathered in Eilat for the first diving safari. We used three desert Jeeps as our vehicles, and each one towed a heavily-laden trailer containing a compressor and enough food and water supplies to make us self-sufficient for several days. Willy Halpert accompanied us as our guide. Like all Israelis, he had to spend some time each year doing military service. These duties often took him into the Sinai. Thus we were able to benefit from his local knowledge and desert experience. He said we wouldn't need tents or even ground sheets. We could just put our sleeping bags straight on the sand and sleep under the stars. We did not drive directly to Ras Muhammed but camped and dived en route. We had breakdowns and problems which were all resolved. But the diving was so superb that none of these difficulties seemed to matter. The closer we got to Ras Muhammed the better the diving became. We were building up to a climax, and Ras Muhammed didn't let

us down.

Because of the strategic importance of Ras Muhammed camping on the beach at night was prohibited. As the sun set an army patrol appeared and asked us to leave. Which we did. When it was dark, however, we crept back in because a number of the group, myself included, were keen to dive at dawn.

When the first crack of pale light appeared in the eastern sky I opened my eyes. As I prepared to dive the eastern sky became suffused with red until it was as if the distant horizon was on fire. Just as the sun emerged above the horizon, creating a path of sparkling crimson light that danced on the surface of the sea, I submerged. Beneath me the sea was mysterious, and deep deep blue.

With my partner we made the long swim to one of the submerged islands off shore — the bearing of which I had taken by compass the afternoon before. I was thankful when we arrived and descended the vertical wall. We were on the outermost tip of the Sinai on the edge of a sheer sea-filled drop into the rift valley. It was a one-way ticket down for anyone who got into real difficulties. We found a ledge on the wall, deflated our lifejackets and sat there, watching the sea fill with light and change from Oxford blue to Cambridge blue.

As the sun rose the sea came to life. Myriads of small fish emerged from the crannies in rocks where they had passed the night. They formed into shoals that drifted like clouds along the reef. That was until a Jack Fish came hurtling along the wall snatching bites for breakfast as he went. When that happened the cloud would explode like a firework and all the fish would scatter — but only for a brief moment. Seconds later the cloud would reform and move gently along the reef as if nothing had happened. Straight out from where we sat the big fish did their daybreak patrol gliding parallel to the reef — effortlessly, smoothly and gracefully. Amongst them were the fish we all wanted to see — Sharks. They cruised back and forth, keeping well clear of us, but obviously aware of our presence. The exhaust bubbles from our aqualungs speeded up with excitement as they passed by. A Turtle, who had remained unnoticed on a nearby ledge until he stirred, flippered quietly but deliberately away and disappeared diagonally down the reef into deeper water.

When our air ran out and it was time to return to the surface the reef had been transformed. The sun was up. Gone were the tensions of mysterious half-light. The place was full of brightly coloured fish going about their daily routine with the almost orderly bustle of office workers arriving in London on a sunny morning. None of the fish seemed to take any notice of the sharks that were still passing back and forth along the drop-off.

It was still early morning when we staggered up the beach and dumped our weightbelts and empty cylinders by the compressor. Most of the other divers had also returned and were talking excitedly about what they had seen. The sun was already powerful and quickly restored lost body heat. Over breakfast the unanimous feeling was that it was the best dive any of us had ever made. Even after breakfast, when we were squatting at the edge of the sea rubbing our plates with sand to clean them, the group was still high on the dawn-dive experience.

On that first major diving safari we had representatives from the media who wrote glowing reports of their adventures. Virtually every member of the expedition took still pictures or cine film of their trail-blazing journey and their dives in the Red Sea. Each one became a disciple, spreading the gospel of the wonders of the undersea world at Ras Muhammed. We had created a new market and Bruce Lyons sent hundreds of divers to Ras Muhammed via Eilat. The big tour operators saw what was happening. One of them mounted a massive publicity campaign and the number of divers visiting the area quickly rose from hundreds to thousands.

The natural inhabitants of Ras Muhammed — the fish — adapted to the invading hordes of divers, especially as many of the visitors came bearing gifts of food. Some of the residents changed their eating habits and developed a taste for the new fast foods. Hard-boiled eggs were in great demand. A diver with a supply of such gastronomic delights could well find himself surrounded by a voracious horde of diners who paid for their meals by the pleasure they gave to the underwater tourists. They also provided a wealth of subjects for the ever increasing number of divers for whom underwater photography became a passion.

Some of the friendliest fish developed quite distinctive personalities. Amongst these were two Bumphead or Napoleon Wrasse, who were later dubbed George and Mildred after two television characters. During my first visit I saw them several times but they were timid and always remained a long way off, no matter how quietly I tried to creep up on them. When these fish discovered that the human invaders at Ras Muhammed did not appear to pose a threat, and they watched other less timid fish enjoying easy meals, greed overcame fear. They approached very nervously at first. But once they got a taste for hard-boiled eggs they were metaphorically hooked. When this happened they forgot all fear of divers. If their addiction was not quickly satisfied they could become quite menacing. As they each weighed 50kg or more, any diver who was fool-hardy enough to hang onto his eggs for too long was likely to find himself buffeted and bullied into quick submission. Indeed, I once saw a diver beat a hasty and undignified retreat when George and Mildred remained unconvinced that their benefactor had parted with all of his goodies and attacked the pocket on his life jacket where he normally carried his breakfast left overs.

The future wellbeing of the friendly fish at Ras Muhammed seemed to be assured when the Israelis made Ras Muhammed a conservation area. Most of the divers visiting the area immediately appreciated the benefits of such legislation and would have voluntarily adopted a conservation code even if there was no legislation to back it up. However the situation changed when the Sinai was handed back to the Egyptians. The U.S. Government generously compensated those who had invested in the Sinai. And most of the businessmen departed leaving just ruins behind them. I was aghast when I heard rumours that the diving at Ras Muhammed had become a shambles. The Egyptian army officer in charge of the area, ignorant of what he had inherited, suggested holding spearfishing competitions at Ras Muhammed on the grounds that this would encourage tourists.

At the time I was leading a campaign to ban all spearfishing competitions, arguing that such events could destroy in a day the trust and friendship the natural inhabitants of the underwater world were building with humans and which took years to establish. Furthermore by eliminating the fish the spearfishermen were destroying what other divers went into the sea to see and photograph. I openly expressed my concern that what I considered to be one of the wonders of the underwater world, Ras Muhammed, should be lost due to ignorance on the part of the Egyptians and selfishness on the part of the undersea hunters.

So when I heard in 1983 that an English businessman, Tony Turner, proposed to set up a new diving venture in the area I was concerned. For it appeared to me that such a proposition called for the kind of commercial courage that would send most bank managers fleeing. But Tony had fallen in love with the Red Sea and was convinced that despite the enormous operational difficulties he could build up a successful long-term diving operation in the Ras Muhammed area with the co-operation of the Egyptian tourism authorities. In 1982 he had sailed his luxury yacht, *Lady Jenny III* from the Mediterranean, through the Suez Canal, into the Red Sea. At

One of the friendly giant Bumphead Wrasse at Ras Muhammed. Is it 'George' or 'Mildred'? (Photo: Horace Dobbs.)

A Lizard fish. (Photo: Horace Dobbs.)

the same time he bought another boat, *Lady Jenny V*. Both boats were based at Sharm el Sheik, near Ras Muhammed.

I had established a reputation for myself as a pioneer in opening up new diving markets. Tony therefore asked me if I would escort a group of journalists and holidaymakers who had paid to dive from his two diving yachts in February 1984. I accepted his offer and agreed to be responsible for the diving as well as providing moral support when necessary.

From Sharm el Sheik we cruised to many locations — one of which was the island of Sinafir which the crew dubbed 'The Museum'. It was so called because of the amphorae there. Amphorae are pottery vessels originally used by the ancient Greeks and later the Romans for the storage and transport of wine, oil and other commodities. The amphora at Sinafir was similar in shape to one I had seen at another site in the same area. That one was of Phoenician origin and pools of mercury it once contained could still be found in depressions in the coral. Nobody has yet put a date on the Sinafir amphora, so I was left wondering if it was Phoenician or dated from an earlier period.

On another site in a completely different location at the mouth of the Suez Canal all of the fine and delicate corals that are so easily accidentally damaged by divers were intact.

This indicated that it had probably never been dived before. On a broad channel on the same site there were so many Grouper Fish of several different species that we named it 'Grouper Gulley'. Nearby we found a cave in very shallow water with seven Sharks sleeping in it. This shark dormitory was so crowded with White Tip Reef Sharks that they were piled on top of one another.

But the highlight of the expedition was undoubtely the dive at Ras Muhammed. Since my first visit to Ras Muhammed a Greek freighter carrying general cargo had foundered on one of the offshore islands. The stricken vessel, called the *Joylanda,* lay on her side with part of the wall of the hull above the surface. We moored alongside and the Zodiac took us to the northern tip of one of the two submerged islands for the classic dive.

We rolled backwards off the inflatable into the deep water. There was a current running along the wall and as we drifted with it I looked out into the blue. I know of no blue anywhere that has the same intensity of colour. The water was extremely clear and from a depth of 30m I looked up and saw my bubbles rising in long clusters towards the silhouettes of divers gliding slowly and silently overhead.

We stopped for a few moments, sat on a ledge and looked out into the ocean which extended miles away from us. I remembered my dawn dive. Now it was nearly mid-day. It was like looking into a highway. But instead of cars, fish from the open sea cruised past. Some were on their own, others were packed into huge shoals. Barracudas, Jacks and a few Sharks flowed by in the non-stop traffic lanes of fish.

As we left the wall, to my intense joy, we were met by the two giant Napoleon Wrasses, George and Mildred. They approached us with the unshakeable authority of two slow-moving Centurion tanks. George's eyes moved independently and swivelled on what looked like ball joints giving him virtually 360° vision. Knowing his reputation I had no doubt what was on his mind. Food. When my partner produced some chicken scraps from the pocket of his life jacket George changed from a slow moving tank to a drag racer. The remains of a chicken carcase, bones and all, disappeared into George's gullet like fluff down the tube of a vacuum cleaner. To another underwater diver we looked like two piscatorial pied pipers — collecting more and more fish for company as we went, when we came to the underwater valley between the two islands we found the *Joylanda's* anchor chain stretched across the seabed. It led us like a road to the vessel itself. The wreck was totally intact, and the underwater visibility was so good we could see it from end to end. Part of its cargo was a container of porcelain bidets many of which were scattered over the reef. They provided props for divers who wanted their pictures taken sitting on a loo 10m down.

Also on the reef, partly unwrapped were some bales of cloth. They were gaudily patterned, of man-made fibre, and showed no sign of disintegrating.

We explored the entire wreck, which was just starting to be colonised with corals. Although it provided another source of interest for the divers I was slightly saddened by its presence because the spilled cargo had turned a small area of the seabed into a rubbish tip. I was partially consoled, however, with the thought that yesterday's junk can become sources of great interest and pleasure to tomorrow's underwater archaeologists.

We finished our dive under the *Lady Jenny V* and surfaced by the diving ladder. When a dive like that is concluded with a hot freshwater shower, followed by a gin and tonic prior to a superb lunch and a siesta in the sun aboard a luxury yacht you can't help wondering if you've had the ultimate diving holiday experience. But when one looks back at memories these trappings are just the icing on the cake — it is that wall of blue sunlit water that leaves the most permanent impression.

The Sinai has been a place of unrest and political strife for centuries. I can see no signs of that situation changing. So in the forseeable future actually getting to Ras Muhammed is going to continue to be an adventure in itself.

I would not recommend it as a destination for those looking for a predictable, Florida-style holiday package. However, for those who want really exotic diving, adventurous travel and are prepared to deal with red tape and regulations which may appear to be utterly absurd and are imposed and administered by officials whose cultural backgrounds have their roots in the pyramids then I would say 'Go to Ras Muhammed'.

Crocodile fish—so named because they bear a remarkable resemblance to the land reptile after which they have been named—spend most of their time resting on the sand. (Photo: Horace Dobbs.)

123

DIVE 14 THE MEDITERRANEAN SEA: Gozo
by Ashley Dobbs

Gulleys, canyons and rocky underwater vistas greet the diver who visits Malta's pretty sister island, Gozo. (Photo: Rico.)

For most Europeans the word 'Mediterranean' conjures up images of sun-baked summer holidays; of arid olive groves and aniseed fields; of aromatic garlic seafood cuisine, and images of a vivid blue sea to be dipped into as your body turns golden brown.

The Mediterranean is a giant open-air playground for Western Europe. It is, however, a very small ocean to support the vast population that taints its rim throughout the summer. As a result the Mediterranean has suffered from pollution and over-fishing. Amongst divers the 'Med' has had a reputation for being clear, warm, and lifeless. Although I

have enjoyed many dives around the Mediterranean I found it disappointing in terms of marine life, seeing few fish more than four inches long. That was until I discovered the island of Gozo.

Measuring nine miles by five the island of Gozo lies in the far south of the Mediterranean, below Sicily and just four miles north of Malta. It stands like a column with tall vertical cliffs that plunge into the cobalt-blue Mediterranean Sea. Gozo is surrounded by deep clear waters which are relatively unexploited. The marine life has flourished, fed by a rich mineral run-off from the fertile land of the island.

In the 8th century BC Gozo was colonised by Phoenicians from Carthage and has been invaded or beseiged by virtually every empire that has influenced the Mediterranean since — the last of these being the British. The result of this very rich heritage is a friendly, mainly Catholic population, who nearly all speak English as well as Maltese — a language akin to Arabic but with Italian and English influences in its vocabulary.

The island has many proud hills crowned by churches surrounded by villages built entirely from golden limestone. Getting around Gozo is easy but slow on the network of tiny lakes, centred around Victoria, that cover the island. They pass through irrigated valleys of green terraced fields producing crops of grapes, olives, tomatoes and onions. Gozo is an unspoilt island — a time capsule of rural Mediterranean life that has been saved from the ravages of mass tourism by virtue of not having an airport. The island, which has 16 beaches, much interesting architecture and numerous excellent restaurants, is already a popular destination for discriminating holidaymakers seeking sunshine but not crowds.

Gozo is also gaining popularity as a diving destination. One of the reasons for this is the abundance of excellent dives that can be made from the shore. There are at least 30 such dive sites, all within half-an-hour's drive from any one point on the island. Thus boat trips, which may add considerable cost to a diving holiday, can be avoided. Such a situation is especially attractive to divers with children or non-diving partners. Underwater activities can be incorporated in a family excursion to the seaside. Added to this are the dives themselves. Dives to all depths are available at different sites, some of which have steep drop-offs to 50m and more. There are entry points on all sides of the island. So should the wind blow hard a sheltered dive can always be made from a lee shore.

The summer in Gozo normally lasts from early March to late October and the climate is warm and dry with a maximum summer air temperature of 33 °C. It would be hotter if it wasn't for the gentle sea breeze that is constant during most of the summer. The weather between November and February can also be sunny and pleasant but there will be showers and the rainfall is quite high.

The maximum water temperature is around 26 °C near the surface. Thus the use of a suit is not essential for those with plenty of natural insulation, but most divers wear at least a shortie wetsuit during the height of summer, especially as the water is cooler at depth. The water is coldest in February when the temperature drops to around 14 °C — which is still quite comfortable if a full wetsuit is worn.

Groupers, John Dory, Octopus and Red

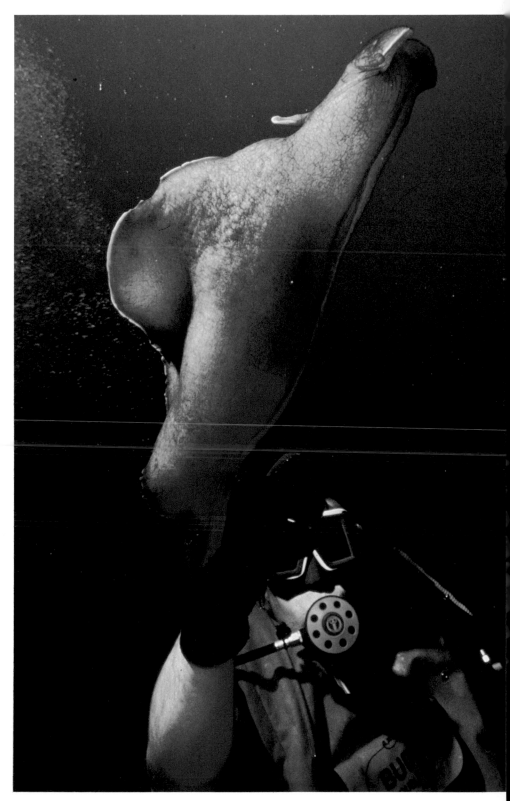

A nudibranch moves through the water with a gentle undulating motion. (Photo: Rico.)

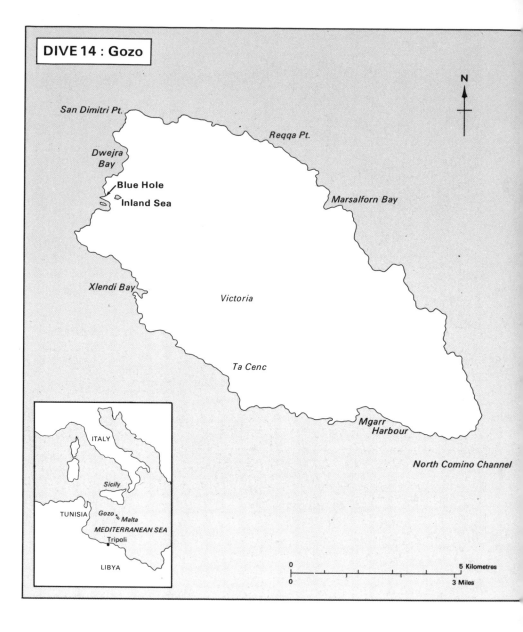

San Dimitri Pt.

Reqqa Pt.

Dwejra
Bay

Blue Hole

Inland Sea

Marsalforn Bay

Xlendi Bay

Victoria

Ta Cenc

Mgarr
Harbour

North Comino Channel

ITALY

Sicily

TUNISIA

Gozo Malta

MEDITERRANEAN SEA

Tripoli

LIBYA

N

0   5 Kilometres

0   3 Miles

Facing page: **Looking up towards
the surface along an underwater
canyon rich with life**. (Photo:
Horace Dobbs.)

Mullet are typical of the life that you will find
underwater. Although the density of the
sub-sea life off Gozo cannot compare with that
on a tropical coral reef there are many
beautiful orange anemones and small purple
corals. However there is one feature of Gozo's
sub-aquatic scenery that is exceptional — its
spectacular underwater caves.

There are several key points on the island
from which most dives are made, they are:
Reqqa Point, Ta Cenc, Xlendi Bay and Dwejra
Bay.

There are two dives at Dwejra Bay that most
typify what Gozo has to offer, and I have
chosen them as the island's classic dives. One is
known as the Blue Hole and the other The
Inland Sea. Both names are self-descriptive.

The *Inland Sea* is a small land-locked lake

situated in a spectacular natural amphitheatre.
This sea-water lake was formed by the collapse
of a huge cave. It is connected to the sea by a
long natural tunnel which is just wide enough
for the passage of the small local fishing boats
that take holidaymakers on excursions
through the cliffs, that tower to a height of
50m above it, to the open sea beyond.
Although a journey through the tunnel is
exciting by boat on the surface, it is much more
dramatic to make the passage underwater.

You can drive right down to the pebbly
beach that surrounds the shore of the lake.
Having kitted up you may either enter the
water directly from the beach, or from a small
jetty in the lake. The lake is 7m deep and the
visibility is usually a cloudy 6m compared with
the 35m plus that awaits you at the other end

126

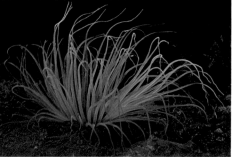

Top: **Flash highlights a diver and reveals the many forms of life encrusting the rocks.** (Photo: Rico.)

Above: **If disturbed, this Cerianthus anemone can retract into its underground tube which may be up to 1 metre long.** (Photo: Rico.)

of the tunnel. The tunnel is about 50m from the jetty. The bottom of the tunnel is strewn with large boulders and gradually drops down to 30m. There are normally shoals of fish at both ends of the tunnel which is 150m long. The tunnel is at first dark and the water emerald. As you swim through, the light at the end of the tunnel turns to an exquisite shade of blue. Illuminated by distant flickering shafts you become aware of the awesome beauty of this vast underwater temple. At the sea-side exit of the tunnel you will be greeted with a dramatic drop-off and often several large Groupers. You may turn either left or right out of the tunnel and swim along the attractive underwater wall. Both directions offer spectacular vistas that can easily lure you into deeper and deeper water. So watch your depth gauge and your contents gauge. Do not stray too far, as the only practicable way back to dry land is through the tunnel.

Limestone is a sedimentary rock formed by deposition of sediments on the sea bed which are then compacted by geological forces. It is a relatively soft rock that is very slowly dissolved by fresh water which re-deposits the mineral

(calcium carbonate) when it evaporates. Thus when limestone regions are thrust up from the sea bed the rain falling on them creates gorges and tunnels which sometimes enlarge into caves in which stalactites may form by evaporation of water dripping from the roof. The Cheddar Gorge is one of the best known outcrops of limestone in England.

The water-laid rocks of Gozo were deposited 40 to 50 million years ago in what is known as the Oligocene period. They first appeared above water about 15 million years ago and joined Europe to Africa. Later this land bridge collapsed leaving Malta and Gozo as islands in the blue Mediterranean Sea. Today evidence of Gozo's sub-aquatic geological origins can be seen everywhere in the stone of its buildings and churches. More obvious, perhaps, is the cave of stalactites and stalagmites called Xerri's Grotto at Xaghra, in the centre of the island. The same processes that gave rise to this inland geological curiosity, now high above the sea, also led to the creation of the coastal features that make Gozo such a spectacular dive destination. For it was the dissolution of the limestone by fresh water, and its subsequent erosion and invasion by the sea, that created the submerged caves and tunnels that divers now enjoy because they provide such exciting opportunities for exploration and photography.

The site I have chosen as my second classic dive on Gozo was once part of a vast underground tunnel and chamber system. Now the land has been eroded, and it has become filled with sea water, you can enter what at one time was a broad vertical shaft connecting to a vast cavern. It is known as The Blue Hole.

The Blue Hole is 300m from the most convenient parking place at Dwejra Bay and it is a bit of a scramble over the rocks to reach. But once you arrive it is a very easy entry.

The Blue Hole forms an almost perfect circle and is separated from the sea by a 5-m wide rim. You can leap straight into the hole where you will immediately find yourself in 20m of clear water. If you are first you can look back to see your buddies descending like parachutists through a black hole in the sky. To the left-hand side is a huge underwater arch which curiously looks like a mirror image of the famous Azure Window which lies just behind it, above the surface. Passing through the underwater arch or 'window' you will find there is a rocky gulley on the left-hand side that attracts shoals of fish.

If you come out of the gulley and continue with the shore on your left-hand side you will find a crack in the wall at 20m. Ten metres into this crack you will enter a large cave. To exit, there is a small tunnel at the back which ascends vertically to a platform in open water at 9m. The sun's rays give the cave a mysterious aura as you enter it.

The safest way out is back through the Blue Hole.

Because the recreations of goggle fishing and then aqualung diving first started there, the Mediterranean has been described as 'The Cradle of Diving'. The pioneer British diver Jimmy Hodges used a Davis submarine escape apparatus, and then an early aqualung when shooting his first underwater films in Malta in the 1940s. Since then the popularity of Malta as a diving location has grown steadily. Although Malta's sister island of Gozo has not gone unnoticed, it has remained relatively unexplored. In addition to the two classic dives I have described there are several others that follow close behind, each offering its own unique diving experience. However, I am certain there are more dive sites, perhaps even more spectacular, still waiting to be discovered.

Top: **Octopuses are nocturnal feeders and are often seen out in the open during night dives.** (Photo: Horace Dobbs.)

Above: **Ashley Dobbs had his first dive with his father in the Mediterranean Sea when he was 12 years old.** (Photo: Horace Dobbs.)

Dive 15 THE NORTH SEA: St Abbs Head by Horace Dobbs

I suppose most people looking at the extensive and varied coastline of Britain would assume that there are innumerable places where a diver could take to the water to enjoy his or her recreation. But this is not so, and it was soon realised by the pioneers of British diving, who discovered that the most popular holiday resorts were generally unsuitable because the wave action on the sandy beaches gave rise to a mass of suspended particles which reduced the underwater visibility. Also, gently shelving beaches meant a diver had to swim out a long way before reasonable depths were encountered. Furthermore, the underwater, terrain in

such areas was generally uninteresting. So the search was concentrated on areas where there was good access to the sea that quickly descended into deep water.

Just such a situation was located on a headland of outstanding natural beauty just south of the outermost extremity of the Firth of Forth. The above-water scenery in the region was magnificent, especially the rocky coastline. Underwater, the seascapes were spectacular. The water was exceptionally clear by British standards throughout most of the year and the region had a rich and abundant marine life. The scene was set for St Abbs to become one of the classic dives of the world.

Its promotion to this status was helped by Norfed, a federation of diving clubs in the north of England. One of the reasons for the setting-up of Norfed was that as a group they could arrange events that were beyond the scope of individual clubs. Also divers with common minority interest could get together and share their experiences.

One such interest was underwater photography. Shortly after I moved to Yorkshire in 1966 I was asked to run an underwater photography course for Norfed. St Abbs was the suggested venue after we had agreed that it should be a practical course in which divers got into water and took pictures as well as listening to lectures on the theoretical aspects of the subject.

As a result I made numerous visits to St Abbs in the early 1970s mostly staying at the Scouts Croft Caravan Park in nearby Coldingham. It proved to be a good base for such ventures because it provided relatively cheap accommodation for the divers who were mostly accompanied by their families. Also there was a compressor on site which made the business of filling cylinders between dives less bothersome than it usually was in the days when compressor stations were relatively few and far between.

Right from the start I was impressed by the number of subjects that offered themselves for photography at St Abbs. Mind you not all of them were as co-operative as I would have liked. Lots of subjects popped out of frame just as I was about to take a shot. The abundant and exotic Powder Puff Anemones were good from this point of view, however, because they were stuck to the rocks and couldn't move.

Of all the dives I made at St Abbs one site stands out in my memory more clearly than all the others. It was called the Cathedral and reference to my diving log book shows that I first dived it on the 27th June 1971 with Ken Crow. The wind was blowing force 4 to 5 westerly, which meant that there were white horses out to sea but it was flat calm in the harbour. We arrived at the rocky outcrop at the end of the harbour wall, fully kitted, complete with cameras and ready to dive at 1.00 pm, in time for slack low water. The water temperature, so my log says, was 50 °F (10 ° C). I took a compass bearing 120°, on the middle rock of the group of three we could see exposed and which would be covered at high water. We scrambled down the rocks and clambered over exposed fronds of kelp plants before we launched ourselves into the channel that led between a large rock called Broad Craig and the harbour wall. The dark green

seaweeds hung motionless in the still water. A Common Jellyfish, *Aurelia aurita* which I identified by the pale violet lines within its almost colourless bell-shaped body, pulsed gently across my field of vision. When washed ashore these primitive creatures are messy blobs of jelly, yet underwater they have a delicate living beauty that is enhanced by their gentle swimming motion. A shoal of Pollack swam ahead of us and then took cover in the kelp when we persisted in swimming in their direction. Sunbeams shone down through the transparent water and covered the rocks and shallow seabed with dancing patterns of pale yellow light. Small fry gathered in tight shoals on the edge of the kelp forest.

An Angler Fish, about 1m long, lay motionless on the bottom. An appendage, that looked like a fishing rod, protruded from the top of its head and dangled what appeared to be a tiny fluttering fish just in front of its closed, well-camouflaged, mouth. Any small fish, taken in by this lure would find itself engulfed in a split second, for these normally sedentary fish can leap forward at remarkable speed to gulp their prey. The Angler Fish themselves rely on camouflage for their own defence and the fishing rod was immediately lowered when our presence was detected. Ken was swimming ahead of me, so I said 'Hello' to the Angler Fish and moved on leaving him to continue fishing in peace when the threat of our presence had passed by.

We were in no hurry and looked at and

The author (right) with one of his pupils on an early Norfed Underwater Photographic Course at St Abbs. (Photo: Peter Duffy.)

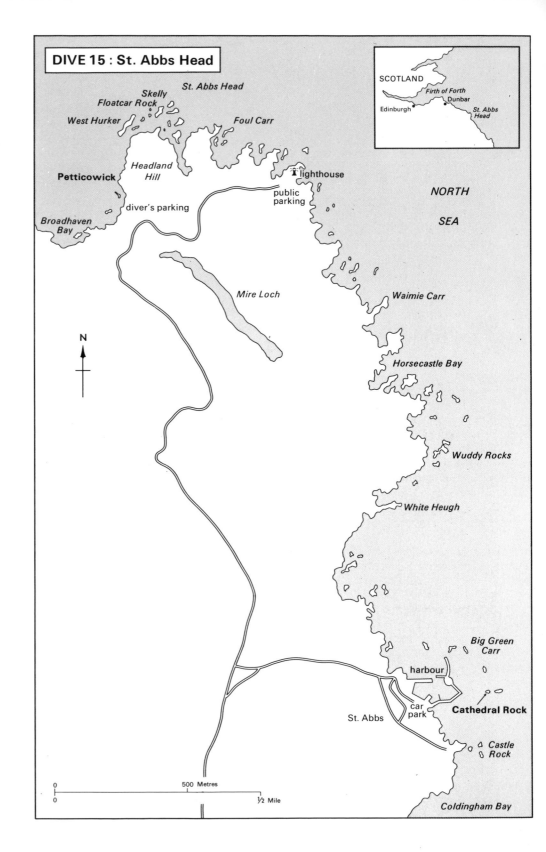

DIVE 15 : St. Abbs Head

SCOTLAND

Firth of Forth
Edinburgh   Dunbar
St. Abbs
Head

St. Abbs Head

Skelly
Floatcar Rock
West Hurker
Foul Carr

Petticowick   Headland
Hill

lighthouse

public
parking

diver's parking

NORTH

SEA

Broadhaven
Bay

Mire Loch

Waimie Carr

N

Horsecastle Bay

Wuddy Rocks

White Heugh

Big Green
Carr

harbour

car
park

Cathedral Rock

St. Abbs

Castle
Rock

0   500 Metres
0   ½ Mile

Coldingham Bay

photographed what we saw en route whilst following a general direction that would take us to Cathedral Rock. Ken knew the area well and I followed him. The water became darker and deeper offshore, especially when we descended below the maximum depth at which the kelp thrived. Here the scenery changed abruptly and the kelp forest gave way to rocks which were covered with marine growth.

We were swimming along one such face when Ken disappeared. He had found The Cathedral. It was a tunnel that passed right through the rock wall. When I rounded the edge I could see my diving partner, silhouetted in black, set against the dark green light that glowed at the far end. There was no current and we easily swam the short distance that took us through to the far side of the rock. We swam slowly and I admired the beauty of the Plumose Anemones and sponges that encrusted the arched stone ceiling over our heads. We continued our exploration on the far side of the rock before retracing our passage to the tunnel. Our time underwater passed very quickly and the tide was starting to run by the time we swam back through the Cathedral. The current, which was almost imperceptible away from the rock increased noticeably when it was forced into the tunnel. The visibility was considerably less on our second passage. The reason for the luxuriant growths within the Cathedral was the current, for it brought with it the microscopic plants and animals upon which the anemones fed — fingering the food from the flowing water with their stinging tentacles which posed no threat to us.

When I returned three years later with a filming lamp and turned it on under the arch the effect was absolutely stunning. The peach-coloured and white anemones shimmered in the bright light which added a thousandfold to the intensity of colours of the sponges and surrounding marine life. I felt as if I really was in a cathedral and pondered on how privileged I was to have seen such a beautiful sight which was denied to man until the invention of the aqualung.

When the wind blows from the south east diving conditions at St Abbs harbour deteriorate. Just such a wind was blowing on the 17th September 1972 when I was running another underwater photographic weekend for Norfed at St Abbs. The sea was rough and the visibility was worsening. So we decided to switch the dive venue from St Abbs harbour to a small cove called Pettico Wick which was on the north side of the headland and therefore sheltered from the wind. My dive partner was a marine biologist, Dave Coates.

Access to the sea was via a stone jetty that ran right down to the water's edge. Its surface was covered with jellyfish. Leaving my young son Ashley to enjoy pottering in the rockpools we slid into the sea. David said he knew of a super photogenic spot and set off like a racehorse to find it. There was a heavy swell that penetrated to the seabed and swirled the kelp back and forth. David was not a

photographer at the time, and didn't appreciate that that particular species of diver usually likes to take things easy. Trying to keep up with him was like running a marathon. On the western side of the bay we eventually found the rock face he was looking for. I needed both hands to operate the camera, and unlike David could not cling to anything solid underwater. But by gripping between my thighs a strong

We found Sea Urchins and Dead Men's Fingers in profusion under the canopy of kelp. (Photo: Horace Dobbs.)

Top: **A detachable close-up lens and flash captured this shrimp on a diver's hand.** (Photo: Peter Duffy.)

Above: **The expression on the face of this Lumpsucker fish is fixed because it is dead.**

Facing page, top: **The walls of Cathedral Rock were covered with a wonderful profusion of marine life.**

Facing page, bottom: **The delicate beauty of the Powder Puff anemone.**
(Photos: Horace Dobbs.)

the seabed. They appeared as a wall when we approached. I watched David swim into the wall — and disappear. I followed suit and he came into vision again immediately. A combination of currents and tides had concentrated the slow-moving jelly fish into a narrow vertical stretch of water until they virtually formed an underwater curtain.

I returned to Pettico Wick eighteen days later and had a completely different dive on exactly the same site. The water was quiet and whilst swimming away from the shore I came across a couple of lobster pots. I did not disturb them and looked at the bait. I wondered how many fishermen really knew how their pots looked when seen from a fish eye view. A large Spider Crab was climbing over one of them looking for a way to get at the food inside. On the swim back to the jetty I came across two Fiddler Crabs, locked in combat. The source of their disagreement was a dead Lumpsucker Fish nearby. I watched fascinated. Eventually one of the two combatants emerged as the victor. The vanquished crab departed, even managing to appear disgruntled, whilst the victor re-attacked the tail of the corpse with his pincers. It was one of those little cameos of sea life that remain registered when so much else is forgotten.

Since St Abbs was first dived in the 1950s the coastline of Britain hasn't changed significantly — but diving and public attitudes towards the sea have. Thus St Abbs still offers arguably the best diving in Britain with direct and easy access from the shore. As a result two hundred or more divers may arrive at the harbour during Bank Holiday weekends. Conservationists realised that if every diver removed just one crab and one sea urchin the area would be changed. After a great deal of lobbying and persuasion it was generally agreed that the whole of St Abbs Head should be made into an underwater reserve on a voluntary basis. A public notice proclaiming this was put up near the slipway and an ever increasing number of diving clubs that supported the principle added plaques bearing their names. It was a generous gesture on the part of the divers who knew that on most days some of the small fishing boats that tied up in the harbour unloaded boxes of crabs, most of which were caught locally. Yet the divers themselves returned empty handed.

The aspiration of many diver/conservationists came to fruition on 18th August 1984 when David Bellamy publicly opened the St Abbs and Eyemouth Voluntary Marine Nature Reserve the aims of which were: to conserve the outstanding biological richness of these inshore waters and to

stipe (stem) of Laminaria seaweed as if it was a rope, I was able to hang on, even though I swayed back and forth with every movement of the sea. I managed to take some pictures, and I did appreciate the beauty of my surroundings but I certainly did not rate it as one of the most comfortable dives I had made.

However, there was one incident on that dive which has remained vividly in my memory ever since. As we made our way back to the jetty we encountered countless jelly fish that hung in a curtain from the surface of the sea to encourage responsible educational and recreational use alongside the traditional commercial fishery, to the mutual benefit of all. H.R.H. The Prince of Wales, a diver himself, added his weight to the proceedings by sending a telegram wishing the venture 'every success in the future'.

I had not been to St Abbs for several years

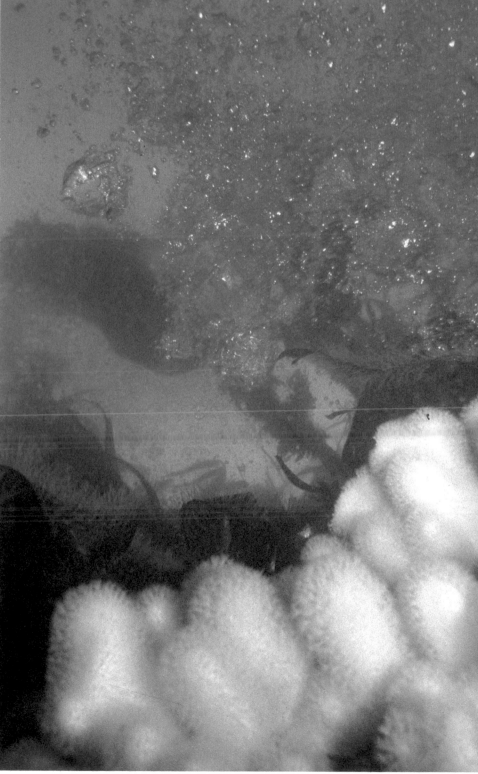

Below: **When I returned to St Abbs after an absence of several years I was able to compare the Dead Men's Fingers around Cathedral Rock with other soft corals I had seen in places·such as the Red Sea.** (Photo: Horace Dobbs.)

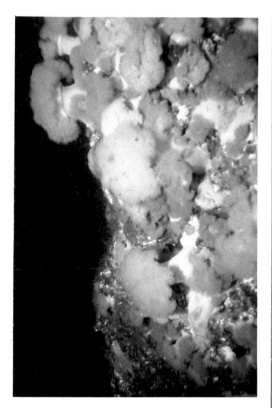

before the official opening of the reserve and, for the purpose of this book, I was keen to see for myself how it was coping with the ever-increasing number of divers who were visiting the area. I was also keen to dive the Cathedral again.

I arrived on the 21st August 1986 on a dull, overcast day. Despite the fact that it was mid-August the car park was almost deserted. It was the day of the highest spring tide of the month with a tidal range of 6.2m. In mid-morning the harbour was dried out and a group of four divers from the Manchester University Branch of the British Sub-Aqua Club were hauling their inflatable from the slipway, across the muddy harbour floor to the water-filled channel that lead out of the harbour.

Before getting changed into my wetsuit I chatted to their leader who dived frequently in the area. I wanted to confirm with him the exact location of Cathedral Rock.

'If you swim out to the rock with two seagulls on top you can't miss it' he said with a twinkle in his eye.

Half an hour later I had rigged up my underwater camera and was fully kitted with aqualung, weightbelt and all the other para-phernalia with which divers bedeck them-selves. I plodded from the car park past the slipway and around the harbour wall to where it forked. There I scrambled down to the rocks that tumbled into the open-water channel that led to Cathedral Rock. As I slid into the water I was immediately struck by how cold it was and felt a dull pain on the small area of exposed skin between the top of my mask and my thick neoprene hood. However that cold

shock quickly passed as I snorkelled out on the surface towards the inner of two small peaks of black rock around which the swell surged. I put the regulator in my mouth and dived down into the gloomy depths. I finned towards the kelp that swayed back and forth with the swirling water. The motion became less as I got deeper. The kelp seemed to pass upwards as I descended, like a passenger going down in a lift. I passed through the depth limit of the kelp and was facing rock. A few seconds later, at a depth of 12m, a green tunnel appeared before me. I had descended directly to the Cathedral.

It was exactly as I had remembered it from my first dive there over fifteen years earlier. Since then I have dived in many of the most exotic seas in the world. Yet swimming into the Cathedral still sent a tingle of excitement and sheer unadulterated joy coursing through my body. The beautiful Plumose Anemonies still hung from the roof like bunches of exotic flowers. Also in great abundance were the flowering stalks of *Alcionium digitatum*. These colonial animals contract to small tough cylinders out of the water and have been given the descriptive common name of Dead Men's Fingers. The spongy body is stiffened with little lime needles, called spicules, which give the structures strength when they are gorged with sea water and the delicate florets of eight feathery tentacles are open like daisy flowers to feed on the plankton soup in which they are bathed. The maximum size of the Dead Men's Fingers that grew on the walls of the Cathedral was about 15cm. However, on that dive I saw them through new eyes because I knew they were closely related to the very exotic soft corals I had seen in the Red Sea and in other warm water regions where Alcionium corals can grow as big as a man. But that knowledge did not detract from the beauty of their small cousins which encircled me as I swam slowly through the Cathedral. On the far side I rose to the top of the archway and peered into another smaller tunnel which also ran right through the rock. As I swam back through the lower larger tunnel I was accompanied by a large Ballan Wrasse and was joined by another one when I reached the far opening. The fish were certainly not as friendly as this on my earlier visits. Broken sea urchin shells on the sea floor nearby indicated why the Wrasse had ho-noured me with their company. They were expecting to be fed. Wrasse, and most other fish, find the insides of sea urchins irresistable.

The flash pictures I took brought the entire scene briefly into brilliant colour. It didn't matter if it was dull above, the undersea world in and around the Cathedral was a beautiful as ever.

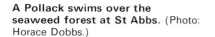

A Pollack swims over the seaweed forest at St Abbs. (Photo: Horace Dobbs.)

DIVE 16 THE ENGLISH CHANNEL: Dolphin Rock by Horace Dobbs

With stories of their close links with man going back over 2,000 years, dolphins are the sea creatures the majority of divers most wish to meet and swim with under the sea. The well documented habit of dolphins swimming in the bow waves of ships underway, coupled with the stories of boys riding on dolphins in ancient times, would appear to indicate that diving with dolphins is easy. In practice it is quite difficult.

On many occasions divers have jumped overboard when their vessel has been accompanied by a school of dolphins, only to find when they've entered the water that the

dolphins have disappeared. There have been cases reported where submerged divers have heard high-pitched squeals and then found themselves in the midst of a mêlée of rapidly moving dolphins who then vanished as quickly as they appeared.

Some, who have made deliberate attempts to make contact with dolphins, have succeeded. Wade Doak, for instance, fitted out a James Wharram Polynesian-style catamaran specifically for this purpose. In his book *Dolphin Dolphin* Wade recounts how he and his wife Jan swam with the same school of dolphins in successive years off the Poor Knights Islands in

The smiling face of Jean Louis – a friendly wild dolphin off the coast of Brittany. (Photo: Georgie Douwma.)

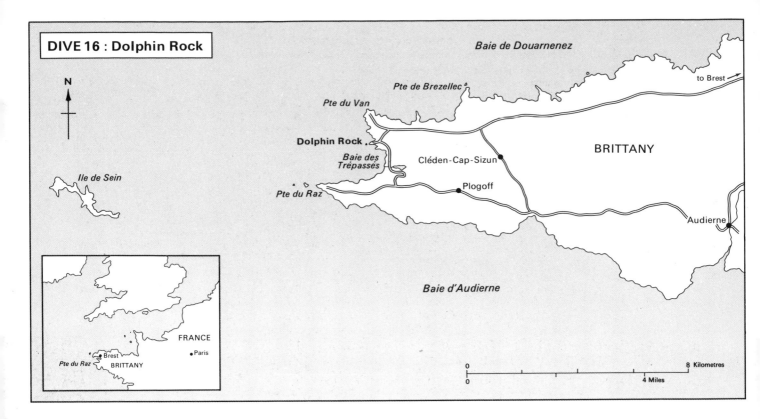

New Zealand. A group of American divers, called Friends of the Sea, have made repeated contact with a school of dolphins in the Bahamas. Indeed, they now run special cruises to introduce swimmers to dolphins, and have been doing so for a number of years.

I have met and dived with a school of dolphins on several visits to Roca Redonda in the Galapagos Islands. I have also swum with schools of wild dolphins in the Straits of Gibraltar. But on all of these occasions I have gained the impression that the dolphins were supremely self-sufficient. Admittedly I did provide an alternative source of interest for a time, but had I not been present I felt absolutely sure they would have been quite happy entertaining themselves without me.

On rare occasions, however, for reasons we still do not know, solitary dolphins leave their school and deliberately seek out the company of humans. When this happens the most exciting and stimulating diving imaginable may ensue. In Britain we have been exceptionally lucky in this respect in recent years because three wild dolphins have chosen to stay around our coast to entertain and be entertained by divers. I have had the good fortune to spend many hours in the sea with all of them.

Donald, a Bottlenose Dolphin, first made contact with divers in 1972 off the Isle of Man. In 1974 I had the ultimate magical experience of witnessing my own 'Boy on a Dolphin' story. I saw my son Ashley ride on Donald in Port St Mary harbour. It was a totally spontaneous gesture on the dolphin's part. From the Isle of Man, Donald journeyed to Ireland, Wales and eventually made his way to Cornwall where he was last seen on 14th January, 1978. In 1983 a dolphin, named Percy, made an appearance in Portreath, which was one of the places visited by Donald. For the next two years Percy enthralled many unsuspecting divers by appearing out of the green haze and watching them intently. Then, for no apparent reason, he disappeared late in 1985. Before he did so, however, yet another friendly wild Bottlenose Dolphin made his appearance off the coast of Pembrokeshire. He was named Simo by the people of Solva who took the dolphin to their hearts. After two years Simo disappeared as mysteriously as he arrived — but not before he had changed the lives of many people, and I had made a documentary film about him with HTV. It was entitled *Bewitched by a Dolphin*.

Thus, over a period of 11 years, I was able to build up a close one-to-one relationship with three separate solitary dolphins, Donald, Percy and Simo, each of whom had a different personality.

Whilst this was going on off the coast of Britain a Bottlenose Dolphin quietly settled off a tiny island close to the Cap du Raz in Brittany. Some fishermen were the first to spot the dolphin, though when they saw a triangular fin cutting a path through the water towards their boat their first reaction was that it was a shark. Jean Louis is the name French fishermen often use for a shark and the name Jean Louis has stuck, even after the fishermen discovered their error.

The place Jean Louis decided to make home was situated in a bay called La Baie des Trépassés, which translates into English as The Bay of Tragedies or The Bay of Lost Souls.

The latter translation would appear to be the most appropriate from our point of view when considering Jean Louis as a dolphin with a lost soul who seeks out the company of humans instead of other dolphins. As events were to unfold, however, the Bay of Lost Souls was to have another, even more sinister, significance. But all that lay in the future when I was contacted in January 1984 by Andy Crofts, a canoeist. He told me that whilst his group had been canoeing in La Baie des Trépassés during the previous year they had been escorted by a dolphin. The dolphin enjoyed playing around the canoes and seemed to get a particular thrill when the canoeists inverted themselves, hanging upside down from their canoes in the water.

It was some canoeists who first drew my attention to the presence of Jean Louis in Brittany. (Photo: Horace Dobbs.)

When the canoeists discovered that the dolphin liked this game they put on facemasks in order that they could see the dolphin more clearly.

The full story of the subsequent events are told in my book *Tale of Two Dolphins*. For instance after two reconnaissance trips to Brittany I made a television film about Jean Louis with John Gau Productions for Channel 4. It was called 'A Closer Encounter' and brought a touch of dolphin magic into many homes when it was first shown on British television on Christmas Day in 1985.

Making a film is a very good way of diving with dolphins for a number of reasons. One of them is that it involves making a very positive committment. Also it can be regarded as work rather than play, and that absolves any question of guilt that might arise in people like myself who have unfortunately been imbued with the work ethic and feel guilty when setting out simply to enjoy myself. Having established that it is definitely work, I can justify going diving — whatever the weather conditions. Also, I have the back-up of a well-paid technical team to help me achieve what I set out to do, which is to interact in a positive way with a wild dolphin.

And so it was, during the summer of 1984, that I spent two idyllic weeks passing as much time as I could in the sea with Jean Louis. During that time I was able to build a closer and closer relationship with the dolphin. It gave me an opportunity to explore a part of the French underwater coast which I otherwise would not have visited. It also gave me a tremendous opportunity to explore the character of Jean Louis. And this led to some surprising revelations.

Firstly, it turned out that Jean Louis was female. From the onset, my relationship with Jean Louis was different from that with all the other friendly wild dolphins I had known, who were all male. Jean Louis was gentle, and with almost mother-like patience, led me slowly away from all of my preconceived scientific studies and gently showed me her territory around the small island which I dubbed Dolphin Rock.

In many ways the underwater scenery around Dolphin Rock was rather like that off Cornwall. The underwater visibility varied considerably from day to day and was very dependent upon the weather conditions, principally the strength and direction of wind. Even a strong offshore wind, which would fetch up white horses on the open sea and send spume and spray rising high into the air around the Cap du Raz, would leave the water relatively unruffled close inshore around Dol-

phin Rock with underwater visibility 10m or more. Even a relatively mild onshore wind, however, would cause the sea to become milky and the undersea world far less attractive from a photographic standpoint.

I also discovered that the weather in Brittany could be as capricious as it is in Cornwall. Indeed, it did range from being flat calm and clear to wild and cloudy during the course of a single day. I dived around Dolphin Rock under all of these conditions.

There is only one sensible point of entry from the shore into Jean Louis' territory around Dolphin Rock, and that is down the slipway from which the fishing boats are launched. The ease of getting into the water depends upon the state of the tide and the direction of the wind.

On one of my early visits to Jean Louis I saw her underwater world in idyllic conditions. The sun was shining and the sea around the entry point was flat. Looking down onto it from above it looked like a pretty underwater garden. I was wearing an aqualung but chose to snorkel out towards the rock in order to conserve air. Beneath me the shallow water seaweeds gave way to a sandy sea bed which had been shaped by the wave action into an irregular pattern of ridges. A Swimming Crab scuttled quickly across the bottom and bravely waved its claws at my shadow as it passed over. Then with a few deft flicks of its back swimming legs it buried itself in the sand and disappeared.

When I reached a plastic marker buoy I removed my knife from its scabbard and hit the hollow ball with the handle. I could clearly hear the sound through the water and hoped that it would attract Jean Louis. When she failed to appear I continued my journey towards Dolphin Rock. On route I stopped again at a small alloy float which I knew marked a submerged wooden crate that the fishermen used for storing crabs and lobsters. The underside of the metallic buoy was festooned with the delicate, pale-green streamers of seaweed. The metallic butt of my diving knife which I used as a hammer sent sound cracking through the water. This time my signal was answered. Jean Louis came into vision, her grey, streamlined body had the appearance of burnished metal. Although it was covered in marks and scars these were lost in the bright sunshine, which, reflected by the wavelets above, played patterns of dancing lights across her body. The powerful, steel-like form looked like a space vehicle as it flowed through the deep blue inner space of the ocean towards me. Closer and closer she came until she was less than one metre from my facemask.

She looked at me with a bright eye and her body quivered. This was no inanimate spacecraft. This was the friendly alien herself. The way in which she wriggled her body was a clear invitation to play. I got the message and took off in hot pursuit as she sped towards the kelp forest around Dolphin Rock.

We then started a game of tag. Of course, there was no way that I could catch her, so she went deliberately slowly and allowed me to approach her when I swam flat out. Then, just as I was about to make contact with my hand she rocketed away and I could almost hear her laughter when she exhaled a stream of bubbles. 'Well, if that's the way you want to play it,' I thought, 'I will try a new tactic'. So I stopped swimming, deflated my life-jacket and allowed myself to sink slowly by gravity into a crevice between the rocks. The canopy of kelp closed over my head and I found myself looking at the stems of the Laminaria seaweed which were like the trunks of trees in a tropical forest. Their holdfasts looked like gnarled roots and fulfilled the same function, anchoring the tough rubbery stems firmly to the rocks, which were covered with encrustations some of which were soft pink in colour. Sea Urchins browsed, like submarine sheep, between the holdfasts of the kelp, scraping encrustations into their mouths on the undersides of their bodies with the chisel action of a series of teeth which fit into a cage-like structure known as Aristotle's Lantern. Sea Urchins are also known as Sea Hedgehogs because their bodies are covered with short spines, the ends of which are fine examples of natural ball-and-socket joints. Tiny white spheres projecting from the hard calcareous spherical body of the Sea Urchin fit into a socket at the base of each of the spines. The spines provide an obvious defence mechanism, but they are also used for locomotion and as spikes upon which Sea Urchins impale pieces of seaweed. The urchins use their tube feet to manipulate the seaweed into position where it affords partial camouflage.

Having looked around the underwater kelp forest I took a breath and held it for as long as I could, remaining totally immobile. Within a few moments a beak burst through the Laminaria canopy over my head. Jean Louis opened her mouth and wagged her head up and down as if she was laughing at my joke.

My studies of Jean Louis provided the basis for a film entitled 'A Closer Encounter' that was first screened in the U.K. on Channel 4 TV and has since been shown in many countries throughout the world. (Photo: Georgie Douwma.)

She then stayed still waiting for my next move. I got a distinct feeling that she was telling me that she had found me and had understood that I had changed from playing tag to hide-and-seek. At this stage I could hold my breath no longer and exhaled violently, before thankfully sucking in a new and deep lung full of air. Jean Louis was vertical in the water with her beak just a few centimetres above my head. The exhaled bubbles gurgled upwards around her body and she quivered, as if enjoying the experience and then swam off quickly with me chasing after her.

It was time to play tag again, but with new rules. Jean Louis decided to show her superiority and no matter where I went she would meet me head-on, swimming over the top of me then disappearing before making her next rapid pass after reappearing in front of me again around the corner of another rock. The next time I saw her she was herding a John Dory fish towards me. The John Dory is a most delightful fish. It has an extremely thin body and swims upright in the water like an Angel Fish, i.e. not like a Plaice which swims horizontally. The John Dory has a black circular patch in the middle of its back and legend says it's St Peter's thumb print. The fleeing John Dory, swimming as fast as it could away from the dolphin suddenly found itself face-to-face with a new predator — me. It could easily outswim me but it certainly couldn't outswim the dolphin. So it foiled both of us by darting into a crevice in the rocks.

I thought I would have another go at hiding and this time I was successful. Too successful. I sat in a channel between the rocks breathing as slowly as possible expecting to see the cheeky face of Jean Louis suddenly appear above me. But it didn't. So I broke my cover and swam upwards, out of the forest. It didn't take long to discover why Jean Louis hadn't found me. She didn't want to. She had found another playmate. A canoeist had paddled out from the beach and was hanging upside down in the water whilst still holding onto his paddle. He could only stay in that position for as long as he could hold his breath. Then he had to roll his canoe back into its normal position on the surface of the sea. This procedure obviously fascinated and entertained Jean Louis. So much so, that when I tried to re-establish my game of tag with her she ignored me and set off after the canoeist when he decided to paddle away.

Such fickle affection is hard on a man's ego. On bright sunny days in the height of summer there are plenty of distractions and I soon learned that Jean Louis was likely to go off at any time for alternative amusement.

However, I do recall another day when I had her entire attention. It was a glowering grey day with a strong offshore wind. Close inshore the sea was flat calm. However, the pelting heavy rain drove all of the holidaymakers off the beach and away from the cove. I had half a bottle of air and I decided to spend it on Jean Louis. It was late afternoon when I slipped quietly into the water.

Under the sea it was strangely peaceful and quiet. I had left the blustery wind above me and when I looked up I could see the rain pock-marking the mercury-coloured pool above my head which seemed to act as an umbrella protecting me from the unfriendly storm. Very shortly after I got into the sea Jean Louis appeared alongside me. She made none of the quivering gestures which indicated she wanted to play. She slowly closed and reopened the eye I could see and with it she conveyed a feeling of gentleness and serenity. So, side by side, we swam over the kelp forest and around our former playground. There was no hurry this time, and I breathed slowly. The two of us were just out for an evening stroll together. I had enough air to circumnavigate Dolphin Rock entirely, and make my way back to the entry point underwater. When I eventually hauled myself onto the rocks I felt very relaxed and completely at peace with the world.

During the night the wind veered and turned onshore. That same wind also blew away the clouds, and when I looked out at Dolphin Rock the next morning it was ringed with a necklace of seething white foam and set in a deep blue sea. I looked everywhere for the dolphin but there was no sign of her. We had a Humber inflatable tied to one of the moorings in the bay and it was bouncing around like a bucking bronco. We decided that we would go out and see if we could find Jean Louis in the wind-tossed sea. So we kitted up in bright sunshine on the shore and then jumped into the sea, finning rapidly the moment we entered the water to avoid being thrown back onto the rocks. Getting out to the inflatable was no problem, and we soon hauled ourselves inboard using the hand lines to lever ourselves over the inflated tubes.

Jean Louis liked the inflatable and usually came to us as soon as we started motoring in the bay. On that morning, however, she didn't, so we moved back towards Dolphin Rock. Close into the rock I saw what I thought was a tree trunk sticking out of the water in the middle of the white foam. Closer inspection showed that it was not a tree trunk at all but Jean Louis. Her head, and about a third of her trunk were above the water, and she appeared

Facing page: **Jean Louis was fascinated by the small folding anchor of our inflatable.** (Photo: Horace Dobbs.)

to be in a spasm of ecstasy in the boiling white foam all around her. The sound of our engine nearby suddenly broke her trance-like state and she dived, appearing alongside our boat a few seconds later. Her message was clear: 'Why don't you come in and join me?'

I put on my fins, mask and snorkel. A few seconds later I was in the water with the dolphin swimming alongside me. She lured me close to the rocks but I was fearful of being swept up on them. So after enjoying being in the waves with her I swam back to the inflatable and asked for my aqualung. Jean Louis became tremendously excited at this turn of events and swam round me in tight circles urging me to follow her and play with her. Like a siren she lured me closer and closer to the rocks. Under the sea the water was full of white bubbles that whirled around as if we were in a giant jacuzzi. The movement of the sea caused the kelp thongs to lash backwards and forwards like palm trees in hurricane-force winds that were forever changing direction. I knew the situation was dangerous but had no

fear. Closer and closer to the rocks we went until we got to a stage where they seemed to rush past at great speed and then stop. An instant later they gathered speed again and would rush back in the direction from which they had come. All of this was an optical illusion of course. Like the one experienced when one is sitting in a stationary train, and a train coming alongside gives one the illusion of moving. In this case, however, I was moving and the rocks were stationary. With Jean Louis beside me I discovered that water doesn't bump into rocks under the sea — it swishes past them. I realised that provided I stayed under water, and didn't have gravity thrusting me onto the rocks, as it would if I was thrown-up on the surface, then I would be quite safe. We played together in Jean-Louis's jacuzzi and began a game of tag. Peter Scoones, the underwater cameraman with the film crew, couldn't resist the situation and joined in the fun clutching his extremely expensive Arriflex camera in its underwater housing. Whilst he filmed Jean Louis in the cauldron of boiling water I took pictures of both of them with my stills camera. Jean Louis loved it.

Playing tag with a dolphin under such conditions is extremely energetic and burns up air at a very fast rate. When I had used up two-thirds of my supply I deemed it prudent to swim well away from the rocks before surfacing and within a few moments of doing so the inflatable was alongside to pick me up. Our boat handler, Georgette Douwma, was very anxious for our safety. However, she need not have worried because Jean Louis had demonstrated how we could survive in a very rough sea. The answer was to stay submerged.

Sadly, whilst we were engaging in this exciting and adventurous dive, a rod-and-line fisherman was swept off the rocks in a nearby cove, and lost his life. That tragic incident was a lesson for us, and reminded us that even though we felt safe in Jean Louis' company we should always respect, and certainly never underestimate, the power of the sea.

I don't know how much longer Jean Louis will remain in Brittany. But while she does, Dolphin Rock will remain a classic dive.

When swimming with the dolphin Jean Louis I often wondered if she was studying me as much as I was studying her. (Photo: Horace Dobbs.)

DIVE 17 THE ENGLISH CHANNEL: The Isles of Scilly by Horace Dobbs

Sunken treasure is often the first subject I am questioned about when people find out I am a diver. I then admit that I have found an old flintlock pistol in the Thames, several old jars and bottles in the River Ouse, as well as a slightly older container, a Roman wine amphora dated 150 BC, which I discovered half buried in the sand under the Mediterranean Sea.

But in many people's minds this is not real treasure. 'Ah, but what about gold, have you found any gold?' they ask.

My answer to that question is, 'Yes'. Before they immediately jump to the conclusion that I

am a millionaire I have to qualify my reply with the comment, 'Just one small piece'.

It happened in 1971 when I took my 13-year-old daughter Melanie for her very first dive in the sea. She had practiced using the aqualung in the local swimming pool before we set off for a family holiday with some Italian friends on the island of Elba. I had made aqualungs for both of my children from old aircraft air cylinders that were called 'tadpole bottles' because of their small size.

We waded into the sea from a beach of very coarse sand. It was flat calm and the water was crystal clear — ideal conditions for a novice to

Jim Heslin and Terry Hiron with coins and pistols they recovered from the seabed off the Isles of Scilly. (Photo: Paul Armiger.)

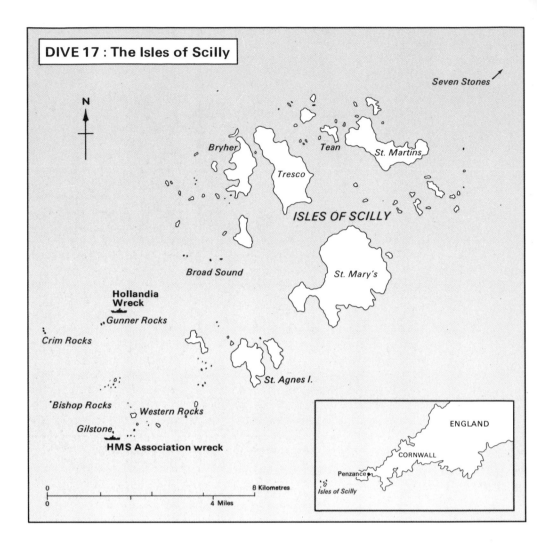

have her first proper dive. I had armed Melanie with a metal rod with a hook on the end with which she could prod things she was not too certain about. We were soon gliding across the seabed towards a small outcrop of rocks where her young eagle eyes spotted an octopus in a crannie. She touched it diffidently with her hook. The startled octopus immediately took off to a safer refuge, propelling itself in spurts with water jets from its siphon, and sending out decoy clouds of sepia ink. It landed back on the rocks and quickly slithered out of sight.

Continuing our submarine journey we saw something glinting on the sand. I picked it up and we both examined it. It was a ring with symbols embossed on it. I knew instantly that it was gold for it was bright and there were no signs of corrosion or encrustation. Melanie slipped it onto her finger and we continued our dive.

When we eventually emerged from the sea Melanie proudly showed the ring to her mother who was sunbathing on the beach.

Naturally she was excited when I told her it was made of solid gold and she decided to keep it. We were concerned that she might lose it. But we need not have worried — Melanie has worn the ring every day since she found it. It has only left her possession briefly to be examined by experts who have been unable to identify or elucidate the meaning of the hieroglyphs with which it is embossed. Furthermore, nobody can tell us the age of the ring. She likes to think it belonged to Napoleon who was imprisoned on Elba. But its origin remains a mystery.

The same cannot be said for the piece of treasure from the deep that my wife Wendy now occasionally wears as a pendant. It is a ducatoon, clearly dated 1739 and came from the ill-fated Dutch East Indiaman *Hollandia*. The *Hollandia* was the pride of the Amsterdam Chamber of the Dutch East India Company when she set sail on her maiden voyage from Texel on 3rd July, 1743 bound for Batavia (today's Djakarta) in Java. The *Hollandia's* proposed 8-month voyage was tragically terminated in heavy seas and poor visibility when she struck Gunner Rock in the Isles of Scilly. Having washed over the rock she tried to run before the wind into the safety of Broad Sound. But with her gun ports open (possibly to fire a distress signal) and her bottom rent out, she foundered in 100ft of water, carrying with her a cargo of 129,700 guilders in silver. The reasons why she ran onto the rocks remain open to speculation.

By 1743 Dutch East Indiamen were beamier, deeper and more sluggish than their predecessors. They were scarcely able to beat to windward. The high standard of seamanship and crewing which had led to Dutch pre-eminence in sailing voyages to the Far East in the 16th and 17th centuries had been lowered by the use of young inexperienced officers and Chinese crews. Whatever the reasons the *Hollandia* was certainly off course and her treasure remained beneath the sea until its whereabouts was located in 1971. Its discovery came about after three years of painstaking research in English and Dutch archives by Rex and Zelide Cowan and the use of a specially developed proton magnetometer installed on an island boat skippered by David Stedeford.

But I did not come by my own piece of treasure from the *Hollandia* until 1979 when I was in the Scilly Isles to film for the BBC TV programme 'Nationwide' the work of Jim Heslin and Terry Hiron who had recovered some 8,000 coins from another wreck — the *Association*. The stories of the recovery of the treasure from this ship are as legion and dramatic as those surrounding its loss.

Unlike the *Hollandia* the *Association* was a British vessel returning home from active service against the Spanish who were shipping home vast quantities of treasure from Mexico and Peru. Loaded with the spoils of war the *Association* was under the command of Admiral Sir Cloudesley Shovell who led his fleet out of the Mediterranean back to England. Because of bad weather taking sightings was impossible. Their position was not what the Admiral thought it was and he led his fleet into one of the biggest maritime disasters England had ever known.

At 8 o'clock on the night of 22nd October, 1707, the 165-ft long *Association*, which carried 96 guns, struck the Gilstone in the Isles of Scilly. Within minutes she broke up and sank. The *St. George* struck the same rock but managed to get off. The *Eagle* went down like a stone with all hands, the *Romney* likewise, followed shortly afterwards by the *Firebrand*. It was all over very quickly. Nearly 2,000 men died with only 23 making it to the shore.

Amongst the bodies found on the shoreline was that of Sir Cloudesley Shovell. Though his corpse was found 7 miles away from the scene

Jim Heslin, on the site of the *Thames* which sank in 1853. The pottery he has excavated bears the crest of the City of Dublin Steamship Company. (Photo: Paul Armiger.)

of the wrecks. Legend has it that he survived the shipwreck and reached land, but was later murdered for the huge emerald ring he wore on his finger. His body was then dumped to make it look as if he had drowned.

When I founded The Oxford Underwater Research Group in 1962 the solicitor who advised us on legal matters raised the subject of Sir Cloudesley Shovell. He informed me about the vast quantity of treasure on board the *Association* and suggested we should mount a project to look for it. But I said we should stick to science — and I led a geological expedition to Cornwall instead. There is no knowing how differently history would have been written if his idea had taken root. But it was to be others who would provide the material for the next chapter in the chequered chronicle of the *Association*.

It started in 1966 when a team from the Royal Naval Air Services Sub-Aqua Club brought up a cannon. Their discovery of the site of the *Association* precipitated a scramble for riches which became known as the 'Scillies Shambles'. No specific group was given clear-cut salvage rights and fierce fights are reputed to have taken place on the land and under the sea. Everything recovered should have been declared to the Official Receiver of Wreck. But all those close to the action knew that much of what was picked up from the sea bed never found its way into his keeping. Amongst those officially involved was ex 'hard hat' diver Roland Morris who had a non-exclusive contract with the Ministry of Defence to salvage the *Association*. So too did Mike Ross

of Blue Seas Divers. However, the fact that these two groups held M.o.D. contracts was of little significance because diving on the Gilstone by any divers was not illegal. Furthermore, a serious question hung over the site which made the legal situation even more complex. Although they were all diving on what was thought to be the *Association* could anyone actually prove it? Without proof of identity the pirates could claim that they weren't diving on the *Association*. After all the first cannons brought up by the Navy divers were not of British origin. Nor was the first gold coin — a Portuguese 4,000-reis piece dated 1704.

The site, where as many as five different teams would be working at any one time, was as large as two football pitches. There were no visible signs of the ship itself, just its contents, such as cannons and anchors, which were scattered over the rocks, such heavy objects naturally finding their way into crevices and gulleys and lodging there. Places on the site acquired names such as 'Cannon Gully' and 'Death Gulch'. 'Aladdin's Cave' was one of the more colourful for good reason. It was a hole under a boulder from which Roland Morris's divers raised 1,400 silver coins in 6 days of diving.

Much of what was found was covered in a concretion known as 'crud' which looked like

rock. On breaking it open, however, the treasure-hunters never knew what they would find. It might be a fused mass of silver coins, a pair of bronze dividers, or an iron cannon-ball. One of the most bizarre finds however was a skeleton — with pieces-of-eight that had come from a mint in South America stuck to the skull.

As none of the items was dated later than 1707 the evidence was strong — but certainly not conclusive in legal terms. In 1969 Bob Rogers and Terry Hiron felt sure they had found the clincher when they managed to extract a cannon from under a boulder that weighed over 100 tons. Most of the other bronze cannons brought to the surface were French but this one was definitely English. It was ornately decorated and bore a Latin inscription which translated as: Charles, Earl of Devonshire and Master of Ordnance. However it was dated 1604 and was probably one of the Admiral's favourite pieces, but it was still not conclusive proof that the site was that of the *Association*.

The evidence everyone was seeking finally came literally to light when the crud was

Top and above: **A fine collection of artefacts raised from ships wrecked in the Scilly Isles are on display in a museum set up by Roland Morris in Penzance. They include a human skull in a** remarkable state of preservation recovered from the Gilstone Reef, and a fine example of scrimshaw art on an ivory tusk. (Photos: Horace Dobbs.)

removed from an object brought up by one of the divers from the Roland Morris team. It was a solid silver plate which, when cleaned up, clearly revealed the arms of Sir Cloudesley Shovell for everyone to see.

Having at last cleared the authenticity of the wreck site, the next problem was to clear ownership of the declared salvaged items. After 18 months of deliberation it was decided that objects that were once Government property, that is, ships fittings such as guns etc., became the property of the salvors — provided they held an M.o.D. contract. Which meant that Roland Morris could keep the three beautiful bronze cannons his team had raised, one of which bore the name *Le Compte de Vermandois*. The lifting eyes of this magnificent culverine, which was put on display at his restaurant, Admiral Benbow, in Penzance, were in the form of two dolphins. Cut deep into the bronze of one of his guns was the word VIGO identifying it as loot captured during the Battle of Vigo Bay in 1702 which was successfully led against the French and Spanish by Admiral Sir Cloudesley Shovell.

The fiasco that followed the discovery of the *Association,* the illegal dispersal of much of its treasure, and the loss of archaeological information upon which no price could be put, will not be repeated in British waters again, for it focused the minds of politicians on the need to reform the. laws governing the salvage of historic vessels. In 1973 The Protection of Wrecks Act came into force and an Advisory Committee on Historic Wreck Sites was appointed.

Cut deep in the bronze of one of the guns recovered from the site of the *Association* was the word VIGO, identifying it as loot captured during the battle of Vigo Bay in 1702. (Photo: Roland Morris.)

When I dived on the classic dive site of the *Association* at the Gilstone in the Isles of Scilly during the summer of 1979 the legal 'salvors in possession' were Terry Hiron and Jim Heslin. They had jointly founded the Underwater Diving Centre on St Mary's where they resided. They provided all the facilities necessary to enable visiting divers to work under supervision on the sites of several historic wrecks — the one selected depending upon the prevailing weather conditions.

In the company of Duncan Gibbins, who then worked for the BBC and was directing our filming, and my partner Chris Goosen, we explored and filmed various wrecks. By the time we had finished, I realised that the Isles of Scilly were a veritable graveyard for ships. So prolific had been the catastrophes that one wreck we filmed had settled on top of the previous ship to founder at the same point.

Even in the height of summer the weather was capricious and I could easily imagine how horrendous the Scilly Isles would be to sailing ships driven before a storm in winter. We waited several days before we could get down on the *Association* site. We eventually snatched a dive when the sea calmed down. It was a heavy grey day and the sky was overcast. The undersea world was gloomy and foreboding.

As I descended I was greeted by waving fronds of olive-green kelp that swayed back and forth in the swell. The deeper we went the darker it became. Beneath the kelp I soon lost myself amidst jumbled piles of sombre, grey-brown boulders. A massive iron cannon was wedged in a crevice in the rocks, a sinister reminder of the events that had taken place in 1707. I swam down to it and examined it in detail. Bracing my legs across the fissure in the rocks I put my hands around the muzzle and tried with all my might to move it. But I might as well have tried to lift the rocks upon which it rested. It was utterly unyielding. Even the fiercest of storms was not going to budge it. It was probably exactly where it landed when it first crashed through the bulwarks of the foundering *Association* to go plummeting through the angry dark water into the depths.

I continued my dive in a random manner, up one gully, down the next, this way and that, looking under rocks and poking into the bottom of channels with my gloved hand.

I knew with my inexperience in treasure-hunting that I would find it difficult to differentiate a ball of silver coins coated in crud from the rocks that were strewn everywhere. After the site had been so intensively scoured by other divers I thought it unlikely, even with my good fortune, that I would uncover a gold coin — which I would recognise immediately. My forecast was correct and after 30 minutes I returned to the surface empty-handed and feeling distinctly chilled despite the fact that I was wearing a thick wetsuit.

After that dive I came back with vivid impressions but, because I had wandered around so randomly, I had no idea of the specific layout of the site. Indeed, I could easily have traversed the same area two, or perhaps even three times, without knowing it. It was an experience that made me realise the immense amount of diving effort that must be put in to survey an archaeological site and put together the information in such a way that it affords an accurate picture for the non-diver.

Another dive on a nearby site added further to my understanding of the persistence and dedication needed to investigate a covered wreck. I filmed a diver working an airlift at a depth of about seven metres. An airlift is like a large underwater vacuum cleaner, with which it is possible to remove an overlay of sand and gravel. High-pressure air is pumped down to the seabed and is allowed to escape back towards the surface inside a larger diameter tube. The rising bubbles carry with them a fast stream of water. When the nozzle of the airlift is placed close to the seabed, loose items are sucked into it and are eventually spewed out with the escaping air. The underwater exit from an airlift looks like the funnel on a steam engine belching forth its mixture of air and debris — which hopefully is carried away by the current and deposited away from the site.

The diver waved the nozzle of his airlift back and forth, a few inches above the seabed. I watched fascinated as the sand and stones underneath it first moved slowly and then speeded up before being whisked away up the pipe. By painstakingly removing layer upon layer the diver uncovered what was hidden beneath the surface. When anything of interest was revealed he proceeded with caution and excavated it using his free hand in association with his underwater suction cleaner. After his allocated time he was relieved by another diver who was already kitted up and waiting to take his spell on the airlift.

When our airlift man eventually climbed back inboard he showed us the result of his hour-long dive. It was a brass plate from an engine, which had obviously been made when steam power had replaced sail. He handed it to Terry Hiron who examined it carefully. It wasn't what he was hoping for and it was not of much intrinsic value.

Its recovery would certainly not cover the real cost of keeping a fully-crewed salvage dive boat on site for a few minutes, let alone an hour. But that was all part of the gamble of hunting for treasure. What is it that really motivates treasure-hunters to spend hours, days, weeks and even years doing what, for much of the time, can be quite boring diving? At first sight it may appear to be simply the prospect of getting rich quick. There undoubtedly is an element of the gambler in all of them; there has to be or they wouldn't do it in the first place. But every successful treasure-hunter I have met, and I've met quite a few over the years, has insisted that it is something else, much more important, that keeps them involved after they have hit the jackpot.

This was forcefully brought home to me well before I met Jim and Terry in the Isles of Scilly. It occurred on 14th November, 1973 when I was in the home of Harry Cox in Bermuda. After a generous libation of local rum, taken from a wooden cask in his garden and run over cracked ice, I sat in his lounge and handled bars of solid gold. I let rubies and emeralds tumble through my fingers. I fingered a double-link gold chain, 4m long, and watched, totally bemused, as Harry manipulated a gold crucifix which opened to reveal a 17th century manicure set with a tongue scraper, an implement for pushing back the cuticles of finger-nails, and a small spoon for removing the wax from the ears. I was handling a fortune in gold and jewels recovered by Harry from the seabed on an offshore coral reef. Then with a great flourish Harry produced his *pièce de resistance*. An insignificant-looking object made of bronze. It was a very early example of an astrolobe which, along with a cross staff, would have been used on the ill-fated vessel for measuring the altitude of the sun and stars to calculate latitude.

Harry's forebears, who came from the West Country of England and landed in Bermuda over 300 years previously, had used such an instrument to navigate their way across the Atlantic. To Harry the historical significance of that particular find outweighed the money-in-the-bank value of the treasure he also had in his possession.

Back in the Isles of Scilly Rex Cowan insisted that it was piecing together the jigsaw of the maritime past that afforded him his greatest rewards. Jim and Terry, with mischievous glints in their eyes, said likewise.